Grandma's Ways
for modern days

Visit our How To website at www.howto.co.uk

At **www.howto.co.uk** you can engage in conversation with our authors – all of whom have 'been there and done that' in their specialist fields. You can get access to special offers and additional content, but most importantly you will be able to engage with, and become a part of, a wide and growing community of people just like yourself.

At **www.howto.co.uk** you'll be able to talk and share tips with people who have similar interests and are facing similar challenges in their lives. People who, just like you, have the desire to change their lives for the better – be it through moving to a new country, starting a new business, growing their own vegetables, or writing a novel.

At **www.howto.co.uk** you'll find the support and encouragement you need to help make your aspirations a reality.

You can go direct to www.grandmas-ways.co.uk, which is part of the main How To site.

How To Books strives to present authentic, inspiring and practical information in its books. Now, when you buy a title from **How To Books,** you get even more than just words on a page.

Grandma's Ways
for modern days

Reviving traditional skills in cookery, gardening and household management

PAUL & DIANA PEACOCK

SPRING HILL

Published by Spring Hill, an imprint of How To Books Ltd.
Spring Hill House, Spring Hill Road
Begbroke, Oxford OX5 1RX
United Kingdom
Tel: (01865) 375794
Fax: (01865) 379162
info@howtobooks.co.uk
www.howtobooks.co.uk

How To Books greatly reduce the carbon footprint of their books
by sourcing their typesetting and printing in the UK.

The paper used for this book is FSC certified and totally chlorine-free. FSC (The Forest
Stewardship Council) is an international network to promote responsible management of
the world's forests.

ISBN: 978-1-905862-35-1

Produced for How To Books by Deer Park Productions, Tavistock, Devon
Designed and typeset by Mousemat Design Ltd
Edited by Jamie Ambrose
Printed and bound by in Great Britain by Ashford Colour Press, Gosport, Hants

NOTE: The material contained in this book is set out in good faith for general guidance
and no liability can be accepted for loss or expense incurred as a result of relying in
particular circumstances on statements made in the book. Laws and regulations are
complex and liable to change, and readers should check the current position with relevant
authorities before making personal arrangements.

Contents

(continued on next page)

Introduction

Anyone wanting to live more of a self-sufficient life in a semi-detached house could do no better than put into practice the things their forebears did. For example, one of our grandmothers had a cheese sandwich for supper every day of her life. She baked her own bread in the morning and at the same time made the cheese she would eat that evening. She never used more than a pint of milk, acidified it with lemon juice, then washed and hung it to drip on the washing line to let the cheese drain. She made scones with the whey, and jolly tasty they were, too. All this happened every day in the industrial centre of Manchester when, during Hitler's war, the people who lived there lived extraordinarily rural lives. Parks were dug up for allotments, there were pigs and hens in the gardens, and goats roamed the banks of the Medlock River. Everyone grew a lot of food and it is repeatedly said that the nation was never better fed.

Our convenience and cash obsession

When we talk to people about living a simpler life, they often argue it is more efficient to earn the cash to buy such and such. In an hour, they suggest, they can make enough money to buy more produce than we grow in weeks. 'Why bother when I can go to the shops and buy stuff?' is a constant refrain. This way of thinking was never in vogue in Grandma's day. And it is undeniable that food grown in the garden, brought to the kitchen and cooked is better for the family and the planet than food shipped in from elsewhere. If we buy provisions from some distant land, they can't be fresh. They have used transport and infrastructure that aren't in any way eco-friendly, and the people who have grown them are forced into a Western monetary system that can't provide them with enough cash to break the great poverty caused by copying the West in the first place.

It might seem more time-consuming and expensive to grow most of one's food, but you do get the *very best* produce. Sure, there are pests and diseases to contend with, the soil has to be fed and it all has to be cared for, but what better 'seasoning' is there than your own extraordinarily satisfying, physical work?

Time for a full life

Interestingly, people with more time on their hands than ever say they wouldn't have the time to bake bread, to repair and make furniture, to grow food, keep hens. 'Why should we relive the lives of a hundred years ago?' they argue. 'We're in a modern age, aren't we?'

We believe that a home with baked bread to hand is a much more satisfying place than one with bought bread in the cupboard. People who cook their own hens' eggs, laid a few minutes ago, are happier than those who buy eggs a month or more old from the supermarket. If time is my currency and I can feed my family and make furniture – and only earn money for the rent and the other financial necessities of life – that makes me a happy person.

Moreover, when our grandparents were around, raising our parents and living their lives, life was not a drudge. There were, in fact, more societies, more sports, more choirs, orchestras and drama groups, and there were certainly more pubs. Grandma (and Grandpa) might have worked hard keeping the home together, but they played hard, too.

Yet, this book isn't really about Grandma. There are no recipes that use funny weights or ingredients, nor are there any old-fashioned plant varieties, and, yes, we do visit the supermarket. There are many things here that you may feel you don't want or need to make. Fair enough; no one wants to force you into making anything. However, you will be able to dip in and out of these pages at various times to create almost everything you need.

More than anything, your own experience is the best teacher, so if something doesn't work for you, then please feel free to modify it. Diana and I would love for you to read between the lines and get involved with the spirit of what we're doing. That way this book will change your life, and as with all life-changing experiences, *you* are more important than this book.

Cooking

Just as it is today, feeding a family 50 to 60 years ago often had to be done on a tight budget. The cook for the family, usually female, had to be creative with whatever was on hand to eat. During and just after the Second World War, many ingredients weren't available, so cooking had to be imaginative and creative; otherwise, meals quickly became very boring. In many ways we are much better off today than in our grandparents' time because we have better equipment for cooking and preparing food. Available ingredients including herbs, spices and a real swing back to growing our own food allow for a more creative and varied menu.

Baking skills are something many of us have forgotten, however. As a result, we've made do with the second-rate taste of shop-bought bread, cakes and biscuits. Yet all the processes involved in creating these at home are made quicker and easier by using modern appliances and ingredients such as a hand mixer and fast-action bread yeast. So in following in the footsteps of our ancestors, we can have 'real' food – and food that is made more simply and speedily.

The principles of husbandry

In those windswept years before 1066 and all that, when the Vikings settled in this country, they introduced a way of living that has stuck in name, if not in practice. The Norse word we know as 'husband' was someone who cared for a house or home, and by extension, his family, crops, animals and the land that gave them life. A husbandman, then, wasn't necessarily male;

the term applied to someone whose primary role was to care for the home, the fields, the livestock… anyone who loved the land and cared for it. That meant a concern for wildlife, too: caring for nature so that nature provided in turn.

Historically, however, a husband has come to mean a married man. Because Viking men often married Saxon women, they used the Saxon word *wif* – now the modern 'wife'. So husband and wife were not just tied to each other, but to the land. This implies that the love they bore for each other also extended to their economic activities: the tilling of land and the keeping of livestock. Consequently, by medieval times this relationship – man, wife, livestock and land – was at its height and became known as husbandry.

The cost of productivity

In this modern age, and for most modern farmers, the maintenance of fertility is an industrial process. Millions of tonnes of agrochemicals, manufactured with the aid of even more millions of tonnes of fossil fuels, are poured onto agricultural land in order to keep production high. However, the actual cost of this fertility is paid for by the planet's ecosystems – and ultimately, by us. Husbandry brings the production of food back down to the family level. Individual families might not make much food in financial terms, but they can cram food production into surprisingly small spaces. Productivity per square metre is very much higher than any farm, agrochemicals or not.

Grandma's Ways is our attempt to bring husbandry – and happiness – back into modern everyday life.

The most important concept

Now, we wouldn't argue for a return to medieval living, with its exploitation, poor sanitation, awful health care and frequently short life expectancy. But (and it is a big 'but') the ideals of medieval husbandry are not out of place in the modern age. There is a lot to be said for love. It is at the heart of husbandry. Love the earth and it will love you back – which may sound a bit 'flower power', but there is an important principle at work here. If we treat the earth with respect, feed it, make sure the land is 'in good heart', isn't drained of nutrients year after year and is not impoverished by neglect, then it will provide for us all.

Throughout every generation in human history, one thing has made people successful. It drives our relationships and guides us into families and groups. It creates both the need for cooperation and invention. Because of it, there is no such thing as 'self-sufficiency', because, in order to be successful, we need each other's help. In all our endeavours, *human love* drives the land, the garden, the home and the family, and to it this book is dedicated.

Diana and Paul Peacock

I

Around the House

Budgeting

Or, how to keep out of debt without living off beans

While no one is suggesting we go back to the days of wartime, if there's one thing a ration book did, it made sure you stuck to your shopping list. With little on the shelves other than powdered eggs, milk and gravy browning, it wasn't difficult to fight the urge to spend more than was in your purse. But with buy-one-get-one-free offers, fifty percent extra free and all the other ways supermarkets encourage us to bulk-buy these days, it's little wonder that we overspend to the point of debt.

Those shiny new credit cards don't help, either: tempting us with pictures of tigers or logos of our favourite football team, and words such as 'zero percent finance' or 'interest-free' to lull us into signing up. Before you know it, you've more going out than you have coming in. Yet there is hope; debt isn't a bottomless pit. It *is* possible to get out of it – and, more importantly, *stay* out of it – through vigilance and a few general rules.

Shopping

For some, shopping is ecstasy; for others, it's that weekly terror that creeps up and knocks you over when you realise there's nothing in the fridge but mouldy cheese and some bizarre bottle of chutney. Supermarkets are specifically designed to pry those hard-earned pennies from your tightly gripped fingers. They employ many innovations for this very task: from the counterfeit scent of freshly baked bread as you walk round the pre-packaged loaves, to the eye-level offers dangling from the ceiling. We have often arrived home after the weekly shop having forgotten half the things we needed while having picked up another twenty items we didn't. So what's the solution?

Start from scratch

Feeding a family with meals cooked from scratch is so much cheaper than serving ready meals, and you have the added benefit of knowing precisely what went into all your food. The salt, fat and sugar content of ready meals are particularly difficult to judge, especially because the information is disguised by clever marketing people who want to keep the unhappy truth from their customers. Of course, you still have to shop for the raw ingredients, and supermarkets are waking up to this, too, with offers allowing you to buy all the ingredients for a meal for around £5–£10. This can work to your advantage; if you build the offer meal into your menus each week, you'll save a great deal.

Make a list

It seems so obvious, but the humble shopping list really does work. Not only does it prevent you from forgetting the toothpaste, but it also keeps you focused. If all you really need is cheese, eggs and milk, writing a list can make sure you walk out of the shop with only cheese, eggs and milk. Knowing what you want to buy before you go into the shop immeasurably improves your chances of sticking to your budget. Because there are better things to be doing than wandering around a supermarket, we make snap decisions to buy things in order to get out before a favourite soap starts or the cricket begins. I can't count the times I've written 'something for pudding' on my list, and then bought three or four items because I couldn't decide between them in the shop.

Plan your menus

Writing menus for the week is a good way of keeping your bills down because it forces you to be specific about what's on your shopping list. Simply decide what meals you will eat each night, then write a list of all the ingredients you will need to cook them. For example:

Day	Meal	Ingredients
Monday	Spaghetti Bolognese (for recipe, see p 214)	Minced beef Tinned tomatoes Garlic 1 onion Red pepper Spaghetti
Tuesday	Lancashire Hotpot (for recipe, see page 198)	Lamb Lamb kidneys Potatoes Mushrooms 2 onions Stock Butter
Wednesday	Fish Pie (for recipe, see page 204)	Fish Mussels Prawns White wine Lemon Herbs Butter Potatoes

The menu-list on the previous page allows you to see exactly what you'll need to buy for three days. Once you know this, you'll know which items you should buy in volume (thus getting the cheapest price per item). In this case, onions and potatoes are prevalent, so buy them in larger quantities.

Putting in a little effort before you go to the shop ensures not only that your bill is reduced, but that your time spent in the shop is, too.

Crack the supermarket code

Ever wondered why the bread is on the other side of the store to the butter, or the milk so far away from the cereal? The supermarket is laid out in such a way as to encourage you *to buy*. If you think of your local store, you can picture the route you walk through it to get what you need. This has been carefully engineered in order to get you to walk around as much of the store as possible in order to bombard you with maximum offers and tempt you to buy that pack of 12 doughnuts or a family-sized box of biscuits. You therefore need to find a way around their sneaky ploys in order to keep your shopping precisely that: *yours*. So how do you do this?

Plan your route. Picture yourself walking round the store; what do you come to first? If you plan your route around the supermarket while writing your list, and put things down in the order that you'll come to them, this will ensure that you'll only search for what you need in each area, rather than browsing through the entire selection.

Stick to your list. It's very tempting to buy things 'because they're on offer', but consider whether you need them and if anything will go to waste. If you stick to your list, you will never waste any food or money, nor will you overspend. If you're really trying to cut back, try writing 'BUY THE ITEMS ON THIS LIST ONLY' at the top as a reminder, or set yourself a challenge to keep your shopping down to a maximum of 20 items.

Never, ever go grocery shopping on an empty stomach. If you do, you'll find that the tempting scents of the bakery department become unbearably delicious. Appetising things will overtake necessities and, before you know it, your basket will be piled high with items you just don't need. If you shop after a meal, however, your head, not your stomach, will be in charge, and it will be that much clearer – and so will your bank balance.

Remember that cheaper foods don't mean poorer taste. Advertisers have done a very good job in persuading us that the more expensive an item is, the better quality it is.

This isn't always true. Of course, it's all a matter of personal taste, but there is very little difference between the premium 'excellence' range and the value brands available at a fraction of the price. Most of the time it's down to how the packaging makes us *feel*.

Next time you shop, replace all the premium or large branded items with the supermarket's own 'value' range and see if you can tell the difference. If the packaging puts you off, think about investing in plastic containers to store rice, pasta and cereals. Not only will you avoid the look of the packets, you'll keep the produce fresher for longer. Of course, if the beans taste like they cost 9p per tin, then don't buy them again, but overall you'll find that the budget versions are just as good as the expensive products – and you'll be so much richer for it!

Take advantage of daily reductions. The time of day you shop can alter the amount you pay. Those handy 'reduced' stickers crop up at certain times as sell-by-dates approach. Shopping later in the day allows you to grab bargains on food items that would be unsaleable the next day, but which are perfectly edible (especially where bread and dairy products are concerned).

Too good to be true?

Like most things in life, a lot of those 'amazing offers' used in supermarkets don't actually end up saving you anything. By learning to read the 'small print', however, you can work out which ones are worth pursuing.

Try a high-tech price check. If you're comfortable with it, the internet can provide you with instant information on the latest in-store prices and offers. Not only can you compare the daily prices of individual items, but you can see who is providing the best offers and points. Buying your shopping online can also take away the temptation the supermarket brings.

Check the price per gram. When shopping in store, checking the price per gram of items allows you to see whether that 'amazing offer' really is the bargain it says it is. Sometimes, items on two-for-one do work out to be a few pennies cheaper than full-price items, but you'll spend more on the initial outlay in order to get the deal. Think carefully as to whether you really need the extra produce for that extra few pounds. It might make the muffins half price, but do you really need to eat 12 of them?

Check the price in all places. Some items are duplicated around the store: either those on offer or items placed together for special occasions, such as chocolates, flowers and wine in a Valentine's Day display. Check whether items such as these are cheaper elsewhere in the store before choosing to buy them from special displays. They may not be exactly the same brand in some cases, but you'll generally find that a good – and cheaper – equivalent exists. This is especially true of items such as raisins or nuts; you'll find them much cheaper in the baking section than the whole-food section.

Get the best out of BOGOF. No, it's not an old-fashioned insult; it's the supermarket (and lots of other high street stores) selling you twice as much stuff as you really need under the guise of 'Buy One Get One Free'. In food terms, this isn't always a good thing, because it usually leads to overindulgence and/or waste. But Buy One Get One Free offers can be fantastic, especially when they offer products that don't have a short sell-by date and that you were going to buy anyway. Things such as shampoo, shower gel, toothpaste and sanitary products are all good bets, although do ask yourself before you buy: 'Do I *really* need all these?'

Be a coupon collector

An ingenious marketing ploy that helps business and consumers alike, coupons are a fantastic way to snip pounds off your weekly shopping. They are so popular in America that they generate around US$3 billion of sales every year. We can learn a lot from those stateside 'coupon kings and queens' by following their example and getting out those scissors when we browse the newspaper.

Keep your coupons somewhere safe, then lay them out when you come to write your shopping list. Do this on the back of a used envelope, and if you have a coupon for something on your list, pop it inside. Then, when you come to the checkout, you'll have everything to hand.

Coupons aren't restricted to the supermarket, by the way. These days almost every website with e-commerce facilities has the option to 'enter a promotional code'. You can get these in a variety of ways:

Sign up to e-newsletters of companies that interest you. These are extremely useful marketing tools. By signing up, you agree to them sending a relevant, monthly advertisement directly to your inbox at very little cost to themselves. These frequently include money-off codes or free postage offers for goods or services.

Refer a friend. Again, this is a useful tool for the companies to get a captive audience for next to nothing, and it usually entails giving a few friends' email addresses away in return for a coupon. Coupons like these are usually quite generous, but tend to be conditional on the friend placing an order.

Take part in online surveys. There are a number of market research companies that pay you for taking part in online surveys in the form of e-vouchers for a variety of companies. Simply create an account, wait for them to send you a survey via email and look forward to receiving your promotional code!

Loyalty cards

'Have you got a points card?'

This is the standard cry from many a checkout supervisor across the land, and it can be fantastically beneficial to the frugal shopper. Yes, such cards can lure you in with bonus-points offers for things you really don't need, and yes, they seem to take an age to build up, but once you do have enough points, the satisfaction in getting something for nothing is immense. I've bought perfume, a foot spa, make-up and countless books and CDs all using loyalty cards – and that is not even counting the vouchers that I've received through the post for money off my shopping.

Loyalty cardholders usually receive postal mailings with extra vouchers and coupons, allowing even more money off and even more bonus points, usually for things you usually buy. So what's the catch? Well, every time you use the card, the company gets valuable information about your spending habits. They get to match up a person's profile (i.e. age, address, marital status) to what they buy, thus bypassing the need to pay for market research, and then send you tailor-made offers that have a bigger chance of being used.

Like the BOGOF offers, loyalty cards can make you buy more than you need, but here are a few tips that will help you get the most from your card:

Keep an eye out for extra-points offers on things you would buy already. If you know what each point equates to in monetary terms, you can then work out how much money off this will give you. Two hundred bonus points can (in some shops) mean £2 in your purse. But only take up the offer if you *would have bought the item anyway.*

If possible, wait to do your shopping at 'bonus' times. Many stores offer double- or triple-points days, allowing your total to build fairly quickly.

Maximise your points. Some stores offer different ways of redeeming your points, so points are worth more under certain schemes than others. Evaluate which scheme provides you with the best-value return.

Bills, Bills, Bills

So you've sorted out your shopping, but what about everything else? There's so much to pay out now, and with direct debits it's difficult to keep track of where and when it all happens. The key was – and still is – simple: be organised. Know what your income and outgoings are, and definitely don't panic. You'll learn that things are never quite as bad as they seem once you've sifted through them.

Income

If you are having difficulties, every little bit helps, so start with the good rather than the bad. Focusing on your income allows you to take everything in, be proud of what you've got and make any necessary changes. Write things down in a notebook so that you know exactly where all your income items are. Keep this 'accounts book' laid out in a clear, concise way. On the left-hand page of your notebook, make four columns, like this:

Date	Item	Gross	Net

Knowing the date you get paid allows you to know when to organise payments for bills. Write down everything you have in date order, including any benefits or bonuses (if you know them – if not, underestimate just to be safe). Including the net and gross amounts allows you to see how much tax and National Insurance you're paying and whether any adjustments are necessary. Don't forget to put down any other items, such as owed monies from friends, refunds, tax rebates, lottery winnings (yes, it all goes in the pot!), benefits, etc. This should show exactly what you have coming in during the month.

5th Jan	Payday (Me)	£ 750.00	£ 600.00
10th Jan	Bonus (Me)	£ 300.00	£ 240.00
15th Jan	Payday (Partner)	£ 800.00	£ 640.00
27th Jan	Family Allowance	-	£ 90.44
Total		£1,850.00	£1,570.44

Outgoings

Now for the tough part. Don't automatically assume this will be terrible. Simply assimilate all the outgoings you have in terms of bills, mortgage or rent, and any loan or credit card repayments you have. Don't include weekly shopping at this stage, as what is left can be divided among the weeks of the month. Ensure that you put down the date of when each item is due in order to pay things on time and avoid undue charges. Similarly, for items due quarterly or annually, split them up into what they would be if they were monthly bills and set this amount aside to ensure that you have enough when the time comes. Include sundry items and regular purchases, such as petrol and school lunches, etc.

Date due	Item	Amount due
1st Jan	Rent	£ 650.00
4th Jan	Council Tax	£ 90.00
10th Jan	Electricity	£ 45.00
15th Jan	Gas	£ 150.00
15th Jan	Telephone/Internet	£ 40.00
15th Jan	Water rates	£ 50.00
18th Jan	Mobile phone bill (both)	£ 60.00
20th Jan	Television licence	£ 10.00
20th Jan	Car insurance	£ 60.00
22nd Jan	Car tax	£ 20.00
28th Jan	Petrol	£ 50.00
28th Jan	Children's lunches	£ 48.00
		£1,273.00

Now you can work out how much you have left over after all the bills are paid:

Income: £1,570.44
Outgoings: £1,273.00
Leaving: £ 297.44

As there aren't *always* four weeks in the month, it isn't accurate enough to divide this by four to get your weekly allowance (which would be £74.36). In months containing 31 days, this could leave you short. Instead, multiply your remaining money by 12. This will give you the amount of money that is your food and household budget for one year. In this instance it yields a figure of £3,569.28. Dividing this sum by 52 will give you an accurate weekly budget based on that month's figures. Based on this information, I have £68.64 to spend each week.

My outgoings are more than my income...

If this is the case, then you seriously need to address both sides of your notebook. Let's start with outgoings.

What don't you need? Are there any areas of your life where you can downshift? Any extraneous bills you don't really need? Television subscriptions can be changed or cancelled; gym memberships can be downsized to 'off-peak'; lottery tickets can be avoided for now.

How can you economise? There are numerous ways of cutting your energy bills. Simple things, such as switching lights off when not in use, changing to low-energy bulbs, switching appliances off rather than leaving on standby, turning down the temperature of your heating, using extra blankets at night… all these can help reduce your running costs.

Switch and save. There are hundreds of advertisements on television citing ways you can switch your energy supplier and save hundreds of pounds. This potential minefield can be beneficial to some customers. Just make sure you check *all* aspects of the switch – and yes, unfortunately, that means reading the small print – and compare companies using one of the various comparison sites online.

Choose more efficient appliances. If making a big purchase, such as a fridge, freezer or washing machine, buy one with an efficient energy rating. New products are labelled with a rating from A to G (A being the highest and best) and are EU-approved. An A-rated appliance uses roughly half the energy of a G-rated one, and, over time, an initial investment can save you money. Consider other products, such as energy-saving kettles, solar-powered phone chargers or wind-up radios to keep your bills down.

Don't make unnecessary car journeys. If you can walk to the shop for the papers, do so. You'll be saving money, helping the environment and improving your health!

Bank accounts

If you're seriously budgeting, consider opening another bank account. Your main account (into which any income is paid), with any overdraft facility, should be used for those items on your outgoings list. This account should not be touched except to pay your bills. Once you've worked out how much you have spare for your shopping, transfer this amount across to another account, which you can use for day-to-day shopping. You may also wish to transfer any sundry amounts, such as petrol and children's lunches, to avoid the temptation of using your bills account for any other shopping.

Paying bills

Gone are the days of sticking stamps to a card to pay your TV licence or water bills. Many companies, particularly gas and telecommunications, now prefer you to pay by direct debit. This can be a mixed blessing, particularly if your outgoings are more than your income. Once you are signed up to a direct debit, the company will take the money out whether you have sufficient funds or not, which can lead to bank charges and further penalties with any company with which you have defaulted. If you have default charges on just one direct debit per month, this could lead to over £400 in charges.

However, if you can afford the outgoings, then direct debits can provide a great, hassle-free way of paying bills. Some companies offer a cheaper rate of service for paying in this way (magazine subscriptions particularly), and with the direct debit guarantee, you know your money is covered if anything goes wrong. Here are a few tips for successful direct debit transactions:

Make sure you have enough money in your account to cover ALL your bills – and a little bit spare in case of price rises or surprises.

Write down every direct debit that is coming out of your account in your notebook, along with the date they will be taken out. REMEMBER: these dates are not set in stone, companies have the right to take things out on, or shortly after, the agreed date. Do not be fooled into thinking you have more money than you thought; the direct debit probably hasn't gone out yet!

Make sure you have the money in at least five working days before the direct debit is due. The banks recommend two, but if you cover all eventualities, at least you'll know you have the money in the bank. Some companies take the money out early (they shouldn't, but it's happened to me), especially around bank holiday times and weekends. Having the money in place well beforehand gives you piece of mind.

If you realise you can't afford to pay a bill, contact the company BEFORE the payment is due and make arrangements to cover the arrears. Most big companies have departments for this and will be open to discussing your financial situation. After all, they want your custom through good times as well as bad.

If it really wasn't your fault, take action! If a company takes the money out too early, thus causing you to get a bank charge, complain. You have an agreement, which it has broken. It doesn't always work, but you can try and get the company concerned to cover the cost of the charge or write to the bank. Similarly, if you can prove it wasn't your fault, speak to your bank manager. I have had bank charges cancelled by doing this, thus saving a lot of time and worry.

Payment cards

A prepayment scheme allows you to keep in control of your bills if you're having difficulty with your budget. Similar to the pay-as-you-go mobile phone arrangements, these cards allow you to pay your bill, usually in conjunction with a meter, at a local convenience store. The price per unit (for example, £ /kWh) is higher than on a direct debit contract, but it at least allows you to spread the bill over the weeks and catch your breath when times are difficult.

Defaulting

If you've been unable to pay direct debits, then you will owe a company an amount of money. If you're quick, you can arrange to pay your arrears directly with them, by telephoning or writing to the credit-control department. However, even small debts are passed on to debt-collection agencies surprisingly quickly, and you'll find that you receive a letter from them threatening a bailiff. There are three things to do if this happens:

Don't panic. Debt collection agencies ARE NOT the end of the world. They are there simply to take away the need for large companies to spend time and money chasing up debt.

Work out what you can afford to do. How much can you pay per month to clear the debt? Go through your finances and decide what you can do with what you have.

Telephone the company and make your arrangement. Be brave! Debt collection agencies can be intimidating and upsetting, but they are not all-powerful. They will accept small amounts of money in order to clear your debt. Make your offer and stress that this is the maximum you can pay. When they have agreed your arrangement, ensure that you stick to it. If you default again, you run the risk of incurring a county court judgement.

Debt advice

Thankfully there are hundreds of websites offering sound advice for helping you get out of debt. If you're struggling, seek out the Citizens Advice Bureau (CAB), which provides official advice on a range of debt-related problems. Ensure that you face your debt rather than letting it pile up. Like illnesses, if you catch it early, it is exponentially easier to cure. Speak to as many people as you can, from your bank manager and the CAB to the companies you owe.

And don't forget: if you can't afford it, please don't buy it!

Make Better and Mend

A guide to keeping the clothes on your back and out of the bin

With international fashion houses selling wildly expensive pieces, high-street fast fashion, and no-frills (forgive the pun) clothes available in the local supermarket for under a tenner, the days of clothes rationing are certainly far behind us. It has never been easier or cheaper to clothe ourselves, but despite this, is it right to throw away our clothes just because of a hole here or a stain there?

Charity shops are a worthy home for items that are too small or ones we really won't wear again, but what about those they won't take? Surely we needn't stick them in the dustbin for want of knowing how to put in a couple of handy stitches? And how do we make the clothes we have last longer? Read on, and we'll show you how a little knowledge and creativity can revolutionise the way you run your wardrobe – and save you a few pounds in the process.

Elegant rations

The rationing of clothes began just after food rationing in 1941 in the UK, and was instituted to save space on container ships and assist the war effort. Forty-eight coupons were issued to keep every man, woman and child to keep them clad for a whole year; bearing in mind a dressing gown alone took up six coupons, it was necessary to make those clothes last, especially where growing children were concerned.

Fashion became more practical, *Vogue* saw its readership soar as women looked to the magazine to escape the war as well as to pick up tips on how to stay well-dressed through the hardships of rationing. The message was clear: 'Clothes must simply last longer than they used to.'

The interesting thing is, as we look back on the era now, we don't think of shabby, patched-up dungarees or threadbare trousers. We think of stylish, elegant people, doing their bit to win the war. That, and legs covered in gravy browning, of course!

Caring for Your Clothes

Today it is possible to buy a pair of jeans for £4. When you take into consideration the profit margins of the shop, the wages of the person selling it to you, the cost of its transportation from who-knows-where in the world, then how much is left for buying quality material and paying the person who made it a fair wage? Even if we leave the ethics out of it completely, the fabric used in the manufacture of your £6 top is not exactly high.

Man-made fibres have revolutionised the way we care for our clothes, leaving out the necessity to boil-wash whites or check our wardrobes for moths, but they still wear out. Here, therefore, are a few top tips for ensuring that your clothes look good for as long as possible.

Don't get stuck on repeat

It's tempting to wear those favourite pair of jeans over and over because of the perfect fit, but they'll only be perfect for so long. Ensure that you wear things in turn in order to give the fibres a rest. One wear a week rather than five will give you five times the length of service. This goes for shoes, too, and changing into 'house clothes' when you get in from work or a special occasion means your better clothes will look good for the maximum possible time.

Hang it up

We all do it: take off the jumper and leave in a heap on the back of the sofa. Well, I do, anyway, but it does the jumper no good. Body heat warms your clothes, and the creases that form while it's still warm are much tougher to iron out, thus creating more stress on the fibres. Hang up your clothes as soon as you take them off, using wooden or (better yet) padded hangers. Fasten any buttons or zips to ensure they retain their shape while hung.

Wardrobe magic

Despite the slight possibility of a magical land at the back of it, the wardrobe is still the best place to keep your clothes. Even T-shirts benefit from being hung straight on quality hangers, rather than being folded in drawers. Make sure you close the doors fully to keep out dust and moths. Keep special garments in suit bags, or use a clean bin liner as a dust cover, piercing the top of the hanger through the plastic.

Stains and dirt

Try to remove these as soon as possible, because prolonged exposure to grease and grime weakens fabric. Brush and polish leather shoes as often as possible and store them with paper or extenders inside to retain their shape. Never let them dry near heat.

Drying woollens

Knitted fabrics lose their shape if hung to dry. To avoid creases, spread them on a flat surface and allow to air-dry.

A stitch in 'grime'

Any pulls, nicks or tears are best mended *before* they are washed. What is a couple of stitches now could be a huge tear by the time it comes out of the machine, so get things mended as soon as they happen. Inspect your clothes before you put them in the washing basket for any split seams or loose buttons – it will save you time and money later on.

How to Sew

Sewing really is very easy, but it can be horribly frustrating at times. The key to sewing is patience, good light (no, really – it makes such a difference) and good-quality materials. Cheap thread will knot (cue angry moment), snap (even angrier moment) and even cause your garment to look worse than it did before (cue meltdown). Making sure your thread is the same colour and type of material as what you're sewing is also a must. Thick thread on thin fabric will be a disaster, so find what you need *before* you start.

I never bother with a thimble as it gets in my way, but you may find them a boon with thick fabrics such as denim, corduroy or tweed. Similarly, I never use a needle threader because I can't use them, but you might like them, so give them a try.

The sewing kit

I have seen kits made from a variety of materials. Some have expensive wooden boxes that open in tiers, with space for thread, needles, zips, buttons, etc. Some are just a small tin that closes with a clasp and only holds needles, small scissors and a thimble. At the moment I'm using an ice-cream tub (seriously: mint choc chip), which I find keeps all my needles (held together on an old bit of card), threads, buttons and scraps very nicely, thank you very much. No matter what kind of sewing box or container you choose, there are some basics you will need to keep in it.

Sewing kit essentials
- A pack of needles of various thicknesses
- A small pair of sharp scissors
- Emergency thread (I find black, white, beige and brown are essential)
- A stock of iron-on mending tape
- A needle threader (if you like them)
- A thimble (likewise, if you like them)
- Dressmaker's pins

The following are also useful:
• An unpicker (I love them; they make unpicking seams a dream!)
• A tape measure
• Safety pins
• A stock of spare buttons

Stitches

There are as many types of stitches as there are types of fabric, but they are all created with the same basic element and motion: needle goes in, needle comes out. Where and when they come out is what is key to successful sewing. The most common types of stitch are presented below.

Running stitch

If you only learn one stitch, make it this one. It will serve you for a large number of mending and sewing jobs, and can be adapted in small ways to improve the strength and quality of a garment. Simply thread the needle, tie a knot in one end, then sew in and out along a line. Easy! This is usually used for seams and for gathering fabric in pleats.

Backstitch

A great stitch for strength and uniformity of style, the backstitch will provide you with a line of stitches that resembles a machine stitch from the front. Thread your needle, tie a loop at the end (a double knot should stop it pulling through) and sew through from the back to the front. Go back out around 5mm below this loop, then return 10mm above this. Go through the original loop and then repeat along your line.

Buttonhole stitch

This sounds difficult, but it is surprisingly simple. Consider your stitch as a backwards 'L' shape. You begin on the outer edge of the horizontal, sewing from the back to the front. Sew across to the topmost point, but don't pull the thread through fully. Sew back to the front on the corner of the 'L', but before you pull, catch the thread in the loop you have made, then pull. This is great for oversewing seams or – surprise, surprise – creating buttonholes.

Blanket stitch

This is a decorative stitch for reinforcing the edges of fabrics. The theory is similar to that behind the buttonhole stitch, only in this case the top of the 'L' is usually the edge, so a loop is made over the top.

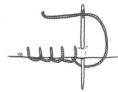

Herringbone stitch

The herringbone is a decorative, neat stitch that gives a sturdy finish to hems. The idea with this one is to work on the wrong side of fabric: for example, when hemming trousers. The stitches on the *right* side should be invisible. Start by sewing a couple of stitches below the line of your hem and tie a knot to secure your thread. Then, working from left to right, sew diagonally up across the hem and collect both sections of fabric in a catch (i.e. pick up only a few threads of the fabric, rather than sewing right through it). Come back through to the wrong side, then sew diagonally down in the same way. Keep your stitches as even as possible to enhance the decorative finish.

Oversewing

A very simple way to secure seams after they have been mended with a running or backstitch. The length of your stitch should be related to how easily the fabric frays. Simply sew through all the fabric from front to back, bring the thread over the raw edge of the fabric and then repeat the process. The closer the stitches, the more secure your edge will be, although keep in mind that delicate fabrics benefit from as few holes as possible.

Satin stitch

Also known as damask stitch, this is a series of flat stitches that covers a section of fabric completely and is used most commonly in embroidery and appliqué (see page 31). The action is very similar to a running stitch, except that the stitches here lie next to each other, rather than in a line. The satin stitch is also best done using an embroidery hoop (see page 32).

Knot your thread and start on the wrong side of the fabric. Sew through to the right side, then out at the point you wish the stitch to end. Come back through a millimetre from the place of the first hole and repeat until your design is finished.

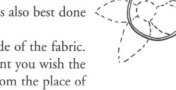

Mending Garments

A quick look at your clothes now will help you identify where any future garments are most likely to wear out. It is quick and easy to take precautions on new items to ensure they last as long as possible. Don't forget to look for:

Area	Precaution
Elbows in shirts and jumpers Knees Seat of trousers Underwear gussets Underarms Inside trouser seams	Sew a patch of lightweight fabric to the *inside* of each area (remember to choose a colour that will not show through from the right side!).
Trouser hem	Sew a piece of tape or medium-weight fabric to the inside of the hem to prevent it wearing thin against the shoe.
Inside thigh	To prevent fabric wearing thin, iron some lightweight interfacing across the seam.

MENDING SEAMS

Seams are the easiest things to repair, especially if there is no fraying or pulling of the fabric, but a few rules are necessary so as not to worsen the problem. Ensure that you use appropriate thread; it seems an obvious rule, but it is tempting to use thick thread on thin fabrics for added strength. If you do this, however, you're more likely to create a hole by using thread that's too wide, so match it to the weight of the fabric. Similarly, a thick needle on delicate cotton will create a hole and, if your stitching is too tight, it will tear.

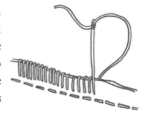

Colours, too, are a problem, so make sure you try and blend the colour of your cotton as much as possible. I have seen bright-pink thread used to darn camouflage combat trousers, which seemed to be missing the point somewhat!

Once you have the correct needle and thread, turn the garment inside out, pin the seam together and sew using a running stitch (see page 20) no larger than 5mm wide along the line of the broken stitching. For added strength, when you reach the end of the tear, sew on a little further, then return the way you came 2mm above it. These two lines of stitching will hold your seam nicely.

To make your seam (almost) indestructible, oversew the edge (see page 21) of the fabric, keeping the stitches no further apart than 5mm.

Mending Tears and Holes

Tears in fabric that are away from a seam are a little more difficult to deal with. If your tear is in an inconspicuous place, such as the crotch, underarm, etc., then you have a little more leeway in the quality of your stitching. Different types of injury to cloth require different types of sewing. Here's how to deal with the most common problems.

 DARNING HOLES

Try and catch them while they are small to reduce the need for patching. Holes need to be darned, which involves creating a small patch from excess thread to cover it.

1. For darning cloth fabrics, find a seam and gather some threads to use in the darning. If this is not possible, choose thread that is the closest match in colour and also material (cotton for cotton, wool for wool and so on).

2. The aim of darning is to recreate the look of the weave of the fabric through stitches, so begin by creating some vertical stitches in the intact fabric about 10mm away from the hole that follow the warp (the lengthwise yarn). Move in closer to the hole with the next layer, and continue up to the hole.

3. When you reach the hole, create a stitch that covers it and then continue with smaller stitches for 10mm.

4. When the hole is covered with vertical stitches, continue to sew into the intact fabric for about 10mm. When this is done, turn the fabric 90° and do the same along the weft (widthwise) threads. When you reach your hole, sew in and out of each thread to create a weave, then continue stitching as normal. This will provide you with a strong and invisible cover for your hole. To strengthen your darn (only appropriate for heavier fabrics), iron interfacing over the stitching on the wrong side.

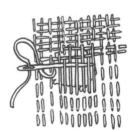

5. A similar method is used for darning woollens. Simply darn matching thread across the hole horizontally, then, catching the loops at the edge of the hole, sew vertically using a chain stitch. This should now resemble a knit.

PATCHING LARGE HOLES

Holes too large to be darned can be patched, either using fabric cut from excess cuffs or turn-ups, or a contrasting fabric, such as at the elbow, made popular by university lecturers throughout the 1970s.

If you can find a small piece of excess (try looking at trouser turn-ups, cuffs, or the underside of collars), snip it out to fit and then pin it in place. Fabrics such as corduroy, cotton, linen and denim can be patched from the inside. To do this, trim any fraying edges, then place the patch inside the garment, with the right side facing out through the hole. Using matching thread, sew the two together using tiny (no more than 2mm) stitches.

DECORATIVE PATCHES

If you can't patch invisibly, it may be possible to create a decorative patch to cover the hole. If the garment is a plain black shirt, for example, the hole can be covered by an embroidered floral patch, either created separately by hand and then sewn over the top, or bought from a craft shop or haberdashery. Similarly, holes can be patched using a plain fabric and then covered by a brooch. Holes in shirts and skirts can be covered by a length of thick ribbon sewn from top to bottom (especially good from the shoulder to the cuff or from the underarm to the bottom hem). If your garment is too holed to be patched, consider using it as patch fabric for other items. I once knew a chap who used his girlfriend's summer dress to patch his jeans. Needless to say, they're not together any more.

Tears

Tears that are not along seams can be mended in a fairly straightforward manner. For straight tears (i.e. a basic tear along a single line), place the garment on an ironing board and close the gap in the tear. Iron mending tape to the wrong side of the fabric. Then, when the gap is closed, darn over the tear using thread in a similar colour and weight. If the fabric has frayed or is wearing thin, it may be necessary to reinforce the mend with iron-on interfacing over a larger area.

Multi-directional tears

These should be mended in the same way. Cut mending tape to fit all the different directions of tears. Darn up in the same way and consider reinforcing with interfacing tape.

New from Old

If your garment really won't stand up to being darned, patched or sewn up, consider what else it could be. One of my favourite (and most complimented) skirts used to be a pair of pin-stripe trousers. And when is a T-shirt not a T-shirt? When it's a bag! Seriously, there are so many ways to reuse, recycle and renovate your clothes, a trip to the tip shouldn't be needed at all. Even clothes that are too small can be modified easily to give you a few more years' use. And they needn't look old-fashioned or eccentric, either, if you don't mix patterns (unless you really want to) or clash colours. There are a million ways to convert old clothes into fabulous new ones; read on for a few ideas.

TIPS FOR RENOVATING OLD CLOTHES

- Ensure the items are clean before you start work.
- Sketch out what you want to achieve before you begin; going in with all needles blazing never produces good results, so plan out your product first.
- Make sure you use good, sharp scissors for any cutting, and spread them out on a flat surface. Go slowly and, if in doubt, use dressmaker's chalk to mark out the line to be cut.
- Gather or buy all the correct threads before use. If using denim, choose heavier needles and threads. If using silks and satins, a fine cotton is needed.
- If possible, take the garment (or a sample of the fabric) to the haberdashery to choose the correct colour. If you don't know which thread to use, ask; they really won't bite!
- Consider the weights of the fabrics you are using; lightweight fabrics such as silks or satins won't stand up to being sewn onto denims or corduroys. Try and keep the weight of the fabric similar when mixing two items to make a new one.

 BAGS

These are the simplest things to make from old clothes, especially if you have a patterned skirt or shirt that you love – and with the decline of the plastic bag, you can never have too many! If you have a sewing machine, you may wish to use it reinforce your seams for carrying heavier items of shopping.

You will need
- Newspaper (to make a pattern)
- Dressmaker's pins
- Sharp scissors
- Needle and thread
- 1.5m length of 2.5cm-thick satin ribbon (in a contrasting shade)
- Fabric

1. Make a pattern for your bag in order to ensure you have enough fabric. Cut out a rectangular shape from newspaper, measuring 37cm x 47cm. Choose the garment you wish to use for your bag, be it a skirt, a shirt, etc. You will need to cut two pieces of fabric from your pattern.

2. If you don't have enough fabric for this, consider using two garments and stitching them together as seen here.

3. Pin together the fabric, with the wrong side of the fabric facing outwards. The pattern has included a 2cm seam allowance so the finished size of the bag will be 35cm x 45cm.

4. Hem down the two lengths and the bottom width using a running stitch (see page 20). Oversew the raw edges for extra strength.

5. Fold the top width back on itself and pin down, ensuring that the top of the bag opens. Press this (avoiding the pins) using a medium-hot iron.

6. Using the herringbone stitch (see page 21), sew the hem down to create a neat finish.

7. On the bottom corners of the bag, push the seam flat against the bottom of the bag as shown. Sew, using a running stitch to create a triangle 3cm from the tip of the corner. Do this on both sides. This will provide the bag with a better shape.

8. Cut two handles from the ribbon to the length of your choice. For a shopping bag, I prefer roughly 50cm each, but you may prefer longer. Pin them to the bag as shown, one handle on either side.

9. Sew a rectangle on each pinned section using a running stitch. To add strength to this, reinforce it by filling in the missed stitches with another section of running stitch. Create a diagonal cross in the same way to ensure maximum strength.

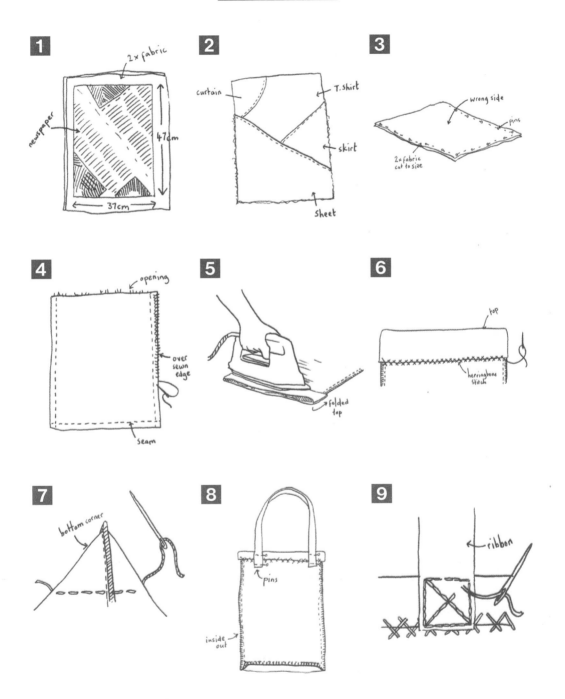

1
2x fabric
newspaper
47cm
37cm

2
curtain
T. shirt
skirt
Sheet

3
wrong side
pins
2x fabric
cut to size

4
opening
over
sewn
edge
Seam

5
folded
top

6
top
herringbone
stitch

7
bottom corner

8
pins
inside
out

9
ribbon

T-SHIRT BAG

This bag is even easier to make because the side seams are already done for you.

1. Simply cut off the sleeves at the shoulder seam; these will serve as your handles. Turn the T-shirt inside out, sew along the bottom seam with running stitch and oversew the edge.

2. Cut along the collar to make the handles thinner. Either leave these as raw edges (T-shirt fabric will not fray) or hem them using a running stitch (see page 20).

 SKIRTS

Here is the well-loved trouser-skirt. I've made five of these so far: one pin-striped and extra-smart pencil skirt, two casual denim skirts and another two denim minis for friends who 'just had to have one'. It's a great way of using trousers that have become ragged round the hem, worn thin or are a bit too tight. You can create either a thin pencil skirt or a more comfortable A-line skirt using the same method simply by moving things out a bit. This is done in no time on a sewing machine, but it is also possible by hand.

You will need
- A pair of old trousers
- A pair of scissors
- Appropriate needle and thread (plus a thimble if your fabric is heavyweight)
- Dressmaker's pins
- Unpicker
- 2m length of satin ribbon in co-ordinating colour (optional)

1. Before you begin, ensure that your trousers are clean and pressed. This really does make life easier.

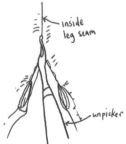

2. If using jeans or trousers made from a thick fabric, begin by cutting off the bottom hem, roughly 1cm higher than the line of stitches. This will make your unpicking quicker and easier.

3. Using your unpicker, undo the seam along the inside leg, right up to the crotch.

4. To flatten out the skirt, you will also need to undo the seam directly below the fly and a little of the way up the back (as shown).

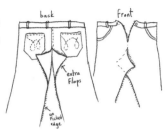

5. Lay the garment on a flat surface and decide the length you require the new skirt to be. If you can't decide, put the trousers on and pin at the length you require. For this type of skirt, the longest that it is possible to create is to around mid-calf, as the bottom of the trousers fills in the gaps. Decide also on the width of the skirt (A-line or pencil) as shown.

A-line skirt

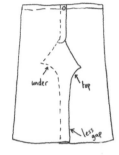

Pencil skirt

6. Cut the skirt to size (leaving 2cm seam allowance) as shown. Do not discard the trimmings, you will use them next.

7. Pin down the remaining fabric so that the skirt is flat. Use the trimmings and cut pieces to fill any holes, ensuring they are slightly larger (for seam allowance), or use a contrasting fabric and pin into place.

8. Using a running stitch (or backstitch; see page 20), sew the seams back down as shown, being careful not to sew through both sides of the skirt. This is best done on a sewing machine, but is by no means impossible by hand.

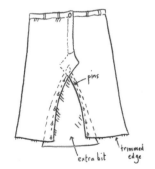

9. Iron the work flat, then fold over the hem and press. Using a herringbone stitch or running stitch, hem the bottom seam. Cover any frayed edges with ribbon as shown, or leave as it is. Denim skirts made in this way do not even need to be hemmed at the bottom.

SCARVES

A scarf is positively the easiest thing to make and is great for using up off-cuts of old clothes, sheets, etc. For the best look, try and keep your 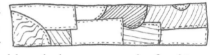 colours/patterns as close and muted as possible, although there are no rules for this.

You need to sew the fabric together to create a length that is approximately 2m (or as long as you want) by 20cm (or as wide as you want). Trim it straight and hem if necessary. Alternatively, use sleeves from silk shirts for shorter scarves or bandannas, simply by hemming round the edge.

Patchworking

The most popular and efficient method of re-using fabric, as the smallest scraps of cloth can be cut to size and used in it. This provides you with a larger piece of fabric that can be used as cushion covers, quilts, blankets, tablecloths and so many other items. The effect can look a little busy, so if the idea of multicoloured blankets keeps you awake at night, keep your colour palette to one or two colours. You can get hundreds of patches from a single garment, so three or four 'ruined' items can keep you warm all winter!

Like most of our renovated clothes, things work better if you keep the fabrics in the same weight and type. Calico, cotton and linen work best, but you can also use denim, corduroy and woollen cloths. The key to good a patchwork is a good template. Work out what shape and size you'd like each patch to be. The most common are square or hexagonal, though other types include cathedral, Somerset star and clamshell.

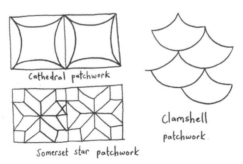

Cathedral patchwork

Somerset star patchwork

Clamshell patchwork

Keep your template under 15cm^2 to ensure you get the most from your garments. Remember, your template should include a 1cm seam allowance all around (so 2cm in total per width).

Getting started

Once you have gathered your fabric together and made your template, wash and iron your garments. Then, using either a tailor's pencil or chalk, trace your template onto your fabric and cut out the pieces using a pair of sharp scissors.

To join, line up the fabric with the right side facing in and pin together. Sew using a running stitch or backstitch (see page 20) 1cm from the edge. When a row has been joined, iron the seams flat. Use the finished patchwork for cushions or blankets.

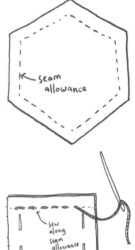

Appliqué

This is basically the act of sewing one piece of fabric on top of another to create a design, and is therefore extremely useful in covering holes or tears that cannot be darned or mended. You can purchase patches from craft shops, or make your own from old garments. Simply sketch your design, make templates and cut them out of the fabric of your choice. You don't need to leave a seam allowance because the edge of the fabric will constitute the edge of your design.

Place your design onto the backing fabric, whether a garment or other material you will make into a cushion, blanket, etc. You may want to use an embroidery hoop to complete this, as the tauter the backing fabric, the easier your job will be. Pin the design into place and, using a small running stitch (see page 20; ensuring each stitch is no more than 2–3mm), sew all around your design.

Alternatively, use a small satin stitch (see page 21) around the edge of your design to prevent the raw edge of the fabric from fraying.

Taking Sewing Further...

If you'd like to know more about sewing or types of stitches, the internet is a great place to start. Sites like videojug.com and YouTube provide practical advice that you can watch directly. Alternatively, a local craft shop will offer a wide range of books and magazines, as well as local libraries, which should also have details on any courses run by adult education centres.

Sewing Glossary

Appliqué A process of sewing one piece of fabric on top of another to create a decorative patch.

Bias A garment cut at a 45° angle to the direction of the weave. This gives a soft drape, and is usually used in ladies' skirts and evening dresses.

Darning A method of sewing to mend holes invisibly, usually with the same thread as the garment or very similar.

Embroidery hoop A wooden or plastic circular device that comes in two pieces and holds your fabric taut while you embroider. They come in a variety of diameters and can be purchased from good craft shops and haberdashery stores.

Interfacing A textile used to strengthen or stiffen another fabric. This comes in iron-on or sew-in form and in many different thicknesses to suit the item.

Raw edge The cut edge of fabric that has not been hemmed.

Seam allowance This is added to the final dimensions of a garment to leave room for the seam, usually 2cm.

Unpicker A tool used to unpick seams and rows of sewing easily and painlessly. Available for a few pounds from a craft shop, they are a welcome addition to any sewing kit.

Glossary items taken from 'Make Do and Mend', published in 1943 by the Board of Trade.

Health and Beauty

Home Beauty Treatments

Through the ages, people have used homemade beauty treatments, from henna and kohl in ancient Egypt to the terrifying use of lead in face products in the eighteenth century. More recently, with the rise of the Hollywood film star, glamour has become even more important to women. Even prior to and during the Second World War, cosmetic houses were bringing out more and more 'must-have products', but during wartime it was very difficult to get hold of simple lipstick, powder or face cream. For this reason, 'make do with what you have' was what women such as my mum had to do.

She was just eighteen years old when the war began, so quickly became an expert at making her own beauty products. This was difficult, as Mum had to use things from the food cupboard and, of course, rations were small, but she, and countless other young women like her, managed to find the ways and means of looking glamorous. Red lips were the trend in those days, but when your prized lipstick was used up, you had to improvise, so my mum and auntie both made a lip stain using beetroot, which Grandad grew on his allotment. They applied it to their mouths, adding a slick of petroleum jelly over for 'gloss'.

These days beauty products, both commercially produced and homemade, are a passion of mine and give me great pleasure. Yes, I do buy moisturiser, lipstick and face colours and a good sun-screen, but other beauty products, such as cleansers, toners and face masks, I tend to make myself. The benefits are many: you know what you are putting on your face; they work just as well as some of the shop-bought products and, best of all, they are much cheaper.

The secret is not to make too much at any one time and have a supply of small, lidded containers available for the potions you do make. Unless you want to try keeping any of these for a long time – and most only last for a few months anyway – there is no need to sterilise your containers; just make sure they have been freshly washed in hot soapy water.

We're very lucky compared with our more recent ancestors, because we have many ingredients available to us, particularly when it comes to essential oils and fresh produce.

When using anything on your skin, whether homemade or purchased, always test a small amount on a small area of skin first to see if you have any allergic reaction to it before using a large amount.

You must also take great care with essential oils: *always* dilute these in a carrier oil or other liquid before use. The recommended dilution is usually on the container, because different oils have different strengths.

Where do I begin?

I started by making face scrubs and masks. Many of the ingredients you need for these are already in your store-cupboard. Here is a checklist of ingredients you may wish to use; these are also useful if you take to making your own soap (see page 57).

General food items
- Clear and set honey
- Fine and medium oatmeal
- Bananas
- Dried milk powder
- Apples
- Lemons
- Eggs
- Olive oil
- Cornflour
- Cider vinegar
- Ground almonds
- Desiccated coconut

Other useful ingredients you may wish to buy, mostly from chemists or health-food stores:
- Aloe vera gel
- Essential oils
- Coconut oil
- Distilled witch hazel
- Sweet almond oil
- Glycerine
- Beeswax

Finally, here are some of the most useful essential oils:
- Lavender
- Chamomile
- Geranium
- Tea tree
- Rosemary
- Thyme
- Rose (this is very expensive, however, and is usually sold already diluted)

Facial Cleansers

Cleansing is so important, especially if you wear make-up. Oils are good for melting away make-up. Don't, however, use the following close to the eyes. All of these cleansers should keep for 2–3 months if you don't use them up within a few days.

Coconut Oil Make-up Remover
This is good for dry, irritated skin.

Makes enough for about 7 days' application

4 tablespoons coconut oil
8 drops chamomile oil
10 drops lavender oil

1. In a spotlessly clean bowl, melt the coconut oil over a pan of hot water; this will happen very quickly.
2. Add the essential oils and stir in very gently so that you don't cause too many bubbles.
3. Pour into a clean, lidded container.

To use
Massage half a teaspoonful of the mixture into your face for a few seconds. Then, use a clean face cloth soaked in hot water, remove all the oil. Keep rinsing the cloth until all the oil is removed. Your face will feel soft and clean. Use within 3 months.

For dry, troubled skin
If you have a dry skin that sometimes breaks out in spots, add 8 drops of tea tree oil into the melted oil for added deep cleansing.

Glycerine and Honey Cleanser
This is useful if you have less dry skin.

Makes enough for about 7 days' application

3 tablespoons cornflour
3 tablespoons glycerine
90ml cooled, boiled water
1 tablespoon clear honey
10 drops geranium oil

1. Put all the ingredients except the geranium oil into a small pan.
2. Stir and heat the mixture until it is smooth and thick.
3. Allow to cool, add the geranium oil and put into a clean, lidded container.
4. Store in a cool, dark place.

To use
Smooth over the face and tissue off.

A Soothing Cleanser
This is a very mild, gentle cleanser and is great if you have redness or an irritated skin.

Makes about 10 applications

3 tablespoons aloe vera gel
3 tablespoons sweet almond oil
8 drops chamomile oil

1. Put all the ingredients in a lidded jar and shake well to combine.
2. This will need to be shaken well before each application as it tends to separate.
3. Store in a cool, dark place and use within 2 months.

To use
Smooth over the face and massage in. Tissue off, or use a warm face cloth.

Facial Masks

This is great fun, and if you get together with a few friends you could have a beauty-treatment party! Some of these are quite difficult to apply at times, however, so be sure to protect your clothes.

Banana Face Mask
This cleanses and softens the skin.

Makes 2 applications

2 egg yolks
1 large or 2 small bananas
2 teaspoons lemon juice
2 teaspoons sweet almond oil
8 drops lavender oil

1. Mash the banana in a bowl. Add the lemon juice and egg yolks. Mix well.
2. Stir in the oils just before application.

To use
Apply the mask to the face, but avoid the eye and lip areas. Relax for 20 minutes, then wipe off with tissues. Splash your face with cool water to get rid of any excess mask. Pat the face dry with a soft towel.

Honey Firming Mask
This seems to tighten and even out the skin.

Makes 1 application

1 egg white
2 tablespoons clear honey
1 tablespoon fine oatmeal
8 drops chamomile oil

1. Mix everything into a thick paste.

To use
Apply the mask to the face. Leave to dry for 15 minutes, then rinse with cool water and pat dry.

Toning Mask
This is a refreshing yet gentle skin-cleansing mask.

Makes 2 applications

Half a small cucumber, peeled and mashed with a fork
1 tablespoon powdered milk
2 tablespoons natural yogurt
10 drops chamomile oil

1. Mix the cucumber with the powdered milk and combine well so that there are no clumps of powder.
2. Mix in the yogurt and oil and apply immediately.

To use
Apply the mask, relax and leave for 20 minutes. Rinse off with cool water and pat dry with a soft towel.

Brightening Mask

The apple in this mask seems to exfoliate the skin very gently
and leaves it looking bright and clean.

Makes 1 application

1 dessert apple, peeled and cored
1 whole egg
1 tablespoon clear honey
1 tablespoon fine oatmeal
2 teaspoons lemon juice

1. In a bowl, mash the apple with a fork and stir in the lemon juice.
2. Stir in the egg and oatmeal briskly. Stir in the honey.

To use
Apply to the face and massage in; a lot will drop off, but if you do it over a clean sink
you can use it again if necessary. Leave for 20 minutes, massage gently for a few
seconds and wash off with cool water and pat dry.

Avocado Mask

I actually don't like eating avocados, but I love putting them on my face.
They soften and cleanse the complexion better than most costly creams and cleansers.

This will make 2 masks

1 avocado, stoned, halved and peeled
1 egg yolk
2 teaspoons olive oil
10 drops of rose oil

1. Mash the avocado with a fork and mix with all the other ingredients.

To use
Apply to the face and massage gently into the skin. Leave for 20–30 minutes –
have a snooze or listen to some of your favourite music. Rinse off with cool
water and pat dry.

Facial Scrubs

Whenever I use a facial scrub, I find it works better if I place a warm, damp cloth over my face for a few seconds beforehand.

Oat and Lavender Scrub

This one is very messy, but it is still my favourite! If your skin feels irritated yet needs a good clean, this does the job on both counts: oatmeal cleanses as well as soothes, and lavender oil is very anti-inflammatory.

Makes 1 application

About 30ml cool, boiled water
1 tablespoon dried milk powder
30g medium oatmeal
10 drops lavender oil
1 teaspoon sweet almond oil

1. Mix the water and powdered milk in a bowl and stir in the oatmeal and oils.

To use
Dampen the face with warm water, then massage the scrub into the skin with circular movements for 1 minute, or until you've given your face a good massage. Wipe off with tissue, then rinse well in cool water and pat dry with a soft towel.

Sugar and Honey Scrub

This is a good scrub when you want to 'glow'. It is a versatile recipe, as you can use either caster sugar or granulated. I stick to caster as it is coarse enough for me, but granulated is good on elbows, knees and heels.

Makes 1 application

2 tablespoons sugar (caster or granulated)
1 tablespoon set honey
1 teaspoon olive oil

1. Mix all of the ingredients together.

To use
To apply, splash your face with warm water, then apply small amounts of the scrub and work it in to small areas of your face. Avoid your eyes and lean over a sink while you do it for ease of use. Rinse well with warm water and pat dry.

Coconut Scrub

A very softening scrub that still really cleanses your face.

Makes 1 application

2 teaspoons coconut oil
1 tablespoon ground almonds
1 tablespoon desiccated coconut
8 drops chamomile oil

1. Warm a bowl under the hot tap and dry it quickly. Put the coconut oil into the bowl; it should melt almost straight away. If not, stand the bowl in another bowl of hot water.
2. Stir in all the other ingredients and allow to cool.

To use
Wet the face with warm water, then apply the scrub. Massage in circular movements, avoiding the eye area. Rinse off with warm water and pat dry with a soft towel.

Moisturisers

You can make a very basic moisture cream at home and tailor it to suit your skin's needs by adding essential oils. There are many others but these are the main ones for general use.

- Lavender is good for calming, cleaning, healing and relaxing.
- Tea tree is good for cleaning because it has strong antibacterial properties.
- Geranium is good for decongesting your pores and relaxing the skin.
- Chamomile is calming and soothing: good for redness and sensitive skin.
- Rose is good for ageing skin and is soothing.

Rich Moisture Cream

You'll only need to use a small amount of this. I find it ideal for the winter months or if I'm out in the wind.

Makes about 6 weeks' supply if used every day

5g beeswax
50ml sweet almond oil
15 drops rose oil

1. Melt the beeswax in a bowl over some hot water and stir in the oils. Beat with a spoon to combine well. Put into a lidded jar and store in a cool place.

Light Moisture Cream

This is better for summer months.

Makes sufficient for about 6–8 weeks' use

20g coconut oil
20ml glycerine
1 tablespoon aloe vera gel
8 drops chamomile

1. Put all the ingredients in a bowl over hot water. When the coconut oil has melted, whisk to combine. (I use a small salad-dressing whisk.)
2. Put into a lidded jar and store in a cool place. It should keep for 3 months.

Toners

Toners are simple to make and you can make them to match your skin type. Because mine changes with the seasons, I find it easy to create my own. Store in a screwtop bottle.

Rosemary and Lavender Toning Lotion
A refreshing, light lotion that tones the skin.

Makes sufficient to last 8–10 weeks

10 lavender flowers
1 tablespoon chopped fresh rosemary
200ml boiling water
10 drops lavender oil
5 drops rosemary oil

1. Put the flowers and rosemary in a small pan and pour in the boiling water. Heat to simmering and simmer for 5 minutes. Remove from the heat, cover and leave to cool completely.
2. Pour into a bottle and add the oils. Shake well before each use and apply with a cotton wool pad over a clean skin.
3. Store in a cool place and use within 3 months.

Witch Hazel Toner
This is good toner to use if you have a slightly oily complexion.

Makes about 8 weeks' supply

60ml distilled witch hazel
30ml cool, boiled water
10 drops lavender oil
8 drops geranium oil

1. Pour the ingredients into a glass bottle and shake well before every use.
2. Apply with a cotton wool pad over a clean skin.
3. Keep in a cool place and use within 3 months.

Hair Beauty

Soap was generally used to wash the hair and scalp in the past. Green soft soap was a popular choice for washing hair because it was so mild; I remember having my hair washed in the green gel and how its fresh, soapy aroma lingered in my hair. Now there are so many products to wash hair with and keep it in 'tip-top' condition that we are spoilt for choice.

I have started to buy basic shampoo bases from a wholesaler on the web and make up my own shampoo recipes to cater for my family's individual needs. It is cheaper and great fun! But you can make your own mild hair wash using soapwort: an old remedy for dirty hair.

Soapwort Shampoo

Soapwort may be purchased in health and herbalist shops.
This recipe is ideal for normal or slightly oily hair.

Makes sufficient for about 6 washes

250ml water
1 rounded tablespoon plus 1 level tablespoon soapwort
1 tablespoon lemon juice

1. Boil the water in a pan and add the soapwort. Cover and simmer on the lowest setting for 20 minutes.
2. Strain the liquid into a bowl and stir in the lemon juice.
3. Transfer to a screwtop bottle and shake well.
4. Store in the fridge and use within 2 weeks.

Variations
- If your hair needs extra scalp cleansing, add 8 drops of tea tree oil.
- To calm an irritated scalp, add 10 drops of lavender oil.
- For dark hair add 10 drops of rosemary oil.
- For fair hair, 12 drops of chamomile oil.

Hair Rinses

Used after washing, a hair rinse can enhance shine and keep hair feeling fresher for longer.

Rosemary Rinse

This makes dark hair shine and smell really clean. It is reminiscent of a very famous dandruff shampoo; rosemary was used in the original formula, so it also helps to clean the scalp.

Makes enough for 1 application

300ml water
2 tablespoons rosemary leaves, chopped
6 drops rosemary oil

1. Put the rosemary in a bowl and boil the water. Pour the water over the rosemary and use a fork to squash the leaves; this will release all the oils.
2. Leave to cool, then stir in the rosemary oil vigorously and leave to settle.
3. Strain the liquid into a jug.

To use
When you have washed your hair and rinsed out the shampoo, pour the rinse over your hair and scalp and comb through. Do not rinse it out.

Vinegar Rinse

Vinegar is a very old hair-shining ingredient and makes your hair soft and easy to manage. Don't worry about the smell; once your hair is dry this will disappear! Most vinegar can be used, but I find cider vinegar best for all types and colours of hair. Red-wine vinegar is wonderful on all shades of red and auburn hair.

Makes 1 application

1½ tablespoons vinegar
500ml tepid water

1. Just stir the vinegar into the water and pour over the hair and scalp straight after rinsing out the shampoo. Do not rinse out.

Beer Rinse

This is ideal for fine hair. Beer has traditionally been used to give hair body and make it more manageable. My mum used it as a setting lotion: she washed her hair, then dipped her comb in some beer and combed it through each section of hair as she put her curlers in. Once her hair was dry, there was no smell and her hair was curly and shiny.

Makes 1 application

100ml beer – any brand will do
250ml cool water

1. In a jug, stir the beer into the water and pour over the hair and scalp after rinsing out the shampoo. Do not rinse out.

Thyme Rinse

This helps an itchy scalp that is prone to dandruff.

Makes 1 application

300ml water
2 tablespoons fresh or 1 tablespoon dried thyme leaves
6 drops thyme oil

1. Put the water in a pan and add the thyme leaves. Bring to the boil. Turn down the heat to a gentle simmer and simmer for 5 minutes.
2. Leave to cool in the pan.
3. Strain into a jug and add the thyme oil. Stir well.

To use
After rinsing out your shampoo, pour the thyme rinse over your hair, being sure to soak the scalp. Massage the liquid into your scalp for a minute. Do not rinse out.

Chamomile Rinse

This is for blondes. My daughter has golden hair and this really makes it shine, but it does dry the hair out so don't use it often. You can buy dried chamomile flowers if you don't have any in your garden. We use chamomile tea bags, as they are easy to handle and have the same effect.

Makes 1 application

3 chamomile tea bags or a handful of fresh or dried flowers
300ml water
3 tablespoons lemon juice
8 drops of chamomile oil

1. Boil the water and pour over the tea bags or flower heads and leave to steep for 3 hours.
2. Strain the liquid into a clean jug.
3. Stir in the lemon juice and chamomile oil.
4. When you have shampooed and rinsed your hair, towel dry and slowly pour the rinse all through the hair, coating every strand. Comb through. If you sit in the sunshine and let your hair dry, this will lighten the hair slightly.

Hair Moisturisers

Deep-conditioning treatments make your hair softer and relieve the dryness at the ends. Homemade moisturisers can be a bit messier than shop-bought products, but they do make a big difference to the condition of your hair.

Avocado Conditioner

Make 1 application

1 ripe avocado
½ teaspoon olive oil
1 egg yolk

1. Halve the avocado and remove the stone. Scoop the flesh out of the skin and put into a clean bowl.
2. Add the oil and mash with a fork. Stir in the egg yolk.

To use
Apply to dry, unwashed hair, massage in well and cover your head with cling film or a shower cap. Leave for at least 30 minutes. Rinse out and then shampoo as normal.

Banana Hair Mask
This softens and smoothes the hair.

Make 1 application

1 peeled medium banana
1 tablespoon clear honey
2 tablespoons natural yogurt

1. Cut up the banana and put the pieces in a bowl, then mash well with a fork.
2. Stir in the honey and yogurt.

To use
Apply to unwashed hair and massage into the scalp and to the ends of the hair. Wrap the head in cling film or use a shower cap. Leave for at least 45 minutes before rinsing and shampooing the hair.

Health Alternatives

Here are some safe household remedies for some minor ailments. They are not meant to be a substitute for medical advice, however, so if a condition does not improve, or if it worsens, see your doctor.

Anxiety or insomnia
• Try putting 2–3 drops of lavender oil on your pillow or on a clean handkerchief tucked into your pillowcase at night.
• Apply a few drops of geranium oil or lavender to your temples and breathe deeply.
• Have a cup of chamomile tea: 1 tea bag in 150ml boiling water. Make your own tea bag by tying about 6 chamomile flowers in a muslin bag. This is best brewed in a teapot and left to brew for 10 minutes before sipping.

Bad breath
Brush your teeth with a teaspoon of baking soda 2–3 times a day. This will clean and freshen the mouth – and it will also help whiten teeth.

Indigestion
• Try sipping 1 cup of very hot water. Be careful not to burn your mouth, though.
• Try 1 cup of peppermint tea, made with 1 tea bag or a tablespoon of chopped garden mint. Peppermint has been used for centuries by herbalists and naturopaths as a treatment for indigestion.
• Put 1 teaspoon of baking soda into a small glass of warm water, mix and drink immediately.

Menstrual pain and discomfort
• For bloating or water retention, drink a cup of dandelion tea: pour 150ml boiling water over a small handful of chopped dandelion leaves. Brew for 5 minutes and drink. Have up to 3 cups of this over the course of a day. Dandelion leaves are a proven natural diuretic.
• For pain, try a cup of chamomile tea: 1 tea bag in 150ml boiling water. Make your own tea bag by tying about 6 chamomile flowers in a muslin bag. This is best brewed in a teapot and left to brew for 10 minutes before sipping. This will help relax you and therefore help relieve the pain.
• Add a muslin bag full of chopped rosemary leaves and 8 chopped lavender flowers to a warm bath. The essential oils and just floating around in warmth will help to relax and comfort you.

Minor scalds and burns (bad burns *must* be seen by a medical practitioner)
• Apply a very cold, wet towel immediately to the affected area or run it under the cold tap for several minutes. If there is any redness, apply a thick layer of aloe vera gel.

Nausea
• Do not take anything without medical advice if the sickly feeling is due to pregnancy. But this did help me: half a teaspoon of grated fresh ginger in 150ml boiling water, brew for 5 minutes, sieve and sip. You can also chew crystallised ginger for the same purpose.
• If your queasiness is due to feeling bloated, try a cup of fennel tea. Either use a tea bag or put half a teaspoon of fennel seeds in 150ml boiling water, steep, cool and drink. Have at least 3 cups of this with a few hours in between and your windy feeling will be blown away.

Sore throats and catarrh
• Pour 50ml boiling water over 1 teaspoon dried of thyme leaves. Leave to cool, then gargle before going to bed after cleaning your teeth and do the same in the morning.
• Salt water helps, but it isn't very pleasant, so gargle with a solution of 1 teaspoon salt in 80ml water. Do not swallow.

Spots
• Mix 4 drops of tea tree oil with 1 teaspoon of cool, boiled water. Use a cotton bud to dab on the liquid and do not rinse. Repeat day and night until the spot disappears.
• Dab on 2 teaspoons distilled witch hazel dabbed with a cotton bud, 2–3 times a day.

Household Cleaners

Keeping your house clean can be a very expensive business. If you believe all the advertisements, then you feel you must have a separate cleaner (or sometimes two) for every job in the house.

I have found that all the cleaners I use to keep the house clean and fresh can be made from a few basic ingredients. You may need to use a little more 'elbow grease' with them from time to time, but they work just as well as the expensive brands and they have less of an impact on the environment and your budget. It becomes very satisfying to sail past the cleaning goods aisles in the supermarket, ignoring the signs that ask you to spend pounds and pounds on all the various bottles. The savings needn't stop at house-cleaning products, either. Even expensive washing powders can be made using a few very basic ingredients.

Cleaning Cupboard Basics

Note: while most of the following items are safe, you should keep *all* cleaners away from children and animals, because some, like the borax and washing soda, are poisonous or caustic.

- Washing soda
- Bicarbonate of soda
- Borax
- Lemon juice
- Salt
- Green household soap
- Vinegar
- Lavender and tea tree essential oils

Instead of buying special cloths and dusters, use old cotton clothes and sheets that have worn through or would be discarded otherwise. You can use poly-cotton, but it doesn't absorb as well as pure cotton. Cut the material you're using into as many useful-sized squares as you can get. I cut mine to about 40cm square, slightly bigger if it is a floor cloth. These can be washed over and over again, so they will last for months, if not years.

Household Cleaners

ALWAYS wear rubber gloves to protect your hands when using any of the cleaners in this chapter, and an apron to do the same with your clothes.

In the Kitchen

The following cleaners are all you need to keep your kitchen clean and fresh.

Universal Liquid Cleaner

This mixture is suitable for work surfaces and cleaning inside cupboards, worktops, tiles, paintwork, drainers and sinks in the home. It removes stains and also has antibacterial and antiviral actions.

50g bicarbonate of soda
50ml lemon juice
1 tablespoon salt
1 litre cold water

1. Put all the ingredients into a clean jug and stir until the salt has dissolved.
2. Pour into a spray bottle and use as you would a normal surface spray.
3. Wipe over with a clean cloth.

Floor Cleaner

This cleans, de-greases and shines large kitchen-floor areas. I add about 15 drops of lavender essential oil for fragrance and enhanced antibacterial action.

50g washing soda
50ml white vinegar
1 tablespoon salt
1 litre cold water

1. Mix together in a jug and pour into a spray bottle.
2. Wipe over with a damp mop and allow to dry. If it dries streaky, polish with a dry mop.

Oven and Hob Cleaner

This is suitable for tough areas to clean on any surface of oven or hob, so long as you use it with a cloth and not a scouring pad.

3 tablespoons washing soda
3 tablespoons salt
A little water

1. In a bowl, combine the soda and salt with enough water to mix into a scouring paste.
2. Use a dry cloth to work the mixture into tough areas of your hob or oven. Leave for a few seconds, then mix with a little extra water to make a liquid and wipe over the whole area using a damp cloth.
3. Rinse with a clean, wet cloth to remove the stains, build-up of grease and the spent mixture.
4. Polish with a dry cloth.

Fridge Cleaner

A combination that cleans and deodorises your fridge and kills bacteria.

2 tablespoons washing soda
2 tablespoons lemon juice
300ml water

1. Mix all ingredients together.
2. Pour small amounts onto a damp cloth and rub over all the surfaces in your fridge.

Washing Clothes

This is something I always used to spend a fortune on. With a family of five that included three rugby players, I was always washing, so I was amazed at the results I had with washing soda, especially on whites. It removes most stains and bad aromas and it disinfects. For a normal family washload in soft-water areas, use 3 tablespoons of washing soda. For the same in a hard-water area, use 4 tablespoons. For all woollens and delicates, I suggest using green soap in warm water as outlined below.

To remove stubborn stains, dampen the area with cold water and rub some green household soap into the stain and wash immediately. For greasy stains, rub first with green soap, then sprinkle on some washing soda also and rub in gently. Wash immediately.

For machine-washable woollens or delicate fabrics, dampen the garment, rub in a small amount of green household soap and wash.

For hand-washing delicates and woollens, fill a bowl or your sink with the desired heat of water and rub the green household soap into the water to dissolve some soap as though you were washing your hands, or grate about a 1–2 teaspoons of the soap into the warm water. Swirl the water to distribute the soap and allow it to dissolve if you're using the grating method. Wash and rinse as normal.

To make scented ironing waters, simply mix ordinary tap water with 8–10 drops of lavender, geranium, tea tree, rosemary or other essential oil (but avoid rose as this is usually mixed with a carrier oil). Mix together well and use as normal.

Simple Fabric Conditioner

2 teaspoons lemon juice
4 tablespoons water
1 teaspoon bicarbonate of soda

Mix the ingredients together and add about 10 drops of your favourite essential oil fragrance. Pour into the correct dispenser in your washing machine.

Washing up

Run water as hot as you normally use for washing your dishes and stir in 1 teaspoon of grated green household soap and 1 teaspoon of washing soda. If washing glasses, add 2 tablespoons of white vinegar to the water to make the glass shine. Rinse as usual.

Window cleaner

All your windows can be cleaned with this amazing ingredient. Pour a little white vinegar into a bowl. Dab a dry cloth into the vinegar and rub it over the windows for shiny, smear-free results.

The bathroom

You can use the Universal Liquid Cleaner on page 52 for most of your surfaces in the bathroom, including the floor.

For tough stains and grime in the sink, toilet bowl and bath

2 tablespoons borax
2 tablespoons bicarbonate of soda
2 tablespoons salt

1. Mix the 3 ingredients together and add a little water to make a paste.
2. Use on a cloth for the sink and bath and on the toilet brush for the toilet bowl.
3. Leave for 2–3 minutes, then rinse with cold water.
4. Polish the sink and bath with a dry cloth if you want extra shine.

To unblock drains in the kitchen and bathroom

For regular cleaning and degreasing drains, mix 4 tablespoons of borax with 200ml water and pour down the drain. For bad blockages, combine 4 tablespoons of washing soda and 4 tablespoons of borax with 500ml of hot water. Pour down the drain and leave for at least 8 hours.

The Living Areas

Carpets

Keep all small children and pets away from carpets when you are treating them for stains or giving them a general clean.

For stains, mop up any excess moisture immediately, then use 6 tablespoons of water mixed with 6 tablespoons of white vinegar and spray onto the affected part. Mop up with a dry cloth.

For bad or old stains, mix 1 tablespoon of borax with 1 tablespoon of salt and a little water to make a thick paste. Rub this into the stain and allow to dry. Vacuum up the dry powder.

To disinfect and freshen your carpet, sprinkle washing soda all over it in a thin layer, then brush it in lightly with a carpet brush. Leave for at least 3 hours, then vacuum thoroughly.

Upholstery

For small areas like arms or backs of sofas. Mix 2 tablespoons washing soda and 5 tablespoons warm water. Dip a cloth into the solution and wipe it over the affected area. Use a dry cloth to mop up any excess moisture.

Air and upholstery freshener

To freshen soft furnishings with a mild antibacterial and antiviral solution, fill a spray bottle with 400ml of water, 15 drops of tea tree essential oil and 20 drops of lavender oil. Shake well and spray directly onto curtains, carpets, sofas and chairs. This may also be sprayed into the centre of a room as an air freshener.

Furniture polish

Use a lidded glass jar and fill it with 50g beeswax and 50ml turpentine or turpentine substitute. Leave to combine for 3–4 days. Stir well and use with a soft, dry cloth as you would other polish. Remember: a little of this goes a long way.

Cleaning silverware

An easy method for cleaning everyday silver items. To clean family heirlooms or antique silver, always consult a specialist.

Put the items to clean in a bowl of tepid water. Scrunch up a 25cm square of aluminium foil and add this to the water, then stir in 1 teaspoon salt. Leave for 20 minutes, then rinse with clean water, dry on a tea towel and polish with a soft cloth.

For badly tarnished items, line a bowl with a sheet of foil, add a tablespoon of salt and the item to be cleaned and pour on hot or just-boiled water. You'll smell this working immediately, but don't breathe in the fumes. Leave for 10–20 minutes, rinse with clean water and polish with a soft cloth.

Making Soap

The invention of soap and detergents goes back into pre-Roman times in the UK, where it is said to have been invented. Most of the ancient world used olive oil to dissolve grease on their bodies, and sweat to make the olive oil come off the skin. This was removed with a stick called a *strigil* and a wash in cold water. However, in ancient Britain there were no such luxuries – but there was lanolin from sheep.

When boiled with wood ash, the mixture created a fat that dissolved in water but which would itself dissolve grease, and soap was born. Nonetheless, it took many centuries and an industrial process before soap became widespread, and it was still common for households to boil their own soap until late in the Victorian period.

Why make your own soap?

The simple answer is pure luxury. Like most of the recipes and processes in this book, homemade soap recipes make a product that is completely different to the stuff you buy in the shops. Homemade soap is a joy to use, nothing else like it exists – or if it does, it is usually very expensive. People who make their own have an experience like nothing else. Sure, you can buy soap that costs pennies, and if you were to earn cash for the time you spend making soap, you could afford to buy a lot of soap – but it will never be *your* soap, and if you can feel pride about a bar of soap, it *has* to be worth doing.

Making soap is basically a chemical reaction between fat or oil and an alkali, namely sodium hydroxide – otherwise known as caustic soda or lye. The major issue with soap-making is learning to handle lye safely. Once mastered, it is fairly simple.

Yet you don't have to start by making soap from raw materials. You can make soap – simple but luxurious soap – at a fraction of the cost you will pay for the same product from the shops by using the melt-and-pour method.

The Melt-and-Pour Method

You can buy ready-made soap in flakes, chips or whole blocks. It is referred to as glycerine soap, which has only to be melted and adapted to make your own personal version. In essence, it is a soap base that you can modify yourself. This way of making soap is not cheating, for you can make quite a number of interesting and perfect-looking soaps that are also available for use straight away, without the need for curing it.

Glycerine soap is made from the commercial soap industry and has to be retreated to turn into soap with a low melting point. It is easily melted in a bowl over steam, and once melted completely, you can add almost anything to it, stir it in and leave it to set.

Using soap base allows you to make speciality soaps without the fuss of using lye, so it is a perfect starting point for first-time soap-makers. Equally, you can prepare soap that you know is ideal for your particular skin type or that of your family members. It is important to seek medical attention for skin ailments, but it is possible to make your own medical soap, such as coal-tar soap.

Setting and thickness

In order to make your own soap from base material you will frequently add liquids, a process that has a tendency to weaken the set of the soap. There are two ways of dealing with this: either add a sheet of gelatine, or add salt.

The simple method

Whichever way you get your base soap, be it flakes or a block, it has to be melted in a bowl placed over boiling water. That's all there is to it. Then you can start to add various ingredients to make *your* soap. You can add food colourings or fragrances. A few drops of each, completely mixed, is usually enough. It's best if you make a weaker fragrant soap at first than a too-concentrated bar that causes you to have skin problems. The process is one of experimentation, although it helps if you know what kind of soap you require.

Disinfectant soap

An excellent melt-and-pour soap to use is lavender or tea tree. For the latter you'll have to buy tea tree essential oil and add a few drops, experimenting to find exactly the right concentration for your skin-type. You can make your own lavender water very easily using a steamer (see below).

Whenever you add liquid to soap, bubbles often appear; these aren't detrimental to the final soap, but they do make it look a bit messy. You can simply scoop the bubbles off or spray them with some rubbing alcohol. It is important to remove the bubbles if you're planning to sell it or give it away as a present.

MAKING LAVENDER WATER

You can mix this liquid with melted soap base to make lavender soap, but you might need to thicken it as described. Usually you have to re-melt the soap and add a spoonful of salt. If it doesn't set then, add a sheet of gelatine or more soap base.

1. Pack the first 'pan' of your steamer with lavender flowers and place it over the boiler section, filled with about 600ml of water, in the normal way. Put the lid on securely and put a cold cloth over it. You need a wet, cold cloth which you are going to keep constantly cool by rinsing it in cold water; this helps the steam condense quicker so that it circulates from water to steam more often, getting more oils out of the lavender. Make sure it cannot be caught out by a flame.

2. Boil the water and set it on a moderate simmer so that the steam passes through the lavender flowers and drips back through them into the reservoir. Continue this for 30 minutes, making sure it doesn't boil dry.

Using moulds

You can buy different types of moulds, but be wary of using glass ones because these can crack if hot liquid is poured into them. We tend to collect the plastic trays that hold products (such as yoghurt) on supermarket shelves, as they often have interesting shapes. Certain chocolate packages have hexagonal bases that make excellent soap moulds, too.

Avoid making huge bars of soap – in fact, the smaller the better. The problem with large bars of gelatine soap is that it can go messy around the edges where water has been left in contact with it, so you need to make sure the soap is stored in dry conditions, especially when it is being used at a sink.

Using Lye

You can buy lye (caustic soda) from soap-making suppliers. You should take all necessary precautions when working with lye in any fashion. You'll need goggles, rubber gloves and old clothes, so be warned: you'll look a little like a mad scientist. In addition, you'll need to dissolve the lye in clean water in a pan that you will, from then on, use for nothing else. Remember, always add the caustic soda to the water – *never* the other way around. Your lye solution is strong enough when you can get an egg to float in it.

Making your own lye

You can also make your own lye. All you need is a barrel with a tap in it and some rainwater. The rainwater is important because it makes the best soap.

In the bottom of a barrel place some bricks, then a layer of straw about 20–30cm deep, and then about 10cm of fine stones. All of this makes a filter. On top of this fill the barrel with wood ash, then pour on about 5 buckets full of rainwater. Leave for a day and pour off. If the egg will float, fine; if not, add more ashes and pour the liquid from the barrel back over them. Repeat this until the egg will float. Don't forget to wear gloves and goggles.

 MAKING SOAP FROM WOOD-ASH LYE

This is the old cottager's method of making soap. They called it 'boiling up soap', and since it took such a long time, you can appreciate how industrial soap manufacture superseded it very quickly. Before you begin, make sure you have used the egg test to make sure there is enough concentration of lye in the soap.

1. Take an old pan and put it on a low heat.

2. Add your fat – you will need about 13g of lye for every 100g fat or oil. This is a good way to use a large piece of pork fat, cut into cubes. You can save the fat from various joints.

3. Over a number of hours, keep on adding small amounts of lye, mixing well. After a while the fat will melt and react with the lye; just keep adding the lye until the fat has changed: the soap will leave marks on the surface. This is called the 'trailing' or 'streaky' stage.

4. Keep cooking the fat, adding lye every 10–15 minutes. From there, once the fat in the pan has changed, turn off the heat and beat with a wooden spoon until you have a well-incorporated mixture.

5. Once cooled you will have soap suitable for washing clothes.

MAKING SOAP FROM PACKET LYE

Packet lye is often sold as drain cleaner, and is labelled 99% caustic soda of sodium hydroxide. Keep this safely locked away from children.

You will need 13g of lye for every 100g fat or oil. **This lye must be dissolved in water at a quantity of 40ml for every 100g of fat or oil.**

Basic instructions

1. Assemble your materials and utensils beforehand, including safety wear such as goggles, gloves, old clothes, etc. Also have a bowl of water ready in case of splashes – especially on your skin.

2. Measure the appropriate amount of lye and water in separate containers. Remember: always add lye to the water – not the other way around – and make sure you don't splash anything.
When you add the lye to the water it will get hot – *very* hot, perhaps even boiling. There will also be fumes, so make sure you do this in a well-ventilated room. Stir with a wooden spoon until the lye is all dissolved.

3. Heat your fat until it is melted and then, by the judicious use of heat or cooled water in bowls, make both the liquids reach 37°C at the same time. When you've managed this to within a degree, stir the fat while pouring the lye into the pan.

4. Keep stirring. You need to stir until the soap thickens. Eventually, having stirred for 5 minutes out of every 10 for an hour, the soap will leave marks on the surface. This is called the 'trailing' or 'streaky' stage, and it means that the soap is nearly finished. At this point you can then add colours and fragrances.

5. Pour the liquid into moulds and leave it to set. If the soap refuses to set, re-melt it and add some salt – usually a teaspoon is enough – and try again.

6. Use a knife to remove any rough edges and cut the soap into bars.

7. Leave the soap to cure. Over a month it will harden and come to resemble 'real' soap. This is achieved mainly by the evaporation of water. The soap will shrink slightly.

Lye Soap Recipes

Simply follow the basic instructions on page 61, using the ingredients listed below. These recipes have proven themselves both easy and safe.

Oatmeal Soap

280ml palm oil
150ml olive oil
¼ cup oatmeal
50g lye
220ml water for the lye

Olive Oil Soap

1.5 litres olive oil
180g lye
600ml water for the lye

Rustic Lavender Soap

500ml olive oil
500ml coconut oil
500ml palm oil
180g lye
500ml lavender water (see page 59)

Lard Soap

This is a basic soap that you can use to prepare numerous homemade soaps.
It will need to cure for a month once set properly. You can add all kinds of aromas to
your soap but don't infuse them with petals. We tried this once, and although they
looked lovely when first made, the end result was always messy. Invariably the petals
went black, and eventually worked themselves loose in the sink.

1.5kg lard
180g lye
500ml water

Recombination Soap

This is the easiest way of making soap because you don't actually 'make it'. Essentially
you take all the bits of soap left in the kitchen and bathroom before they vanish away
into uselessness and pat them dry. Collect them until you can simply melt them all
together and make a new bar.

This is an ideal way of making green washing soap. A lot of people used to buy
green soap and grate it to melt with collected soap at a ratio of 50:50. Since green
washing soap is very mild, you can use it as a basis for treatment soaps. For example,
you can melt it down and add some concentrated lavender water. Mix it carefully; most
of the water will evaporate in the melting and you will be left with a medicated bar.

Another soap we've made in this way consists of adding some oatmeal to the
melted green soap. This gives it some abrasive qualities. I've used this soap at the rugby
club for years. It is especially good for getting mud out of stud wounds – but you have
to close your eyes and rub!

II

In the Garden

Grandma's Garden

Although we grew up in an inner-city area, we used to be fairly self-sufficient in vegetables, eggs, chicken, and rabbit; some of us even kept goats and pigs. Our family used to have two dustbins. One of these was literally a dustbin, because whatever packaging there was on our shopping ended up keeping us warm in the fire, and the ashes from this bin were usually used on the garden.

Our other bin was known as the 'swill bin', because it held all the scrapings from our plates, and it was collected once a week by the swill man. This went to feed pigs at the local pig farm, and we got a capon each Christmas as payment.

Legislation today

How this world has gone! For a start, you cannot get capons – castrated cockerels – in the UK any more because the way they were produced has been outlawed. A capon was created by injecting a cockerel with a pellet in the neck, which chemically castrated it; this had the function of making it grow unusually large – which, of course, meant more meat on the table.

On top of this, it has become illegal these days to feed *any* animal on scraps. Even your backyard hens aren't exempt from this regulation, which was originally designed to keep the possibilities of spreading foot-and-mouth and other diseases to an absolute minimum.

Finally, you're not allowed to keep certain livestock in an urban setting any more at all. You need permission from the Department for Environment, Food and Rural Affairs (DEFRA) to keep goats and pigs – something most of us with an urban council house could never hope to gain. Such DEFRA licensing numbers are only issued to people with land that has been defined as having 'agricultural access' and this doesn't include domestic gardens, no matter how self-sufficient we can show ourselves to be.

The outlook for local livestock

Many councils around the country are using by-laws to prevent people from keeping livestock on council land, with the result that today, most allotments do not allow hens, bees, goats or pigs to be kept there.

While one can see a certain amount of sense in these laws as they apply to hygiene and human and animal health, as usual, they have been taken to extremes in many cases. Because of this, Diana and I are campaigning to allow people to keep a minimum level of livestock on their land – two hens, a couple of ducks – and a wider range of livestock on allotments: a couple of goats and a pig for each one.

All this is a long way off, of course, so in this book, we have concentrated on what you can (legally) do at the moment. We do look forward, however, to amending a later edition!

What you can do

Even given the current restrictions, you can still do an awful lot towards feeding yourself and your family, and, to be honest, the fewer animals you keep, the less land you need. Besides, you can always get some meat if you have a friendly field nearby and permission from the landowner to shoot the odd rabbit.

When it comes to any livestock, you must always be professional in all you do – even more so if you live in an urban environment. Don't just take this section of the book as a guide to how to perform various livestock functions such as feeding and housing; you must also learn how to kill your animals properly, whether for food or out of mercy if they are suffering in any way, from someone who really knows how to do it and can talk you, show you and watch you through the process. It is important that you can do it properly, and like everything else, you cannot learn these things with one eye in your book and the other on your task.

Finally, be discrete. Even if you are killing your chicken because it is irrevocably ill, make sure that you have somewhere you can do it without prompting the neighbours to call the RSPCA.

More than anything else, never lose the wonderful fact that as the world turns, summer and winter it is bursting with life at every stage. The fact that you have wonderful bounty from the garden because of the sun and rain is marvellously satisfying – a fact that should be remembered and celebrated at all times.

Growing Herbs

No kitchen garden would be complete without a constant supply of herbs. If you're to be truly self-sufficient, or simply want to do more for yourself just as your grandparents did, you need herbs: for teas, for flavour, for health and for use in all kinds of remedies and potions for use around the house as well as around the body (see pages 33–50).

There is a tradition of growing herbs as near to the kitchen as possible, partly for convenience and partly because of the aroma. This stems from the time when people believed that disease was caused by bad air, and thought herbs somehow made the air good. The idea of growing herbs by the kitchen door is fine – *if* you have space for them. Otherwise, anywhere will do so long as you don't have to travel a long distance with them. On a hot day, herbs can become less than appetising in a few minutes, so use them as soon as possible. One of the best way of bringing cut herbs home from an allotment is to wrap them in a wet towel.

Seeds or plants?

It is possible to grow many herbs from seed, but it's probably not practical. Many nurseries sell good-quality plants that you can grow on in pots and borders. This is probably the best way of making a good herb selection for little cost, because you know they are all healthy, good-quality plants.

You can also buy a limited selection of herbs from the supermarket. Most sell them as 'living herbs', usually chives, basil, mint and a few others, and they are usually of pretty poor quality and flavour. Pot them on to a larger pot, or better still, put them in a bed of good compost, however, and within a couple of weeks they will be running away with themselves.

Sowing herbs from seed can be a bit hit-and-miss in some cases, but plants such as rocket and dandelion are very good at germinating and reliably giving you a good crop.

Why bother with herbs?

This might seem like a silly question, but many people genuinely have forgotten how to use herbs in their daily lives.

First of all, there's the issue of flavour. Herbs make the difference between a simple flavour and a fuller-tasting, delicious, more correctly seasoned food. You might be able to make an omelet just using eggs, but one with chives added to it is so much more appetising. A casserole without bay leaves is all right, but add a couple of bay leaves and there is a difference: it might be subtle, but it is there. The difference herbs make to a meal can be just as much about educating your palette. Herbs are tasty!

They're good for you. Herbs are almost as important as medicine when it comes to keeping you healthy. (If you're ever ill, of course, don't just run to the herb garden and treat yourself, expecting miracles; always seek medical advice.) What herbs are excellent at is *keeping* you healthy. Garlic is a case in point; it has been proven as an antiseptic, antibiotic and antiviral. It has been shown to reduce high blood pressure, decrease the blockage of arteries and improve blood circulation, it helps the heart and was responsible for saving countless thousands in the First World War because the government made field dressings impregnated with garlic, which significantly reduced infection.

They make life sweet. Herbs such as sage and lavender are good at dealing with aromas around the home. The kitchen and bathroom are made so much sweeter – and safer – by the use of an aerosol spray of disinfectant lavender water.

Growing Herbs

Any plant that gives off strong aromas or has bright colours, or both, is usually hungry for nutrients. Herbs should be grown in beds of deeply dug soil that is enriched with a 50:50 mix of compost and really well-rotted manure. I have found that a 2m x 1m bed is ideal for a mixed herb bed, and to this I would add a full wheelbarrow of this compost mix.

Of course, you can grow herbs in containers of all kinds. As a general and very rough rule, only grow plants so that they achieve a height equal to the height of the pot plus its diameter of the pot. You will not go too far wrong using this as a guide. If you're growing herbs in a pot, then fill it with a 75:25 mixture of compost to very well-rotted manure.

Herb starter kit

You can easily buy plants, more or less at any time, that are not only easy to grow but will really increase not only your knowledge and culinary experiences, but your confidence. As a starter, try lavender, thyme, parsley, lemon balm, sage, chives and garlic. Others to try, which need a little more attention and are more difficult to grow, include rosemary, basil, coriander and marjoram.

Sowing

Nearly all herb seeds are sown in the same way. Plant them in modules filled with John Innes No1-type compost. Plant two seeds per pot and select the strongest-growing plant. If you can use a propagator lid, then do so until the seedlings become established. I tend to water with a spray in the first week, but once they have germinated, just moisten the compost to avoid fungal infections.

Planting on

When the plants are as big as their container, they can easily be potted on to their growing positions. Harden them off over a week, preferably at least after the third week in May, when the danger of frost is past.

Give them plenty of water at this stage to enable them to cope with the shock of being transplanted.

Caring for Your Herbs

Obviously, all plants have different requirements. Some, like sage, prefer to be dry in the summer, but it doesn't matter that much if you water them. Generally keep all your herbs reasonably moist, but not wet. You should give them a feed with liquid manure once a month. In winter, cover with a cloche or horticultural fleece and you will have some leaves available for use.

When pot-grown herbs get bigger than the height plus the diameter of their pots, transplant them to the next-sized pot – but never put a small plant in a large pot.

Basil

This is an easy-grow plant. It needs a rich soil and sunshine, and that's that. Simply sow three seeds in a 8cm pot of moist compost and keep it around 16°C. They will germinate within a week or so and you should prick out the fastest-growing ones. Pot on in May or plant in a border. I always sow fresh to use on a constant basis; basil will outlast the winter if pampered, but I just don't think it's worth the effort. Water only the roots, or at least water just the soil around them and don't drench the plant in order to avoid fungal problems.

Chives

You should grow chives everywhere. Line borders with them, grow them among your potatoes and in between rows of other vegetables. This can be grown from seeds (simply broadcast), or bought in pots and broken into clumps. Divide them in the spring and again in the autumn, increasing your crop. They overwinter well as long as they get some respite from driving cold, wet winds.

All the chive is useful and good to eat. It is packed with sulphonamide molecules, which are good antibacterial agents. The roots are supposed to be good for decongesting the lungs, and the flowers are pretty as an edible garnish. Besides, they look pretty!

Coriander

Coriander is a member of the carrot family, an annual, so it goes to seed quite easily. Don't worry; just keep taking the leaves and then take the seeds when ripe. The seeds are used in curries and have an astringency; steep a few in boiled water and, when cooled, you'll have a good mouthwash.

Sow outdoors in May in well-prepared soil and 3cm drills. They usually germinate in a couple of weeks and when they have pushed themselves through the soil, thin them to 20cm apart.

Dill

You need dill seeds to make pickled gherkins. This member of the carrot family is fun to grow, and I just love salmon with dill sauce – it's wonderful!

Sow in April in a drill, or in modules indoors in March. Dill is not happy with frost, but if you grow it in pots, just bring them indoors for a winter stock. Keep moist but not wet, and if you do grow this herb in a pot, make sure the pot is at least 45cm deep, because once the roots reach the bottom they stop the plant from growing.

Lavender

We've been growing lavender in a large tub for ten years. The plants generally like full sun and dry conditions, but they don't mind a drop of rain.

You can grow them from seed, sown in April and kept at room temperature. If you buy lavender as a young plant, however, it is easier to grow because it can be frustratingly slow at reaching a plantable specimen when grown from seed. Each spring, give it a good mulch of rich compost and during the summer give it some liquid tomato feed. Trim the plant in winter and you will be rewarded with many fragrant flowers the following summer.

Mint

Mint is one of the most invasive plants in the garden. Plant it in one spot and it will be turning up all over the show. For this reason I usually grow it in a pot – actually a number of pots. You can bury this in the ground if you like, so it looks like the rest of the border, but I have grown it in hanging baskets and growbags with great success.

There are more varieties of mint than any other plant we eat. Apple mint tastes of apple, spearmint is generally used for topping ice cream, peppermint is the hot one that makes the best mint tea. So long as you keep it moist and the soil rich, your mint will grow, whatever type it is. Replace your stock once every three years. You can divide the plants, or take cuttings in the autumn.

Parsley

Like mint, parsley is a hungry plant. Insects don't like it, so grow it in pots everywhere to keep them at bay. Curled-leaf and flat-leaf parsley are treated the same in the garden, and have very similar flavours. They also have similar use in the kitchen. Flat-leaf parsley chops up better in a salad. Seeds take a while to germinate, and most people simply start their stock from plants.

If you persevere with seeds sown in modules, however, you can get a large stock of plants in only a few months. Collect seeds from old plants for next year. Once in compost, it grows well. Feed monthly and do not pick any leaves until the plant is at least three months old.

You can divide in autumn to increase stock.

Rosemary

Rosemary prefers a sandy soil. Use 50 percent compost, 25 percent sand and 25 percent well-rotted manure. Rosemary is best grown from bought plants in a very sunny spot. Pot on to a large pot in the first year and then place them in a sunny border. They will stay here for about twenty years.

Between May and September, water if the soil is bone-dry, but otherwise leave them alone save for a liquid feed once in June and once in August.

In October simply trim the plant so that it keeps its shape and doesn't become straggly and unruly.

Sage

Sage takes about a fortnight to germinate and from there is fairly slow-growing until it needs to be planted out. But it is quite a strong plant and produces great-flavoured leaves and exquisite flowers. It is such a lovely plant that I am amazed we don't grow it for its looks alone.

All this plant needs is good sunshine. It is helped by a monthly feed from liquid fertiliser, but from there it simply has the summer to grow and produce a wonderful flavour.

Sow in April and harden off in June, then pot on or place in borders. In the winter it will die back a little, but if you protect from frost you will have a supply throughout the colder months. Divide the plants in autumn or take cuttings.

Apart from stuffing and flavouring many dishes, sage is an antibacterial plant that can help with all kinds of illnesses. Sage tea is made by dropping a few leaves in boiling water, steeping for about 5 minutes, then flavouring with lemon and honey if desired. This was once a Greek remedy for T.B., but it is actually very good for a sore throat due to its antibacterial properties.

Tarragon

Tarragon has been grown in the UK for centuries and is used to flavour seafood and chicken dishes as well as omelettes. It is slow-growing but will reach a height of 1m. Because of this, the plant is best grown in a border.

Buy young plants to start off – it's much easier – and transplant them in May. You can take cuttings in autumn; keep them in a cool, frost-free place and plant them out in the following May.

Thyme

Thyme is not the easiest plant to grow because it likes a hot, dry climate. It can become twiggy and sparse in a British summer.

Thyme grows to a height of about 30cm with a spread of around the same dimension. While it may not be the easiest to grow if planted out in the UK, it is actually ideal for pot growing and will remain good to harvest for several years, as long as you allow it good sunlight and not too much moisture.

This is one of the herbs best bought as a plant and transplanted. You can increase your stock by taking cuttings in the autumn.

The Kitchen Garden

There is such an elegance to be experienced in the growing of vegetables and fruit. Flowers are exciting and beautiful and all that, but you don't get the grace of the leek or the expectation of the swelling pod, or the purely unknown results of pulling carrots. Vegetable gardening has, for the purist, elements you just cannot get from the flower bed. But then, you do get to eat what you grow!

Enough to eat

In the UK we used to have an understandable fascination, almost a national worry, that we were going to get enough to eat each year. Would the potatoes last until next summer? Were there enough peas or carrots or, worse still, would the onions stay fresh? This psyche has its origins in bad times, when common land was taken to support the rich and when farming began shedding its workforce to the towns.

As the eighteenth century passed, the only reliable source of much of the food for townsfolk was the garden. Great tracts of land owned by the church were given over as allotments, and people survived on these. Until the 1950s, half of everyone's food was home-grown.

Today we don't depend on home-grown food. Instead, it is grown in every corner of the world. Where once we didn't eat a tomato from October to June, these days they are plentiful every month of the year. This bounty comes because the tomatoes are shipped from Brazil or Kenya, and it may not be costly in terms of money, but it is very expensive for the environment.

So the greenest thing you can do for the environment is to grow some food in your garden, on the footpath, the balcony or even the roof, for that matter, but think quality over quantity. By giving your attention to detail to make brilliant tomatoes rather than just tomatoes, not only will you have the best produce, but the quantity will easily increase so that you have enough to last the year.

How much do I need, then?

If you reckon that a plant needs half a square metre, on average, to provide a crop, then you can work out the area you need, especially since you can more or less say this space will provide a family of four with two meals.

Consequently, half a square metre of carrots might yield nine carrots, a single potato plant will provide between five and ten good-sized tubers, and so on.

If you multiply your favourite vegetables in this way you should have a very rough idea of how much to plant. For example, our family – a very hungry family, I must add – eats the equivalent of one potato plant a week, so I grow thirty of them, which is around five rows at about 4m long, spaced around 75cm between the rows. In this I plant first earlies and then maincrop potatoes, and they last probably until Easter because there are always some losses to fungus, vermin and so on.

Grandad's Techniques

The way we garden these days has changed out of all recognition compared to that of yesteryear, a number of traditional techniques we're not used to using are still worth thinking about. For example, hardly anyone these days would know what a riddle was or how to use it. We use modules to sow seeds in, whereas our grandparents used trays of compost and pricked out the seedlings to successively bigger pots. Cloche gardening – covering plants with glass – was not only time-consuming, but expensive, as each 'merry tinkle' indicated that yet another pane of glass had to be replaced. With horticultural fleece and polytunnels, the modern gardener has a lot of aces up his sleeve when it comes to growing, but none of these improve gardening more than bagged compost and growbags, which allow you grow food practically anywhere.

Trenches

Trenches are dug for a number of crops that have a heavy need for nutrients. A trench is simply a long hole, often as much as 5m long and around 60cm deep and across. The lower half of the trench is filled with fresh peelings and other material you would normally compost. When half-full, you simply cover with soil to fill in the rest of the hole. The material will rot down, releasing its nutrients to the soil. You have to prepare a bed like this well in advance of its use, maybe as much as six months earlier, but you do get very rich soil. As the material rots, the level of the soil might lower, so you'll also have to fill in any excess.

Sowing seed

Sowing in a tray is the starting point because all you learn here is transferable to other methods. In Grandma's day they used wooden seed trays which looked a little like the tangerine boxes you see these days. You can still buy seed trays, and because they are made from plastic, many also have propagator covers to keep the wind away from the germinating seedlings. Use good-quality seed compost when filling a tray, and fill it to just below the lip. Use a piece of wood that just fits inside the seed tray to tamp down the compost. This makes a firm substrate that looks very neat. The neatness is actually an important part of the process, because it encourages accuracy and cleanliness.

Open your seed packet in such a way that it can be resealed easily and pour some seeds into your hand; hold these palm up, so that the seeds rest in the fold of your palm. Use a piece of cane to mark off a strip at one end of the tray, then, with your free hand, carefully tap the seed-holding hand so that the seeds drop one at a time onto the compost and you have an even spread. Move the cane down a little and repeat again and again until you have gone down the tray.

Sprinkle some compost on top of the seeds and firm down, then finally give them a watering from a can with a fine rose. If you have a propagator lid, fix it in place.

Sowing in modules

When you sow in a tray, the seeds grow en masse and you have to prick them out into pots (see next page). Growing in modules is different because you sow a couple of seeds in a tray that has up to 24 separate compartments. Fill and firm these with compost in the same way as above, and sow two seeds in each compartment. As the seeds grow, you'll have to decide which one to discard. Always choose the strongest.

Nurture the growing plants until they are large enough to be pushed out of the module into a bed or larger pot.

The advantage of the module is you don't have to handle the plant at the seedling stage and thus get a much stronger plant when you pot it on.

Temperature and damping off

Most seedlings will germinate at around 15°C. Any temperature above 10°C will promote the growth of fungal spores and your seeds may get a messy disease called 'damping off'. Control this by keeping the humidity as low as possible. If you have a propagator lid, then remove it for some time each day, and don't overwater the seedlings. If you can, water from beneath by dipping the tray in water.

Some seeds will germinate only at higher temperatures – certainly some of the more exotic plants, such as chillies. The higher the temperature, the greater chance of damping off, so work hard at keeping the humidity down.

Sowing in drills

A drill is merely a straight line. Prepare your soil and mark out a line with a garden string. Normally drills for sowing are a finger's depth. Use a hoe to create a small 'V' in the soil and sow in this. Once sown, the soil is simply folded over using a garden rake and then firmed down by a gentle tapping with the back of the rake head.

Pricking out and potting on

We hardly ever prick out seedlings these days, but it is a great technique if you have to handle seedlings in general. There is one fundamental concept to keep in mind, however: NEVER TOUCH THE STEM OF A SEEDLING.

Usually seedlings are sown in a tray of compost and, having been sown roughly, will germinate and grow, but too close together. You have to remove them and put them into individual pots so that they can grow normally without any encumbrance from near neighbours. Prepare where they are going before you prick them out – this is usually an 8cm pot of compost. Fill the pot with compost and firm it down. Use a small dibber (generally a pencil) to create a hole to take the seedling.

Using the same pencil, push in next to the seedling and, *holding the leaf*, lever the plant out of the compost. Do not pull up by the leaf; just hold it steady.

Use the pencil as a guide, gently insert the root into the hole you have previously made in the pot. Firm in gently with the pencil. Give your new plant a good watering and place it in a cool but sunny spot to recover from its ordeal.

'Potting on' is self-explanatory. As the roots grow inside the pot, they begin to need more room. The plant needs either to go into a second, larger pot, or into the soil of a bed or border. If the next home for the plant is to be a pot, make sure it is the next size up from the original; it's not good enough to pot a plant directly from a 8cm to a 30cm pot in one jump.

Put some crocks for drainage on the floor of the bigger pot, followed by some compost. Then put your hand over the top of the pot you're transplanting from, and, with the plant held securely but gently between your fingers, turn the pot over and give it a sharp tap on the base. This should dislodge the plant, compost and all, and it will now be held securely in your hand.

Place the plant in your new pot, and add fresh compost all around it. Firm this in and water well afterwards.

Hardening off

You might sow seedlings at 25°C, and once the seedlings have germinated, have to plant them outside at temperatures that are much cooler than this. In the normal course of things, the plants will be fine at daytime temperatures, but the night can be much colder. I remember recently the temperature reaching -1°C in June.

Hardening off acclimatises young plants to growing at local temperatures. If the day is pleasant, put the plants outside during the day and bring them indoors at night. Repeat this for a full week, and when you're sure there will be no frost, let them stay out at night, too. Then, after a couple of days, you can plant them in their final growing positions.

Compost

These days there are many different ways of making compost. Most of them add up to different ways of spending money on all kinds of paraphernalia. Basically, all you need is a receptacle – one that 'breathes' – and that's it. I know that those systems that use worms make something like compost, but if you feed them something full of bacteria (*E. coli* is a common example), the resulting compost will have even more bacteria in it than when you started.

In my experience, aerator compost drums don't work. They never really get hot enough and are very expensive for what they do. You can buy many hundreds of bags of compost for the cost of one of these.

Good old-fashioned compost heaps have three needs: heat, air and water – nothing else. Maintain the heat portion of the heap by insulating it, or having it so large that the outer portion of the heap acts as insulation. Get the heap hot and what you have left behind is germ-free and weed-free.

Grandad's composter was made from what were then 'newfangled' (he used that word a lot) pallets that seem to be everywhere these days. He had two of them with the wood nailed together in the shape of a large letter 'E'. It gave him two bays: one he was making new compost in, the other was a receptacle for 'turning' the compost.

When the compost was ready, he put it into a large bin, again made from pallets, as a reservoir of material to use. From this he made all kinds of mixtures of soil and sand and peat (although we don't use peat nowadays, of course).

What to compost

Everything except:

- Meat, fish and gravy or bones or anything animal-based (these attract rats)
- No perennial weeds unless you have completely killed them beforehand
- Nothing diseased: nothing with blight or any visible diseases on it

You'll hear a lot of talk about getting the mixture right when it comes to composting, as though it were some sort of garden cooking. The truth is you should be able to compost anything with one proviso: if using grass cuttings, mix them with newspaper to soak up the liquid. ('Don't mess with it, lad. Just get on with it!' I can hear him now.)

Make sure that any material added to your compost remains warm. Throw old carpet, bubble wrap, plastic sheets over the heap – anything you have on hand to insulate it. Collect a bucket full of scraps to compost and add this to the heap in one go rather than adding a little each day.

Water

Your heap needs liquid. You can use rainwater, urine … anything, really. About a bucket every two months keeps the microbes working, because as they reproduce, the heat kills them off in the centre of the heap.

Turning

After about five months you will need to refresh the air in the heap. This is best done by shovelling all the contents of the heap from one receptacle to the next. After this, the heap should get really hot and will be finished in approximately another two months. You can tell when compost is ready because it is friable, dryish and has a wonderfully earthy smell.

After you've turned your heap, start another in the first bed. By the time you've used your finished compost, you'll be ready to turn the first bed again.

What to do with your compost

Grandad was a great believer in John Innes compost. It wasn't a product, but a recipe. John Innes was a merchant who bequeathed land for a horticultural research station. They needed a growing medium that would always remain the same, whoever used it. The John Innes Centre produced four recipes:

- John Innes Seed Compost, for sowing the majority of seeds (but no one uses this much today)
- John Innes Potting Compost No 1, for sowing large seeds and pricking out the majority of seedlings
- John Innes Potting Compost No 2, for potting on young plants into larger pots
- John Innes Potting Compost No 3, for final potting of mature plants

Unfortunately, you simply cannot get many of the constituents of the original John Innes No 1 compost (hoof and horn are generally impossible to get these days). But to make a close approximation, add 1kg of all-round fertiliser to the modern John Innes No 1. This compost will do for most situations.

Why use John Innes-type compost?

I cannot count the number of times I've bought so-called organic compost, or special 'super compost', only to see my plants rotting away in a product that is obviously not fit for its purpose. The problem is that we have become lazy and no longer recognise good compost when we do see it. Making your own John Innes-type compost is about the best (and only) way to ensure a perfect product.

Leaf mould

Fallen leaves make an excellent compost. You should collect as many leaves as you can and compost them. Grandad had a wire basket he used to push leaves into, but these days a string net will do just as well. To compost leaves, you need lots of air. Just pile them up and you will have a great seed compost a year later, no turning needed.

The composting conundrum

If all you ever do is to compost material grown in your own garden, your fertility will diminish year on year. There is no such thing as a free lunch and if you eat crops and do not bring anything in from outside the plot, your soil will deteriorate – even if you grow 'green manures'.

Leaf mould is an excellent way of bringing in nutrients from the outside; so is the sensible use of mineral fertiliser. In Victorian times, they used crushed rock, and you can still get this material today. You get an enormous increase in productivity in the garden with the application of crushed rock, but don't make the mistake of thinking this is all you need; your soil needs organic matter, which is why the John Innes compost is made from both organics and minerals.

The hot bed

This is a trench dug deeply to 75cm and can be as large as you can afford. Half the soil is mixed with compost, and the rest is placed elsewhere in the garden. Fill the trench with fresh cow manure as deep as 45cm, then fill the rest of the hole with soil. The manure will begin to rot and get hot. In this soil/compost mixture you can sow seedlings early in the year.

Many gardeners in Grandma's day would have seedlings in the ground as early as January in a hot bed covered by a cold frame or in a greenhouse.

Tools

A working garden needs a couple of spades, a hoe, a general-purpose garden rake, a trowel, a garden fork, a garden line, a pair of secateurs, two very sharp knives (one penknife and a larger one), hundreds of canes for support and a wheelbarrow as an absolute minimum.

Getting a tool that suits you

Buying a spade is a personal thing. It should be wooden-handled, with the grain running down the shaft, and there should be no nicks or pinches to catch your skin along the shaft. The handle, regardless of whether it is a 'D a 'T' type, should not pinch or force you to hold it in any way that is uncomfortable. There should be no rivets protruding a long way, and where the shaft meets the blade, the join should be seamless.

When you hold it in your hands it should have a pleasing balance and be neither too heavy nor appear weak. If you've not had any exercise before and have just decided to dig, buy the smallest spade that is practical and fits you well. Then buy a larger one in three months' time, when you've gained strength as a digger.

Care of tools

You will no doubt remember your parents telling you to look after things. Today we're expected to use something until it becomes unfashionable, then throw it away and get another, more fashionable one. The same principle drives all businesses, and garden tools are no exception. In Grandma's day, however, everyone knew how to recognise a good tool and how to look after it and the pride was in making it last a lifetime – maybe two – rather than how 'up to date' it was.

Nearly all garden tools are used for cutting through soil, and it is important that you keep them up to scratch during their lifetime. One of the first things to do when you've finished using a tool is to wipe it clean. You need somewhere to keep your tools out of the wet, and you should always endeavour to return them. It doesn't have to be a shed, either. On my allotment I had a hidden box secreted away under my muck heap. People would break into the shed, which I eventually just left open to avoid the damage to the door, but they would never think of looking under the muck heap for anything valuable.

I also made a large wooden box, about 60cm square, without a lid. Filled with sand and about a cup full of motor oil dribbled over the surface, this makes the ideal finisher and lubricator for all your cutting tools. Once you have finished with them, wipe them clean and give them a few plunges into the oily sand.

You will find digging much easier if you keep your tools sharp. Go over the cutting blade at least once a year with a good metalworker's file. This will sharpen it and save you at least five to ten percent effort when using it.

Grandad's Digging

There are a number of interesting digging techniques we hardly ever do these days. Digging a deep hole for trenching is quite hard work, and you therefore need to know how to dig with as little effort as possible.

Firstly, if you're new to digging, limit yourself to 15 minutes a session. This will save your back. You can increase the number of sessions daily, but do not exceed three per day for a couple of months. Protect your back; it's no use digging all day and then being laid up for the next fortnight with a bad back.

Don't put too much on the spade. If you dig a piece of earth and then try the Herculean task of lifting it, especially if it is nearly all clay, you will not be digging for long. Never try to shift much more than half a spadeful at any one time. Two digs well within your capacity are worth one dig beyond it any time.

Dig with your arms and legs. In all circumstances dig with a straight back. Don't lean over your spade; stand tall next to it. Lift and twist with your arms, and with anything heavy, either don't attempt it or keep your arms and back straight and lift with your legs with a standing motion.

Why dig at all?

There are many people who suggest that the non-dig garden is the way of the future. By placing compost on the ground, growing in containers and various other methods, you cut down the amount of digging. However, eventually you have to dig round and through the compost you've made and laid on the ground, and in order to make compost, either you or someone else has to do some digging.

Digging does a lot for the soil. If it's heavy, digging breaks it up. It allows you to treat the soil at various depths, exposing pests to the frostiness of the air and all kinds of grubs to the greedy bills of garden birds. Digging allows you to get fertility and organic material deep into the soil and it increases the surface area of the soil to the improving ravages of wind and weather.

Double digging

This particularly English way of digging gets nutrients two spades down, encouraging roots to go deep, collect water and nutrients, and promote lush growth. Grandad would double dig his potato patch in the cold days of January and plant with potatoes by St Patrick's Day (March 17). Essentially, you dig a trench one spade deep, keeping the soil to one side. Then dig another spade deep, keeping the soil.

Half fill the trench with very well-rotted manure, then dig another trench, piling the soil on top of the soil of the first trench. Half-fill this second trench with well-rotted manure and overfill with soil from the next one, and so on until you have dug over the whole bed.

The last trench you dig out is topped off with the soil left over from the first. Because you've put in a half trench's worth of manure, you've raised the level of the soil, so you should be left with a well-dug mound.

Preparing a fine tilth

This is an important job if you're going to sow seeds directly into the soil; carrots and turnips come to mind. You need to dig over the soil and, while you're doing it, incorporate some compost into it. If you are going to grow cabbages or any brassicas, then add a trowelful of lime per square metre.

Rake over to level and then get out the hoe. A Dutch hoe has two uses: weeding and making a crumbly soil. It has two blades: one for the push stroke and one for the back stroke. Lay the blade quite flat and, with a rapid backwards and forwards motion, cut through the soil. You are looking for a crumbly soil, one that is light, fluffy and warm – the kind of material seedlings would have no problems pushing through.

Crop Rotation

What follows is an explanation of why crop rotation, followed blindly and without thought, can be a bad thing for the garden. Already I can feel your hackles rising as a generation of poor teaching has led everyone to believe that, to maintain fertility and keep pests down, you have to practise crop rotation.

The major problem stems from the confusion caused by transferring what is done in farms at the field scale into the small scale of the garden or allotment. In the field, crop rotation works to add nitrates to the soil, thus rejuvenating it. The normal action of acidic rain on gaseous nitrogen in the atmosphere is to cause a small amount of it to turn into nitrite, which is now easily turned into nitrates in the soil by microbes. This is improved during a thunderstorm. If you simply leave a field to its own devices, it will regain some fertility from this source alone. Grow some plants such as clover and the soil will get an even bigger dose. Consequently, the crop-rotation system became an agricultural norm from the late Middle Ages onwards.

However, in the garden we add fertility in different ways. We add a lot more nitrates from a single barrowful of compost than we could by any green manure or nitrogen-fixing plant. So now we have to think about soil-borne pests, and rotating can be a good and a bad thing. Every allotment in the land has been infected with clubroot because of crop rotation and people walking on their soil. It is a certainly good idea to follow potatoes with cabbages and carrots – but there is one crop that Grandad would never rotate.

Every year we had a bonfire on the onion patch. In fact, we had many. We always grew onions in the same bed every year and the key to our success was the bonfires.

There are a lot of nutrients present in wood ash. It was the mainstay of agricultural fertiliser for a long time, and onions in particular love to grow in soil rich in wood ash. Whether you sow seeds in December or buy onion sets in March, you will find they grow best in the same bed year after year. The bonfires increase the fertility and at the same time deal with soil-borne pests of all kinds in the top 30cm of soil.

I'm not suggesting that you stop crop rotation altogether, but you should think carefully about it. If you have four large beds, rotate three of them and leave one just for the onions.

Above all DON'T WALK ON YOUR SOIL, and be sure to keep the fertility up with plenty of well-rotted manure and compost.

	Year 1	Year 2	Year 3
Area A	Cabbages	Roots (Potatoes, etc.)	Peas & Beans, etc.
Area B	Roots (Potatoes, etc.)	Peas & Beans, etc.	Cabbages
Area C	Peas & Beans, etc.	Cabbages	Roots (Potatoes, etc.)

Catch crops

If you go for a walk in the countryside, the deep country you might call wilderness, you will never see soil. Unless eroded away or ploughed up by man, the bare earth is always jam-packed with living plants. Nature will never allow good resources to go to waste because something is always ready to exploit bare earth and the resources beneath it.

We grow our food plants in neat rows with bare earth between them, and the result is that weeds come in to fill the gaps. We spend most of our time hoeing up the weeds only to expose bare earth again. So why not grow a secondary crop between the rows?

Catch crops are an example of how you can grow between plants to get something extra to eat. Catch crops include dwarf beans, spinach, lettuces and any number of salad leaves. Anything can qualify as a catch crop, but they tend to be shallow-rooted plants that don't compete with the main crop in the ground.

Propagation

The process of propagation is how you make more plants for next year – and, as usual, there are many ways of doing this.

In Grandad's day, gardeners didn't waste anything that could be grown on. These days we have the attitude that once a plant has finished, we are doing a good thing by composting it and then buying another. This would never have been affordable years ago, and any opportunity to increase stock for free was taken – just as it should be done today.

Propagation by division

Say you have a pot of chives and there's no room for any more, or you have a rhubarb that is old and stuffed full of stems. You can divide these and many other plants simply by taking them out of the soil (or container) and breaking them apart by pulling – be careful not to damage the intertwined roots and rootlets too much, however. You can easily get four groups of plants where you had only one by using this method.

Pot or plant these and you will have four more plants which, over the year, will increase in growth. Large plants can be divided by using two garden forks 'back to back' to lever them apart.

Propagation by cuttings

There are two different types of cuttings you can make, depending on the nature of the plants involved.

Hardwood cuttings

You can take cuttings of fruit bushes such as blackcurrants. Choose a branch that has grown this year and, in the winter, cut it into lengths that each have three or four buds on them.

Dip the lower end of the pieces into rooting powder and plant them in a 30cm pot filled with a mixture made up of half soil and half compost. Keep them cool but frost-free over the winter. Hopefully about three of them will take root and can be potted into a 30cm pot of their own to grow out in the next year.

Propagation by softwood cuttings

Follow exactly the same process as with hardwood cuttings, except use the tips of new stems that have grown during the last summer. Cut lengths, including the tip, that have around five buds on them and repeat as above. These cuttings are best stood in individual pots of compost as above, and by the spring around half of them should have taken root. This is also a great way to propagate vines.

Growing Vegetables

What you grow depends largely on your needs and tastes (obviously). However, how much to grow and how to store it depend on other things, such as available space, and your ability to keep some foods dry and vermin-free. What follows is a concise and brief guide to growing and storing a number of vegetables and fruit.

William Cobbet, my local MP of some 200 years ago, wrote the original book on self-sufficiency and suggested that a large family could obtain nearly all its food from a quarter of an acre – about an eighth of a football pitch. He didn't actually say how this could be achieved, but this amount of land is equal to around five ordinary allotments, so he probably wasn't far off the mark.

The following vegetables are the ones I grow more or less each year and is by no means exhaustive.

Artichoke

There are two kinds of artichoke: globe and Jerusalem. They are both plants that add culture to the garden, although they are completely unrelated.

The globe artichoke, also known as the French or green artichoke, is a tall thistle that has large flowers. The flowers are harvested when small and tight, boiled and used to dip in a mayonnaise sauce. They are elegant in the garden and the kitchen. If you let the flowers open a little, they become too tough for use, but they can still be whizzed in the food processor for soup.

Buy them as roots, which you plant in a trench (see page 75) with a lot of manure incorporated in it – they are hungry plants. Don't let them dry out in the summer, and in the winter mulch them with compost. Harvest when the flowers are cold. After four years replace your stock by dividing the roots and growing on.

Jerusalem artichokes have nothing to do with Jerusalem at all. They grow from tubers which should be placed in a light, sandy soil in full sun early in March. The plants grow well with some water and a monthly feed of liquid manure. In November the leaves die back and should be removed. Dig up the tubers to eat as you need them. They aren't easy to peel, but they are well worth the effort once roasted or boiled.

Asparagus

Getting asparagus to the stage where you have a good crop is such a thrill. Everyone should grow this plant.

Make a trench (see page 75) in September, and in March dig out the top 15cm. You need to make a little mound along the centre of the trench and spread the roots of your crowns on top of these. Fill in with soil and water. In the first year a flimsy plant will develop. Mulch this with a mixture of good compost and manure and keep well-watered.

The plant will die back in winter and should be cut back. In the following year, it will come through and should be left alone, and fed and watered as the first year. The next year take ten percent of the spears that appear by cutting them with a knife just below the soil surface. The following year take no more than twenty percent. After that take no more than half, leaving the rest to grow and keep the plant strong.

Beans, Broad

These should be sown in a double row: two rows 30cm apart and then another double row 60cm further on. You can sow in October for a crop that will produce beans in May. Future sowings can be made every fortnight until June, and you will have fresh beans right through to the beginning of October.

Beans, French

You really can grow French beans anywhere, in large pots or beds. They can be had all the year round, making this a brilliant vegetable. These days, we basically sow them in April and harvest them as they appear in July or August. However, in Grandad's day, they were sown all the year. if you make a sowing in October under a cloche you will have late-spring crops; just make sure you protect them constantly with the cloche. If you sow in August, you'll have autumnal and winter crops.

Simply sow them in drills around 15cm apart. The soil should be fairly rich and moisture-retentive.

Beans, Runner

These are sown in a trench (see page 75) as early as March under cloches to get them going, or you can sow in modules in February indoors and transplant them to their final positions in May. Runners are traditionally grown on a trench dug the previous year. Remember: this crop is hungry and thirsty, so from the end of May, water daily and feed with liquid fertiliser once a week. Sow them once a fortnight to have a long period of cropping.

The easiest way to preserve them is to cut them into finger-sized pieces, blanch them in boiling water for 30 seconds and then freeze. Grandad's method was quite different: he used to put a layer of salt in the bottom of a large earthenware pot, then top that with a layer of beans. He continued these layers until the pot was full. The beans were preserved in the salt and when you wanted to cook them you had to soak them in several changes of water to remove it. They retained their flavour quite remarkably, however!

Beetroot

Every garden should have beetroot. They're very easy to grow, so long as the soil is not too full of nutrients. Sow in drills under a cold frame in a hot bed (see page 80) in January, then grow in rows to have an early crop by May. The secret is always to thin the beetroot so that there is a hand's breadth between each. If you let them grow closer together they simply produce smaller beets.

Sow outside from April to June and you can have beets all year round.

When pulled, they should be boiled and pickled as you would red cabbage. We buy industrial-sized jars from chip shops which still sell pickled eggs; they make great jars for storing pickled beets, so long as you pick them small – less than 5cm – when they're at their best anyway.

When you harvest beets, lift them from the ground with a trowel rather than pulling them by the leaves.

Broccoli

In essence, you should treat all the brassicas (broccoli, cabbage, swede, sprouts) in the same way, and the reason for this is a disease known as clubroot. Most growers in Grandma's day never saw any clubroot, but try and find a parcel of ground without it these days!

The disease affects all brassicas and is caused by a fungus that is spread around the garden on the soles of your shoes – so don't walk on the soil if you can help it. It makes the roots become gnarled and significantly reduces their ability to feed the plant, which doesn't grow as well as it should. Thankfully, the fungus does not affect humans at all. Clubroot doesn't do well in lime, and this, alongside modern sowing techniques, gives us a chance to work around the disease organically.

Sow broccoli seeds in April in modules of compost, each of which has half a teaspoon of lime added. Grow the plants until they are quite large, about 15–20cm tall. This will mean watering regularly and one addition of liquid fertiliser. The root systems should be very well-developed by now.

In late May dig out large holes, three times bigger than the modules, and line each with a trowelful of lime. This large quantity of lime will keep the fungus at bay. Fill the hole with a 80:20 mixture of fresh new soil (even if you have to buy it in bags, or sterile soil) and lime. Transplant them in this; they should be 60cm apart.

Heel them in strongly so they will grow upright and not fall over. All brassicas like to be firmed in strongly, particularly broccoli and sprouts. If you don't, the heads will be loose.

Sow again in August and overwinter them. This way you'll get heads from September to March.

Brussels Sprouts

Treat these as though they were broccoli, but make sure the soil is rich, with manure dug in. Sow in March, plant out in very late April or early May.

Cabbage

Treat as broccoli (see previous page), but sow summer cabbage in March/April, winter cabbage in June, and spring cabbage in August. This way you can have cabbages all the year round.

Carrots

I reckon carrots saved my grandparents' marriage. They were both equally vocal and stubborn, and whenever there was 'trouble brewing', Grandad would go out and hoe some land for carrots.

They need a very fine tilth: the soil has to be chopped and chopped until it has the consistency of cake mix. They don't need much in the way of nutrients, but all stones need to be removed. Otherwise, the carrots will simply make funny (and frequently rude) shapes, which might be amusing but are all but impossible to cook.

There is no reason for missing out on carrots. You can grow them anywhere so long as you stick to the basics. An old grower's tip is to grow them in drainpipes. Cut the drainpipe into 1m lengths, then saw down the middle lengthways. Tape them back together and fill with compost. Sow carrots in these and water every few days and feed monthly. When you think the carrot is fully grown, about four months later, cut open the pipe and carefully wash the compost off the carrot. You should have very long carrots with a very long, tapering root that would win any prize going.

Traditionally carrots were grown in a frame with walls 60cm high to exclude the carrot root fly that appears mostly in May and June. These days, however, simply cover them with horticultural mesh to foil the flies.

Cauliflower

People think cauliflowers are difficult to grow, but they're not. Treat them as broccoli (see previous page), making sowings in modules every fortnight from mid-February to late April. You can sow again in October in modules and keep them in a cool, frost-free greenhouse ready for planting out in April; these will yield some summer heads.

Plant out as they attain the correct height as per broccoli, and firm them in well. By September, they should be producing heads. Make sure they don't dry out and protect the heads with leaves by snapping off any big enough to fit over the head and using these to cover it.

Celery

This hungry crop is easy to grow if the soil is moist and very well-fed. Sow in modules in March at a temperature of 21°C. Transplant to a previously dug trench in May, about 45cm apart. Instead of fresh material in the lower part of the trench (see page 75) half-fill it with well-rotted manure. Keep the plants well-watered and feed monthly with a liquid fertiliser. Harvest individual stalks when they are 2.5cm across.

You can blanch (whiten) celery stalks, if desired, by drawing earth up around them, or by making collars out of drainpipes – anything to cut out the light.

Chicory

A few chicory plants are good in the garden, especially when you want to flavour a salad or create some brilliant roast-chicory heads. Our grandparents used the root, dried and ground, to make drinks, and as a coffee substitute and 'filler', but I can't think why: it tastes awful!

Sow chicory in April in a simple drill, and thin the plants to 45cm apart. In September, start to blanch (whiten) plants you are going to pick by putting a flower pot over each head. It takes two weeks in the dark to remove the bitterness to an acceptable level.

Kohlrabi

This ugly plant came into its own after the Second World War because it grew so well and produced a substantial vegetable for the little room it took on the ground. The other thing is that it enabled you to grow turnip-like vegetables right through the winter because it didn't need any frost protection.

Sow kohlrabi in drills in March for a supply throughout the summer. Thin to 30cm apart, then repeat again in June and July for autumn and winter supplies. They need reasonably good soil.

Leeks

These are great plants, completely perfect for winter and great fun to grow. They are simple and will reward the grower with a fantastic vegetable, just as useful as onions but with less peeling!

Sow leeks in modules indoors in April. Keep them going in the modules; you can probably afford to have three or so plants per compartment. In May, harden them off, then prepare them for growing on. Remove the plants and wash off the compost from the roots. Use a bulb planter to make holes 45cm apart to receive the young leeks. Line up the leeks together and cut off two-thirds of the root and the top fifth of the shoot. Now you have uniform plants. Pop one into each hole and fill it with water – nothing else.

They will be ready in November through to January and beyond. Once the plants have filled the hole they will grow steadily until November, when they will simply maintain themselves.

Onions

The traditional way to grow onions is to sow the seed in pots on Christmas Day. I'm not completely sure I've ever managed this (!), but in any case, onions are best grown in a rich bed, and fed with wood ash year on year (see page 84) and some well-rotted manure.

Sow them in modules and grow them to a few inches high. Transplant them into their bed in late April. You can also buy onion sets, which are temperature-treated bulbs that will not run to seed. Again, plant these in April. They need to be around 30cm apart.

Keep the rows weed-free and they will grow rapidly once warm days arrive. Make sure the bulblets do not push themselves out of the ground a week or so after planting, as their roots grow.

Plant Japanese onion sets in August or sow seed in July for a late spring crop. You should also broadly sow onion seed in August for use as young onions through the winter.

Curing In late August or early September, the leaves will begin to fall over. Pull your bulbs up with the help of a trowel and leave them in the open air, out of the rain, so that their outer skins dry and harden.

Parsnip

This crop is a long time in the ground. You have to treat parsnips exactly like carrots (see page 89), only they should be sown in early April and pulled the following January onwards. Unlike most garden crops, a frost does them good, and actually improves their flavour.

Peas

You can sow peas in almost any soil except heavy clay. The earliest are had by sowing in a cold greenhouse in early December. Plant six peas per 30cm pots and they should be hardened off in March to be planted out in early April.

Sow in March out in the open every two weeks until July and you will have a succession of peas to pick until September. If you grow old-fashioned varieties such as Giant Exhibition, they will need to be supported by canes. The standard variety is Kelvedon Wonder, which is suitable for sowing more or less any time from early spring to summer.

Potatoes

Potatoes need a rich soil that can be dug deeply and a prodigious amount of well-rotted manure – at least a spadeful per square metre. Depending on the variety, they need between 15 and 25 weeks to bear a crop.

Place them in a trench (see page 75) about 20cm deep and 75cm apart. They come in groups: 'First Earlies" 'Second Earlies' and 'Main Crop'. I only ever grow First Earlies and Main Crop because my new potatoes last until the Main Crop ones are ready.

Plant by St Patrick's Day (March 17), and leave them alone for a couple of months. As the vines appear, draw soil around the plants. This is called 'earthing up' and stops any emerging tubers from becoming green and poisonous. Water only at ground level, and don't splash the leaves if you can help it.

Blight On rainy days from July onwards, following a few days of really hot weather, a fungal infection called blight may devastate your potatoes. Black spots appear on the vines, and within 24 hours the whole crop can be ruined. You can keep this to a minimum by only watering at soil level, cutting out some of the vines to decrease the humidity and keeping a close eye on the crops. You can also grow blight-resistant varieties, such as:

- Earlies: Colleen, Karlena, Orla; and
- Maincrop: Remarka, Robinta, and Stirling

Harvest with a fork, tentatively at first, 15 weeks after planting First Earlies and up to 25 weeks after Maincrop. Do not be tempted to plant supermarket potatoes, nor should you keep stock from last year. Always buy fresh seed potatoes each year; this way you will have a better harvest. Always try to grow potatoes on fresh land each year if you can, over a three-year cycle, to reduce the blight spores in the soil.

Rhubarb

What a plant this is! You can usually 'borrow' a crown from a neighbour, plonk it in the ground that has been prepared with lots of rotted manure (as for potatoes actually) and you get a wonderful crop year on year.

Plant crowns 30cm deep in April and leave them untouched for a year. The following winter mulch with a lot of well-rotted manure and take a few stalks the following spring. Increase your harvest the following year, and after four years divide the crowns to increase your stock. Do not eat the leaves and do not harvest after mid-July.

Shallots

Treat them as onions (see page 91), only once you've harvested them, divide the crop into two piles. One is for curing and saving to make great sauces, especially with beef meals. The rest can be peeled, soaked in 300g/litre salt solution for 24 hours and then pickled in vinegar. Nothing is better with strong cheese at Christmas!

Tomato

No garden should be without tomatoes. You can grow a couple of varieties, Gardener's Delight and Moneymaker (though it never made me any money!) indoor or outdoors.

Sow in 8cm pots in March indoors at around 20°C and grow until they can be potted on at around 20cm high. Grandad used to pot on into progressively larger pots, but these days there is no need to bother.

You can put them into growbags in the greenhouse in May. Alternatively, use ring culture pots (these have no bottom and are filled with compost). Those for planting out should be put into 30cm pots in an unheated greenhouse.

The plants will grow in size over the next six weeks, and by the end of June they will start to bear flowers. At this time, never let them dry out and give them a weekly feed of tomato food.

Where a leaf leaves the stem a small shoot will appear; this will grow large if you let it, so pinch these all out unless your seed instructions indicate otherwise.

You'll need to support the plants as they grow, usually with canes, although string suspended from the greenhouse roof will do. Plants destined for outdoors can be hardened off in the first week of June.

When you have four trusses (sets of flowers), pinch out the growing point and no more flowers will appear. On average, a truss will bear 500g of fruit, so you can judge how many you need to grow.

Ripening takes place in late August and September. I used to try to force them, but in the end, Diana makes chutney with any green ones, so I no longer worry too much about it!

Turnips

These are the easiest plants to grow. Treat them like carrots (see page 89), sowing from late March to September, and you should have turnips for most of the year, except in the winter. Late-sown turnips are ideal for giving the hens a treat!

Growing Fruit

It is surprising how just a few plants can produce such a commotion in our house. Strawberries are fought over when they appear in June – supposing, that is, that the slugs haven't got them beforehand. Even in the smallest gardens you should always find space for some fruit. Either in tree form, bushes or smaller herbaceous plants, fruit is nothing short of flavoured sunshine. You don't even need to plant a lot of it because, thankfully, there is always some out there in the wild to collect.

Select the right fruit for you

From a self-sufficiency point of view, fruit is a boon. It makes the most wonderful jams and preserves and it can also be stored frozen in ready-made pies and such. There is little need to 'hard store' fruit in the same way as you do vegetables. Fruit can also be juiced, or successfully made into wines and beer, so the possibilities are endless.

In our current home, I limit our fruit-growing to strawberries, apples, gooseberries, cherries, blackcurrants, pineapples and grapes. If this doesn't sound like a lot, I happen to have a hedge at the bottom of the garden which has elderberry that provides both flowers and fruit, and nearby there are wild raspberries and blackberries to be had. Within a mile of us are some plums that remain from a derelict house, and on top of this there are crab apples, rowan berries, sloes and redcurrant, all growing neglected but free in nearby hedges.

Which just goes to show: before you start growing every fruit there is to be found, have a look what you can find for free.

Bare root or ball root?

Most fruit trees come in one of two forms. Bare-root trees, as you find in most nurseries, are delivered in the winter while the plant is dormant. Because their roots are wrapped in a little compost but mostly wet newspaper, you must plant the specimen before the first leaves appear in the spring.

Ball-rooted plants usually have their roots wrapped in quite a lot of soil surrounded by a net, or sometimes they come in a container. Ball-rooted plants can be bought at any time of the year and planted more or less in every season, except when there is a drought.

Planting a fruit tree

Whether it is bare- or ball-rooted, planting a fruit tree is fairly straightforward. Dig a large hole, at least three times the volume of the ball of roots, or at least 60cm^3 if it is a bare-rooted tree. Line the bottom with 15cm of really good compost and mix some slow-release fertiliser. Mix the soil you dug out 50:50 with compost.

The tree will need staking, so hammer this in place to give the young sapling support before you plant it (otherwise you might damage the roots).

Put the tree in position and evenly but firmly fill the hole all around it with the soil/compost mixture. You should have the tree positioned so that the scar where the plant was grafted onto a rootstock is just slightly above the soil.

Firm the tree in with your boot and give it a good, long drink of water, then fasten it to the stake with a rubber tie in a figure-of-eight fashion to prevent the trunk rubbing against the stake.

It takes most fruit trees at least three years to produce a crop. Try not to allow fruit to set in the first two years, but mulch with good-quality rotted manure each spring. Look out for pests in the spring, and spray accordingly. Thankfully, these days you can usually find good organic sprays without too much trouble. If you can't source any locally, you should be able to find them easily on the internet.

Apples

There are hundreds of apple varieties to choose from. Modern varieties are self-fertilising, older ones are not, so if you opt for the latter you'll need more than one tree. You can buy apple trees in many sizes: from dwarf rootstocks that fit on a patio in a pot to large, expansive rootstocks that will produce a huge plant.

To save space, think about training apples against a fence by tying the branches to wires and forcing the plant to grow along them. Secure three parallel wires set off the wall or fence at 60cm intervals along which to train the branches. Prune the central branch to the level of the top wire. Where convenient, tie branches to the wires on either side of the main branch. Remove all the other branches. Side shoots will push out lateral spurs which bear fruiting buds.

In the winter, the length of the side shoots should be reduced by a third, or to the boundary of your space.

Harvest

As I mentioned, it will take three years to get a decent crop, but once you have, you'll want to know when the fruit is ready. To test for ripeness, hold an apple in your hand, and if it falls off the tree easily or falls after a half twist, it's ripe. Otherwise, don't try to force it off the plant.

June drop

Apples put out a lot of flowers, far more than they can mature to fruit. Generally in June the ones the plant cannot handle are shed, and you should not try to stop them. This is a natural thinning process, and an important time for an apple tree.

Storage

Apples should be stored with air all around them in a cool, frost-free place. Otherwise, juice them by running them through a juicer or chop them into small pieces and give them a blast in the food processor. The slurry can be put into a muslin sack, or pushed through a clean pair of tights. You can put this pulp into a press to provide the best juice you've ever tasted – or better still, the best cider.

Blackcurrants

These are easy plants to grow if you have a lot of sunshine and good, rich soil. Site plants in a hole and fill with a 50:50 mix of soil and well-rotted manure.

Care

Each spring mulch with more well-rotted manure – but make sure it doesn't touch the stem. Feed the plant during the summer every month and be sure the soil never dries out.

Blackcurrants are ready a couple of weeks after they have turned black and you will need to protect them with garden netting to keep birds away.

Pruning

When the plant is two years old, cut out any crossed stems and prune to make the plant open out so that air can circulate easily about the fruit.

Figs

You can buy fig trees in supermarkets these days, but until recently you were considered an expert gardener indeed if you could grow them. Mediterranean in nature, these plants will get through the UK winter if you keep the worst of the weather off them and you will get great, sweet-tasting fruit.

Strong sun

Make sure fig trees are planted in the sunniest spot you can find. If you can grow them against a south-facing wall, then all the better.

Fruit

Figs are normally pollinated by wasps, who burrow into the stem where the flowers are hidden, but most of them are self-fertilising these days, so the wasps are not needed. The plants set fruit in August and it takes the whole winter and spring for them to be ready the following summer.

Care

Add a good mulch of compost in the spring and then feed with liquid fertiliser once a month from June to August. Take out the most crowded branches in the spring, creating a plant which is open to the air, allowing moisture to be blown away.

Gooseberries

These great plants provide more fruit per leaf than any other. They are always full of sugary juice, from which you can make fantastic wine, or just eat them from the plant. They are not bothered about soil quality so long as the drainage is good.

Buy them as plants to be planted in October to January. Usually you can get them for free on allotments. Take cuttings or divide the plants in autumn

Pruning

The problem with gooseberries is that they produce so much fruit and so many branches that the wind does not penetrate into the innermost stems. For this reason, on hot days they can get very hot indeed – and this is when fungal infections abound. To counteract this problem, in the winter (preferably in late January), prune the stems back so as to produce an open plant. Remove any dead wood and then have a look for any crowded branches.

Grapes

Grapes are much more successful these days than they ever were. At one time the only grapes we could grow here in the UK were 'Black Homberg', but there are now dozens of varieties. All you need to remember is that they don't mind cold winters, but they do not particularly like cold, driving rain.

Fruit is produced on one-year-old growth, so the vines you grow this summer will bear fruit next summer. Only ever prune the vine in the winter, when all the leaves are off the plant.

Feed vines in spring each year with a mixture of compost and well-rotted manure.

Training single-cordon vines

Traditionally, the grape has been grown outside a greenhouse and trained inside through a window. It is usually trained high into the roof as a single-cordon plant, or maybe two as a maximum.

Buy your vines in May and plant them either outside along a fence or in a greenhouse as described above. Pinch back all the lateral branches off what you will later train as the main cordon, to about five leaves.

When the leaves have fallen off in winter, cut back the main shoot by just over half and cut the laterals to a single bud each.

The following summer, treat the plant like you did the previous summer; tie in the main shoot and build your frame of wires. Take out any flowers that form. The following winter cut the main shoot back to old wood and the laterals to a strong bud each.

The third summer allow one bunch of grapes per lateral shoot to form, and keep any sub-laterals that form down to a single leaf. In the winter, when the grapes are taken and the leaves have fallen, cut the laterals to two buds. It is these buds you will use next year and so on.

Care

Keep the plant moist. Remember, plants with large leaves like a lot of water. From June to August, feed once a month with tomato fertiliser. Collect your grapes once they are full and sweet. Don't leave them on the vine because they will get fungal infections. For every bunch you remove, it is better for those that are left behind. Make sure the greenhouse is well-ventilated.

Melons

You can treat melons a bit like squashes, in that you grow them on mounds of rich earth in a very sunny spot and sometimes add a cloche to get the temperature up.

Sow two seeds in a small pot of compost in April and keep only the best-growing plant to prick out.

Planting out and care

Harden off in June. Dig a large hole, 45cm x 45cm and fill with a mixture of 75 percent good compost and 25 percent well-rotted manure. Plant in this, and make sure your plants are at least 1m apart. Cover with a bell cloche if you can. You can also make a tent out of plastic sheeting to make mini greenhouses over the plants.

Water every third day and put some tomato fertiliser in the water every second watering. In really hot times, water every day. Pollinate the plants by hand, by pushing male flowers inside the female ones as the female flowers appear. Only grow three melons per plant as a maximum. They should simply fall off the plant when ripe, and you can smell their ripeness.

Pears

You can treat pears almost exactly like apples. They are planted and fed in the same way (see 'Planting a fruit tree', page 95), but are much easier to prune in that, although you do it in the same way, they are much more forgiving.

An espalier pear is beautiful to look at, and the best fruit garden I ever saw had a wire fence around the border with apples, pears and plums trained around it.

Raspberries

Raspberries are one of the best choices for beginning gardeners because they are very difficult to kill unless they find themselves waterlogged. They do like a lot of water, but aren't happy if left standing in it, so make sure they are grown on free-draining soil. Otherwise, the plants will give you excellent fruit year on year right through the summer and autumn.

Summer-fruiting raspberries

Dig a trench about 60cm wide and 45cm deep and half-fill it with compost; fill in the rest with soil. In October, plant raspberries at 45cm intervals. Cut all the canes back to 20cm and tie them to a wire framework to hold them in position.

In spring, mulch the canes with compost and some organic fertiliser. Leave them to grow this year and cut out all the flowers. Next year you will get fruiting canes, which you harvest as soon as they are sweet and big enough to eat.

Tie in any canes that have not fruited and cut out the fruiting ones at the bottom. Repeat the spring feeding and pruning regime.

Autumn-fruiting raspberries

These are stand-alone plants and need no support. Dig a hole as per gooseberries (see page 97) and plant from October to March, avoiding the coldest of the weather.

Pruning should take place in February, not in the summer as for the summer-fruiting varieties. With these canes, all you do is take all the growth back to 15cm and the new growth will provide next year's flowering shoots.

This type of raspberry should be fed each spring with a mixture of bonemeal and compost as above.

Strawberries

For a plant that is so delicate in flavour, the strawberry is actually as tough as old boots. You only ever get a problem with them if they are growing new shoots in frosty conditions, and even then you'd hardly notice any real trouble.

They are called strawberries because they were traditionally grown with straw under the leaves so that, when the fruit formed, it was clear of the soil and pests such as slugs and didn't spoil.

Planting

Buy strawberry plants in April and May, or later in the year in September. Simply dig a hole with a trowel, add a little compost and plant on top. You can grow them in all kinds of containers: pots, hanging baskets, even in the holes in hollow concrete blocks.

Plant the strawberries so that the crown in the centre of the plant is at the soil's surface. If you plant them too deep, they will be susceptible to rot; put them in too shallow and they will refuse to grow at all. The plants need to be watered every couple of days when first planted, but after that, weekly should be fine unless there are some serious droughts.

Runners

One or more side branches, called runners, will grow out from each strawberry plant, and at intervals along the runner a little plant will appear. If you take this plant, while it is still attached to the runner, and place it on the top of a pot of compost, it will send out roots.

Once the roots have appeared, cut it free from the parent runner and you will have a brand new plant. Keep the runners in a cool but frost-free place and plant them out next year.

Diseases and longevity

Strawberries have all manner of problems with viruses and deteriorate in three years. By the fourth year, they should be removed. You can replace a third of your stock with new plants taken from runners as above, however, and you will have an ongoing supply of brilliant plants.

Keeping Hens

My grandfather used to keep poultry. He had chickens, mainly, and nearly all of them were Rhode Island Reds (RIR), although he did have others he had swapped for some that weren't. We used to eat the non-RIR birds, but he wouldn't let us touch his favourites. He had a window-cleaning round, and many's the time he came home with a chicken in lieu of money for his services. Once he himself paid for a new ladder with chickens.

Only recently have chickens decreased in value. In our grandparents' time they used to be an excellent commodity, a rarity on the table because at the butcher they would cost as much as ten shillings (50p in today's money) – way beyond the means of most people. Only after the 1950s did chicken meat really start to fall in price. By the turn of the millennium, you could buy a chicken for not much more than they were fetching a generation previously.

This drop in value of chicken meat has come about because of two things: the intensive-broiler system and a huge amount of imports from abroad. Sadly, these savings have been made at the expense of poultry welfare the world over.

My grandfather's point of view was that you should never keep an animal unless you were quite prepared to look after it properly. This also meant being able to kill it properly, either for food or as an act of mercy if it was unwell. In this country there is a measure of hypocrisy in that we complain about the plight of chickens in battery farms and broiler sheds, and yet sales of really cheap chicken have risen steadily. In my book, and I dare say in my grandfather's book, anyone who keeps chickens in their garden is doing bird-kind a favour.

Keeping a henhouse

Before you consider housing birds, you need to be sure that your deeds allow you to keep poultry on your land. One of the restrictions devised in the 1930s stated that if you lived in a suburb, you shouldn't really spoil it for everyone by keeping chickens. ('Mr Worthington has travelled to the City all week and needs his peace and quiet, so he certainly doesn't want to be woken by a noisy cockerel…') It's a real shame that some five percent of properties in the UK still have this restriction. You can find out if it applies to your home by checking your deeds.

If you live in rented property, you may well be refused permission to keep chickens, so you have an important decision to make: should you ask permission and get refused, or should you go ahead and get chickens, then risk getting into trouble with the landlord? It's your call. But if you keep only a couple of hens – and keep them well and clean – you should be fine.

Neighbours are the key, and a few eggs every now and then will do great things for your relationships with them.

Where to put hens

When I was a boy, we kept 30 hens in an old air-raid shelter and they terrorised the garden – and the neighbours, too. In fact, we had some hens roosting in our shed that actually belonged to next door, and visa versa. However, these days you wouldn't be allowed to have so many hens in one garden.

Yet however many hens you plan on keeping, you need to be sure that the garden is secure, that cats and dogs (and children) cannot get to the birds, and of course, that the hens cannot get out of the garden and into the street.

Chickens do best in a space where there is plenty of light but also shelter from wind and rain. In particular, they should be kept away from overhanging trees, and if they haven't got the run of the garden, then their run should be secure, with a wire roof above it.

The henhouse should be built off the ground in order to prevent rats and mice from burrowing underneath it. Likewise, all chicken feed should be presented in such a way that it can be brought indoors at night, away from vermin. This is particularly important if you live in the city. In the country, where you generally have more room between yourself and your neighbours, you might leave the hen food outside. In the city, however, being accused of attracting rats would probably be the death knell for your poultry-keeping activities.

After a while, and if they are on grass, you should move your hens to stop the build-up of parasites in the soil. Slugs in particular (but some insects, too) pick up these parasites, and if they are eaten by the hens, the latter can then get sick, especially if there are other stresses in the flock, such as a prolonged period of bad weather. If you move hens to another patch of grass every three months, however, you should not get this problem.

The henhouse should be roomy enough to keep the appropriate number of hens. Do not overcrowd them, as this only leads to bullying and feather-pecking and ensures that, once one hen is ill, the rest will become ill, too.

A run attached to the henhouse should be large enough to allow the birds to fully stretch their wings; therefore it needs to be about 1m wide, and around 60cm tall. It is probably best, in the city at least, to have 5 square metres per pair of birds.

The inside of the henhouse needs cleaning regularly to remove parasites and keep it fresh. The birds should be able to perch on poles that are no more than 5cm in diameter and that positioned from 7–30cm off the ground, and the henhouse should be lockable at night. The structure of the henhouse should be permanently checked. If there are loose or weathered boards, predators will eventually get inside.

The nest box

Somewhere in the henhouse there should be a place for the birds to lay. This is known as a nest box, and should be around 30cm square and filled with straw. The nest box will also act as a stimulus to the birds: they cannot help sitting in it because the nest box rounds out the straw and presents a really inviting place to lay.

You can help get your hens' hormones going by placing an egg in the nest box. This will stimulate the birds, assuming they are at 'point of lay' (around 22 weeks old), to start laying.

At first you will get small eggs with interestingly shaped shells, but they soon improve and get larger until they reach their full size.

What do hens give us?

It is not surprising that people who have looked after hens for some time don't want to kill them for meat. And anyway, besides meat, hens give the gardener an awful lot. Eggs are an obvious bonus. You can turn a handful of mash, a few leaves and a few scraps into an egg a day. If you let chickens roam, they will lay eggs on a diet of slugs and snails, earwigs, spiders and a lot of grass.

Hens have all the eggs they will ever lay present in their ovaries. Poultry have 'strings' of eggs, which they lay in succession. The first string might have 300 eggs, which will be laid at the rate of one a day, give or take the odd barren day. After this, the hens will moult for a month or two before the second string of eggs will come into play. There are fewer eggs in the second string. This can continue annually for five or six years, and the hen's last string might have only 50 eggs on it. The number diminishes with every moult.

Once you have tasted an egg that has popped from the hen's bottom minutes earlier and has been cooked straight away, you will never want to go back to buying them from the supermarket.

Another gift the hens give is their manure. They provide many a hundredweight of manure each year, which should be composted and used in the garden. If you buy food for your hens, you'll get back adequate manure for an average garden. It is also, once composted, the best material for growing mushrooms. This manure alone is an excellent reason for keeping hens.

On top of this, hens are wonderful creatures to keep and have around. They provide an excellent opportunity for young children to learn about caring for animals and to find out about their ways. Hens make perfect pets and can become completely engrossing.

The cockerel

It is an advantage to keep a cockerel, especially if you want to raise your own chicks. They take on the role of bossing the hens, which stops them from bullying each other and maintains order – rather like a sergeant-major. However, cockerels *are* noisy and so probably aren't suitable if you live in a town or urban environment.

Buying hens

For the purposes of this book I am going to assume that you fancy keeping a few hens for eggs and nothing more. You can buy hens in various ways. Some companies sell them along with henhouses; this is usually the best route for finding hens for the beginner because then you'll know exactly what you are buying.

Buy the largest henhouse you can afford and fit two or three birds in it. It is a good idea to set up the henhouse and run a couple of days before you introduce the hens to it, so that they can go straight into the henhouse.

Ask for point of lay (POL; see page 103) pullets; a 'pullet' is simply another word for a young hen, usually under a year old. It is surprising how long a bird that is described as being at POL takes before it starts actually laying. Be warned: if you buy them over the internet, you have no real way of checking their status.

If you want to raise chicks, you should choose pure-strain birds, because hybrids do not breed easily. Something like a Wyandotte or a Rhode Island Red will produce chicks each year for a long time.

Another good way of buying hens is from a society such as the Battery Hen Welfare Trust. This charity is dedicated to rehousing former battery hens. These birds have finished laying their first string of eggs but with a bit of care and attention they will soon come back into full bloom. It is a truly wonderful experience to watch a hen with few feathers regain her dignity. These are *not* sick hens, however. Normally they are very well; it is only the rigours of living in a cage that has been hard on their appearance.

Feeding your hens

It is actually illegal to feed livestock on kitchen scraps in the UK, but the law turns a blind eye in most domestic situations. Each hen needs a daily ration of basic food, and on top of this they like as many scraps as they can manage to munch through.

You can buy layers' pellets, which are made up of a balanced mix of feed that is perfect for laying hens. They will eat their fill of this stuff, but no more. Hens aren't greedy. Don't feed them anything other than pellets in the morning, but in the afternoon let them have whatever scraps you have available.

They also need good, fresh water and plenty of it. Why should they drink water that you wouldn't drink yourself? The provision of good, fresh water is probably the most important way of keeping hens healthy. They need a regular supply of grit as well. Hens eat their food and 'chew' or grind it in an organ known as the crop. This has stones in it which grind the food and make a sloppy mix that enters the long stomach.

Manure (again)

A hen's manure should be somewhat solid and 'fluffy'. Keep your eyes on the poo and you will be able to assess a chicken's health. An animal whose poo is very runny might only be slightly off-colour, but if there is blood there, then you should assume something is wrong. Keep an eye out for red mites, which rest on the perch away from the light, and chicken lice, which can be found at the base of the feathers. You should worm your hens every three months, and at the same time dust them with mite powder.

Finally…

If you notice that your birds smell, then your neighbours can probably smell them, too, and might have cause for complaint. Check the state of your birds every day and clean out the henhouse and chicken run regularly. Healthy birds shouldn't smell, and keeping them clean ensures their good health – and yours.

Keeping Bees

What follows is a descriptive 'taster'. It is not designed as a guide to beekeeping, because if you're serious about beekeeping, you really must learn the craft properly at a local beekeeping association. There are many reasons for this, not least being that, once you're involved with a hive of many thousands of bees (and there can be 30,000 of them in the hive in the summer) you may find you don't like it. They might intimidate you for one thing – although this is, really, all in the mind.

So why become a beekeeper?

Becoming a beekeeper is one of the most relaxing things you can do. To be good at it, in fact, you have to be calm. Bees, to a certain degree, respond to you and your moods. If you're calm and peaceful, they will be, too. The way bees orientate themselves and manage their affairs is inspiring and, of course, there are the products you get to steal from the hive, such as honey and beeswax (see below). On top of this, a beehive on an allotment or in a garden can increase your produce yield by around 30 percent, so there are very good economic reasons for keeping bees.

The bigger picture

There is a much more important reason for keeping bees: bees are having a bit of a problem these days. Colonies are collapsing, bees are dying and everyone is worried about the future because honeybees are so important as pollinators of most of our crops. Some pundits suggest that we might not last long as a species ourselves without bees – and they might be right. However, this situation is not new. Around 100 years ago, almost all the bees in the UK died out because of a 'mystery disease'. This condition, caused by the acarine mite, was not understood for some twenty years after most of the bees died, yet here we are, with bees and every hope of understanding what is happening this time around. We know that the varroa mite is one of today's big problems for bees, although it by no means explains the collapse that is happening on such a large scale.

One thing is certain: for every new beekeeper, there is more hope for bees because there will be more colonies, and therefore an increased gene pool. Sexual reproduction is about getting new genes into the gene pool – what Grandad would have called 'better blood'. Every time an organism reproduces sexually, the offspring will have slightly different genes that might be more useful in the future. Perhaps there is already a colony out there with varroa mite resistance, or one more able to meet the challenges of a changing climate.

What bees give us

Honey Bees make honey by collecting nectar from around the district and transferring this into cells in the hive. This is mixed with enzymes and then evaporated until the honey reaches 80 percent sugar, when it is ready for consumption. At this strength, honey lasts almost forever.

Not only is honey a nutritious substance, it is also very healing. A teaspoon of local honey will inoculate you with local pollen, which actually gives you a measure of protection during the hayfever season.

Propolis Propolis is a substance that can best be described as 'bee glue'. Any space in the hive that is smaller than a couple of millimetres is glued together with this substance. Any dead animals – mice, for example – are also covered in it. For humans, propolis makes an extremely effective antiseptic, and is excellent for treating sore throats.

Wax Everything from candles to furniture polish, lipstick to face masks are made from beeswax. It is highly moisturising and has been the basis of a lot of household uses for centuries. Bees make wax to draw out the combs in which grubs grow and in which they keep honey. Beekeepers sell wax to beekeeping suppliers so that they can make foundation sheets to go in new hives.

The Hive

What people once recognised as a beehive, with sloping sides and a pitched roof, is hardly seen these days. These days, almost all the world uses the US Langstroth hive, but we Brits use the National, which looks just like all the others but is a slightly different size.

Hives are placed on a stand that keeps the bees off the ground. The stand should, if possible, be fixed into the ground so it cannot be pushed over. The hive itself is made up of a number of boxes.

On the stand is a floor. This is made from mesh so that any varroa mites falling off the bees end up out of the hive. In the old closed-floor system, the mites simply crawled back into the brood box, reinfesting the bees. This way they cannot get back inside the hive.

The lower box is known as the brood box and contains eleven full-sized frames. It is a larger box in which the queen lays eggs, the workers tend the young and the queen, and also store honey.

On top of this you'll find what are known as super boxes. None of these have floors and lids, and they stack on each other exactly. Supers are half the depth as brood boxes and therefore contain eleven half-sized frames. Between the brood box and the super box is a special grid, known as the queen excluder. This prevents the queen from getting into the supers, but the worker bees are able to squeeze through easily.

In the super boxes workers store honey. When the honey is just right, they seal it with wax, securing their supplies for later. Bees need one super box full of honey, plus whatever stores there are in the brood box, to get through the winter. As a beekeeper, you may keep as many supers on the hive as you think fit. It is not uncommon to have three or even four stacked up.

On top of the super boxes you'll have a crown board, with a special device called a bee escape, which allows the bees to go only one way through it. So when you want to collect honey, a couple of weeks beforehand you clear the bees from the super boxes by putting a solid board between the brood box and the crown board, and the bees eventually crawl out of the top part of the hive but cannot get back inside.

Bee Society

There are three types or 'castes' of bee: the queen, the worker and the drone.

The queen

The queen has two basic functions. Firstly, she gives off a pheromone that gives all the members of the hive an identity. Bees know they are from a certain hive partly because of this pheromone.

Her second job is to lay eggs. Queens mate on a single day; following this, they retain the sperm that will last them a number of years. A single queen will lay more than a thousand eggs in the height of the season and then stop laying altogether later in the year, around October. As she lays her eggs she will fertilise them from her supply of stored sperm, and when this runs out, the workers will begin to make another queen.

The workers

Workers are all female and live for three sets of 22 days. The first is the 'egg and grub' set, for they only emerge from the cell on day 22, when they start to wander around, getting to know the orientation of the hive. For the next 22 days, workers will do a number of jobs, from cleaning, wax-laying, caring for the grubs and the queen, and being a guard bee to standing at the entrance ventilating the hive by flapping their wings.

The final period in a worker's life is spent foraging, and she will literally wear herself out collecting honey and pollen. She will travel many hundreds of miles and not only collect food, but will tell others where she is going.

The famous 'waggle dance' is only a part of the way in which a worker bee communicates. Bees coming back to the hive with a good source of nectar will communicate this fact to the others, and when there is more than one source, they will make a clear decision about where to collect first. Bees are clever!

Drones

Unlike workers, drones have only one function: to mate. When a new queen emerges, she will fly out of the hive and the drones will follow her. This nuptial flight might last for some time, and more than a few copulations will take place. Drones die in the act. In the late autumn the female workers throw any remaining drones, who have no sting, out of the hive to die in the cold. They are not allowed to overwinter.

What you need

1. Bees of course! The best place to get a colony of bees is by joining your local beekeepers' association. They come in a box called a nucleus ('nuc' for short), inside which are five frames of bees, a queen, and (hopefully) eggs and grubs on the frames. These are transferred to the hive and fed with sugar syrup.

2. A bee suit, which is easy to clean and has a mesh veil built in to keep the bees away from you. You should wear boots and a pair of beekeeping gauntlets. Many beekeepers of yesteryear, Grandad included, went into their hives with bare hands. I don't like being stung, and am actually pretty scared of bees, so I wear gloves.

3. A smoker is an important tool because the bees think there is a fire and dive into the hive to fill up on honey. The smoke clears them away, and when they return they are much less able to sting. Being full of honey placates them somewhat.

4. A hive tool is an ingenious device used for levering out the frames from inside the hive.

5. Insurance: if you keep bees you can get third-party insurance to cover anyone being stung or property being ruined by swarms and so on. If you live in a populated area, this is probably a very good idea.

6. Buckets and boxes: invariably you remove wax and propolis from the hive every time you go into it. This needs to be preserved, collected and modified for sale or use. At the same time you need to be able to extract the honey, which is done by either having a rotating drum extractor or by gravity into a bucket. All in all, beekeeping is an expensive hobby, with the hive, bees, suit, etc. costing around £350 and up. The expense, however, is offset by the fact that local honey is sold for around £3.50 per 450g jar, and in a good year you might get something like 100 jars per hive.

Disease control

A bacterium reproduces every twenty minutes, and in a day there can be many generations. A honeybee reproduces once every three years or so. The ability of the honeybee to evolve its way out of disease problems is severely reduced and is partly why today there are no reports of wild colonies in the UK. They seem to have died out, and bees that are now managed by man will succumb to varroa mite and other problems. The same goes for a beehive in the garden. Unless you actively keep them alive, they will die. Bees are in intensive care and simply cannot be left to their own devices.

Keeping bees, therefore, is a function of your ability to keep them alive. You will need treatments for varroa mite infestation, and the ability to estimate the numbers of mites inside the hive. You have to treat the bees in such a way that you do not impart chemical resistance to the mites and at the same time do not overburden the hive with poisonous chemicals.

On top of this, treatments for other diseases, stopping the bees from swarming, making new colonies, and coping with awful, washed-out summers where there is hardly a flower in sight make beekeeping an interesting but demanding pastime.

Is it worth it?

At the end of the day, and despite all the hard work involved, beekeeping is an important activity for anyone contemplating self-sufficiency. With your own supply of honey, you break the stranglehold of the supermarket, because without it, you always need sweet stuff.

All of the brewing and baking activities of the house are enhanced by the use of honey – as opposed to sugar – and without it, you cannot make mead: possibly the most wonderful drink in the world (see page 317). And, as everyone knows, thirst is a terrible thing!

Keeping Ducks

Ducks are the funniest and happiest of animals, and you can successfully keep them in the garden. They do need water, but less than you would think; certainly you don't need a lake to have ducks – although they will love it if you do! They do, however, need to be able to wash their faces as a minimum because they can, from time to time, have problems with sticky eyes.

If you can provide flowing water, all the better. This washes away the droppings they produce near the water's edge and provides a constant flow of clean (hopefully) water for drinking and their general use. If all you have is a bathtub sunk in the ground, be sure to change the water at least every third day – it gets really messy.

Like hens, ducks come in hybrid and pure-breed form, and they have the same range of types: from meat breeds to good egg-layers to dual-purpose breeds. A Khaki Campbell or a modern Indian Runner, for example, will lay as many eggs as a hybrid chicken – up to 300 a year.

It shouldn't be underestimated that ducks can be kept just because they are fun animals to have around. They make fantastic pets and can easily be happy around other pets and children. Their endearing ways make them completely ideal for an urban garden.

Buying ducks

Find and get to know a breeder of the type of duck you're thinking of buying. This is by far the best way of getting both good advice and, at the same time, some excellent ducks. You can find the breed society on the internet or in your local library and ask for a list of respectable breeders in your local area. The British Waterfowl Association (www.waterfowl.org.uk) is an excellent starting place, and you will find a breeder's directory on the website.

Local markets sell all kinds of poultry by auction, but you need to be sure exactly what you are buying. Take someone with you who knows about the animals and can tell if you're bidding on something that will turn out to be a waste of time. Importantly, when you buy from a breeder you can find out if the ducks in question have been inoculated against disease and things like *E. coli*, and you can be sure about their parasite status. This is all but impossible to do at auction.

Some specialist companies will also sell you ducks and their housing, and these are usually good sources of animals that are clear from disease and parasites. And at least you can take them back…

Housing

In many ways, keeping ducks is similar to keeping chickens. In fact, ducks can easily live alongside hens, and will share living quarters. They have little need for perching but they will use it if there is easy access to it. Ducks are not good jumpers or climbers, and they will not simply hop onto a ledge like a hen; they need ramps to waddle up to their sleeping quarters.

Housing must provide ducks with protection from predators on all sides, including top and bottom. Foxes will dig under chicken wire to get to ducks; unfortunately, they seem to be their favourite food.

An ordinary chicken house will suffice. During the Second World War, ducks were kept in large cages with something like a tin bath sunk in the ground so that the birds could bathe, but cages are too open to the weather. Despite their oily waterproof feathers, ducks need some protection from the weather, and they particularly dislike having their feathers ruffled by wind-blown rain. It is interesting that although ducks appear to live in water, they don't like rain that much.

Feeding

Use a hopper feed system to feed your ducks, because they are really messy otherwise. They must be fed pellets just like hens, but they are partial to a lot of 'extras'. You can buy wildfowl pellets for the various stages of a duck's life. Starting with 'starter crumbs' to 'finisher's pellets' the range of food is very similar to that used for hens and it is possible to feed both species together, especially if you are feeding mixed grain.

Ducks need a clean supply of drinking water beyond their needs for generally getting wet and washing their faces. They love to forage and eat up leaves, and more than anything they adore slugs. They are not so heavy on garden crops as chickens, and because of this, they are described as 'the gardener's friend'.

A wide variety of food will prevent your birds from getting bored and therefore also prevent squabbling and bullying.

Cleanliness and eggs

Duck eggs are more porous than hen eggs and therefore absorb aromas and taints from their environment. For this reason, you need to be careful how and where you store them, and you should also try to use them as fresh as possible because they lose moisture more quickly.

Ducks lay all over the place, particularly near the water, or even in it. The porosity of duck eggs means these eggs, unless you catch them straight away, can actually be dangerous to eat. The answer is to eat only those eggs you know have been laid in the nesting area. Unfortunately, ducks don't like nest boxes, so the floor of the hut needs to be covered with straw. Eggs should be collected as soon as possible after laying, as ducks seem to like to move their eggs around a lot – and they get messy!

Once you know they are laying, you can try to keep ducks locked in to lay, and only let them out later in the morning.

Even though ducks don't need a drake to produce eggs and will happily lay without being fertilised, if they have been bred they don't make particularly good mothers, and must not be allowed to range with their young, because they will probably forget them or wander them through impossible terrain. It is best to keep ducklings in a small coop until they are grown.

Illnesses

Ducks suffer from the same range of parasites and illnesses as chickens. If you introduce ducks into an environment where there are a lot of hens, you might find they succumb fairly quickly.

Maintain active cleanliness and be sure to move them around the garden or paddock so that parasites cannot build up. Perhaps the most important thing you can do is to find a vet who is good with ducks. These are quite rare, so if you're contemplating buying ducks, you might look for a suitable vet first.

Killing and Dressing Poultry

If you wish to kill your birds for food, this is up to you. I'm not going to enter the argument for and against killing animals for food. However, even if you never intend to eat your animals, you still need to be able to kill them humanely if they are suffering distress from illness or injury.

Grandad used to take a bird's head off with an axe, and that was that. However, there are many reasons why this isn't a good idea. Firstly, you might need more than one hit, and the bird will suffer. Secondly you might hit your hand (Grandad did), and then *you* will suffer. What you need is a way of killing the animal quickly without hurting it unduly, and neck dislocation is the most common way I know of doing this. In my opinion, wall-mounted or handheld plier-type neck dislocators are too harsh for the bird not to feel pain, and inverted 'killing tubes' can cause a degree of stress.

Killing by neck dislocation

Regularly handle your birds so that they are used to being picked up and will come to you without any fuss. If you're going to kill a bird for food, separate it from its fellows and deny it food for 24 hours, but give it plenty of access to fresh water.

The same method is used for killing both hens and ducks, only you will have to work harder with ducks because they are a good deal stronger. Gather up your bird gently and calmly and hold both legs in a firm grip with one hand. The head should be held in the other hand between the middle fingers, pointing outwards so that the back of the head rests in the palm of the hand. Push down on the head end and twist sharply. You will feel the bones break and the animal will begin to flap violently. Within 30 seconds the flapping will stop and the bird will be dead when the convulsions cease and the eyes close.

Plucking

Hold or hang the bird upside down for the blood to fill the void in the neck, or cut through the neck to allow the blood to escape.

Carefully pull out the flight feathers. Some people dip the bird in hot water – around 60°C for a minute – and pluck it wet. This can help speed up the process, especially with bigger birds.

Plucking is done by rhythmic sharp tugs at the feathers 'against the grain' – that is, in the opposite way to how the feathers lie. When you get used to it, a bird can be plucked in ten minutes.

You can compost the feathers, but they have all kinds of uses, from pillows to adding to mud to build pretty strong walls.

Dressing a duck

1. Completely pluck the bird as soon as possible after it is killed.

2. Remove the head with a cleaver as close to the bottom of the neck as possible. Chop off the feet. Open up the skin around the neck.

3. At the other end, cut around the anus, or vent – being careful to avoid cutting through the guts. If that happens, you will have a proper mess to sort out.

4. Pop your fingers inside the skin and open up a hole; use scissors to make the hole bigger by snipping at the skin, making sure (again) that you do not pierce the guts.

5. Place the carcass on some newspaper and get your fingers – or the whole hand – inside and draw out all of the insides. You should have drawn the livers, heart and lungs out, too. Keep the liver and heart if you want, either for gravy or for the dog.

6. Pull out the crop at the head end, and any associated bones. Make sure you cook the animal as soon as possible after you've dressed it.

Foraging from the Wild

It is quite remarkable how much we used to rely on the hedgerow harvest in this country – and how much we've forgotten. In our case we lived near Europe's largest aniline factory which made everything blue and smelly, so for us in the 1960s, foraging meant a bus ride to the far reaches of the city where the water in the rivers and the air were fresher. It was good to get out into the countryside, have a day out and bring back a basket full of blackberries – which used to leak and drip on the bus journey home!

These days you cannot see pollution so much, but it's still there. Gone are the days when cars spewed lead in their exhausts, making roadside foraging unhealthy as well as dangerous. But most rivers in the city are still polluted in one way or another, rendering their fish impossible to eat. I can catch trout in every river in Manchester, but I wouldn't necessarily eat them.

Which all goes to prove an important point: be sure about your foraging. If you're not completely happy about the state of the land, field or stream, then simply pass it by. Don't be tempted to collect any vegetable material such as dandelions from pavements, either. Councils regularly spray them with insecticides and herbicides, and dogs do the same with urine.

It's not a supermarket

On supermarket shelves you expect to find perfect fruit and vegetables that need little washing. In the field you might find a perfectly edible specimen that had been found by some creature before you. For example, common earthball mushrooms are devoured by many more species than just us humans, as you will see when you cut one open – dozens of tiny insects might be lurking inside. This is one of the main reasons for washing your food, but get the bugs out and what is left is perfectly edible – and enjoyable, too.

Be prepared to cut off 'bad bits' and collect only those pieces you would be willing to eat, but do collect them all the same. This mostly applies to mushrooms, but it is equally important when it comes to collecting fruit.

Don't take everything

There is a temptation to stock up and be sure we have enough food to eat. But, if you take, for example, all the wild garlic from a wet river valley, there will be none left for next year. If you only take ten percent, the plants will reproduce in order to replace what you took.

You should approach foraging and growing in different ways. When you grow, you want to maximise your crop. When you forage, you become a part of nature, sharing in a real way with rats and mice, pigeons and sparrows. Don't take everything because once it has all gone, it probably won't return.

Whose field is it, anyway?

Just because you have a right to roam does not mean you have the right to pick. Theoretically, you have the right to take a few leaves from a plant, although certainly not from any of the protected plants in the country, but you certainly do not have the right to collect a harvest on someone else's land.

It might not matter if you're simply raiding a few hedgerows, but you might find yourself in trouble with the landowner if you pinch his wild mushrooms. The law changed about 150 years ago, making it illegal to forage on private land. Even the biblical practice of gleaning the fields to get some corn stopped unless you had specific permission from the landowner. There is a good side to this: if you simply walked into any old field to forage, you could get into real difficulty if there happened to be a bull about.

Similarly, sheep can be quite dangerous, and the act of asking permission will clear up any such dangers. By the way, never enter a field unless you have a stout stick in your hand. Rams are particularly fond of running up behind you and butting you over before trampling on you. The stick is for self-defence.

Be sure of what you are doing

The countryside isn't there to provide you with everything you need for the home. For example, it's illegal to uproot any wild flower in the countryside. So if in June you come across some beautiful red and unusual flowers that would look lovely in a vase, leave them alone! It is best to decide what you are foraging for, and stick only to that.

Seasonality

No matter what time of year, there is always something you can eat in the wild – if you know what to look for. Of course, fish and game have their seasons, and many country- and townsfolk alike waited with eager anticipation for the 'Glorious 12th' when, at last, they could bag some food. For many with hungry mouths to feed, however, a rabbit was just as edible in April as it was in November, and thus the game laws were enforced to ensure that a species could raise its young before being killed.

Around a town, however, there is still a constant supply of food to be found – if you know where to look. The following are a just a few examples:

Winter
Mushrooms, Rose hips, Dandelion, Chickweed, Mahonia, Rowan berries, Hawthorn berries

Spring
Wild Garlic, Watercress, Fat Hen, Mushrooms, Nettles, Dandelions, Chickweed, Hawthorn leaves, Elderflower

Summer
Lime, Seaweed, Walnuts (young), Blackberries, Mushrooms, Cherries, Sorrel

Autumn
Nettles, Elderberries, Apples, Crab Apples, Sloes, Chestnuts, Walnuts, Cobnuts

Ten Plants to Harvest

This is not meant to be an exhaustive list, but is a cross-section of the plants we harvest from time to time, or have experimented with on occasion.

In recent years humans haven't had to rely on foraged food; perhaps we will in the future, but in any case foraging is a knowledge that can make the difference between starvation, poisoning and plenty in hard times. Even in the modern world, it can add a delicious variety to your diet.

Bistort

This plant looks a bit like a plantain. It has knife-like leaves and a central stalk which, to the passerby, make it look like grass. In late spring, the central stalk boasts a flower head with very tight pink and white flowers on it. The flowers look like someone has chewed gum and pasted them onto the plant.

Bistort's leaves are a bit spearlike and should be mixed with others to make a proper meal (eating only bistort leaves would feel like a bit of an imposition). Traditionally they were used in a Lenten pudding called Easter ledger. To make this, you need a handful each of bistort, nettle, dandelion and flowering currant leaves.

Soak them in water overnight and chop them finely. Drain and mix with a cup of oatmeal and a finely chopped onion. Bake at 180°C/gas mark 4 for 20 minutes, then break an egg into the mixture to cook as it cools. Makes four portions.

Bramble

This mass of prickly plant is found on waste ground and in woodland. In Georgian times brambles were planted over graves to keep the dead in their coffins. These days you have to stop them from growing – they cause such a tangled mess! However, it is interesting to know that if you find brambles in churchyards, they could be at least as old as the church: sometimes several hundred years.

Their fruit, the bramble or blackberry, can be collected from July to September. It is said that Satan urinates on them on Michaelmas (29 September), so don't collect them after this date if you're superstitious! In truth, any fruit still on the plants at this time is likely to be of inferior quality.

In order to harvest brambles effectively you need a pole with a nail half-knocked into one end. Thrust the pole into the thicket and pull out a branch so that you can easily pick out the fruit.

Blackberries freeze well and, as well as jam and jelly, you can make apple and blackberry pies and crumbles from them. It's a shame that these two plants don't always ripen at exactly the same time, but if you freeze some, then you get the best of both worlds.

By far the best use of brambles, I think, is the three or four gallons of bramble wine we brew each summer. It takes ages to collect enough for that much wine, but in February, with a glass in your hand, it really is worth it!

Crab apples

Crab apples are hardly edible but still more than worth collecting because you can use them to make the best apple jelly there is. Crab apples look like tiny apples, and there are a lot on each tree. Collect them in autumn or winter.

To make apple jelly, chop up the apples and cover them with water in a large pan. Boil until they are soft and strain the liquid into a bowl through a muslin cloth or jelly bag. Don't squeeze the pulp at all.

Measure the liquid and add 1kg of sugar for every litre of juice. Boil until you get a setting point (see page 266). Stir and ladle into prepared, sterilised jars (see page 266), screw the tops on immediately and label when cool.

Dandelions

The word *dandelion* means 'lion's tooth' because of the serrated edges of the leaves. It is possibly one of the healthiest plants you can eat. The Latin is *Taraxacum officinale*, which means official cure for ailments. In particular it is good for kidney and urinary problems because it is a natural diuretic.

Use dandelion leaves in a salad and take them in the early spring when the leaves are small and sweet. Later in the year you can put a plant pot over them to blanch the leaves; cover the drainage holes, too, with pebbles. In addition to draining the colour out of them, this serves to make them less bitter. You can also roast the roots; they have a bitter flavour – a bit like chicory.

Nettle

This is one of the best plants in the service of mankind. The leaves can be eaten, the stems can be made into rope or fashioned together to make cloth. Theoretically, you could eat nettle soup while wearing a nettle suit!

Nettles grow best where animals have urinated, but don't let that put you off. We all know about the sting and think this is to stop us from eating nettles. However, once picked and cooked in boiling water, the sting is no longer a problem – just be sure to wear gloves while you're picking them.

Pick only in the spring and early summer, or if you must take leaves later in the year, then pick only the topmost and youngest.

Rinse and drain them. After a few hours most of the stings will have gone, and you can bash them about with a towel, which will finish off any stings. Cook them just as you would spinach or any greens, and also use in soups or casseroles. We freeze parboiled leaves in an ice-cube tray and add them to everything from curries to omelettes.

Rose hip

When rose hips are in the hedges in the autumn, we collect a lot of them. There is more vitamin C in rose hips than any other plant on the planet. You can collect any rose hips – none of them are poisonous. Just make sure you wear gloves when you do so.

To make rose hip syrup you need 1kg of rose hips and half as much sugar. Remove all the stalks and brown bits and chop the flesh into small pieces. You can put them into the food processor if you like. Cover with boiling water and simmer for 15 minutes. Remove from the heat and leave the hips to steep. Strain the liquid into another pan and cover the remaining pulp with water and boil for another 10 minutes. Add this liquid to the first, then discard the hips.

Boil this liquid until it has reduced to 1.2 litres, then add the sugar, stirring until it has all dissolved. Allow to cool, then bottle it in sterile containers (see page 266). This is a brilliant tonic, and it is also fantastic for getting yeast going for brewing.

Sloes

The blackthorn is a hedgerow plant, the one with the spines as big as a hairgrip that pierce you every time you go near them. Sloes can be recognised because they look a little like plums in the hedge: quite small and in little bunches. The very best use for them, apart from making sloe jelly, a little like the crab-apple jelly above, is to pop them in a sealable container of gin.

Sloe gin is the very best start to Christmas celebrations – but brandy will do just as well!

Wild garlic

Imagine you're walking along a riverbank in woodland and a strong aroma of garlic hits your nostrils. Nearby, probably on a hillside, there will be a number of plants all clumped together with pretty white, star-like flowers. This is wild garlic, otherwise known as ransoms. It is completely edible. You can tell these from any other woodland plant by their strong garlic aroma. If it doesn't smell of garlic and has white flowers, leave it alone!

Simply snip the plant at the base and use it as if it were regular garlic. Don't uproot it, however, because the small bulb will send up a new stalk next year. Finely chop the stem, leaves and flowers and use as you will. It has all the health benefits of ordinary garlic.

Rosebay willowherb

Also known as 'fireweed', these tall plants with pinkish-red flowers on the top can be eaten so long as you are careful. Some people can be allergic to the juice that comes from the cooking process. Collect the small, spear-like leaves and boil them like cabbage, then strain them from their water into a colander. Rinse them with boiling water and then they make an excellent cabbage alternative. The young shoots can be taken whole and eaten as though they were asparagus, for which they do make an excellent alternative. Again, wash all vestiges of the cooking water away.

Lime leaves

The lime, also known as the linden tree, bears flowers on its leaf bracts, and was the mainstay of country parks of the eighteenth century. Its leaves are excellent to eat when the plant is young. In the spring, gather some new leaves and boil them like greens. They can also be eaten raw in salads, and both blossom and leaves make a restorative tea.

Collecting Wild Mushrooms

There are more wild mushrooms eaten these days than ever, and more people are joining foraging groups and getting out there to enjoy these fantastic organisms. I say 'organisms' because modern science believes fungi to be neither plants nor animals. Some of the biggest animals on the planet are fungi, living in soil, measuring many miles and weighing many tonnes. You simply don't see them because their filaments are microscopic.

Collecting mushrooms in the UK can be hazardous, however, so I am deliberately steering away from giving you a definitive and foolproof guide to the ones you can eat because you should learn these at the hands of an expert who knows the nuances of mushroom identification. The Destroying Angel and the Death Cap, for example, are pretty similar to ordinary button mushrooms, so you need to be absolutely sure of what you're collecting in order to be safe, not sorry.

A good trug

Once you have learned at the hands of an expert and are ready to collect, keep mushrooms in a trug, which is a basket made out of wood, and never collect them in plastic bags. They break easily and should be handled carefully. Use a sharp knife and cut the mushroom just above the surface, and do not pick them from the soil by hand. Ripping it up damages the mycelia, or filaments, under the soil. Also, if it happens to be poisonous and you've picked it by mistake, you could get it on your hands.

Five edible wild mushrooms

The penny bun is sometimes called the cep, which is its French name. Found on the woodland edge, the penny bun mushroom has a brown cap between 5–12cm in diameter and is brownish. Underneath, it is yellow or greenish/cream. Under the cap there are no gills, just tiny tubules, but the stalk has some veins just under the skin. If you tap the skin under the cap, it doesn't bruise, like many poisonous types. It is brilliant grilled – with or without cheese!

The birch boletus grows exclusively with silver birch trees. Its stem is composed of lots of scales and the mushroom darkens with age. The cap, which is about 12cm across, is coloured many shades of brown. It starts like a penny bun, but flattens out in time. The stem is really rough and looks a bit like used sandpaper. This mushroom is the one people dry, then put into soups and stews. Actually, it is very good in a stir-fry. To dry it, cut it into thin strips and leave in a dry spot, or use a desiccator.

Puffball There are many types of puffball, including the poisonous earthball. You tell the difference by slicing them. Only ever eat the pure-white ones. If you see blackness, it is poisonous. Puffballs are found in woodland and, as their name suggest, they look like a ball so are easy to recognise. When you slice them, wash away any insects that might have taken up residence, but then simply chop them into cubes and fry in butter.

Morel The most wonderful mushroom. Morels have a creamy white stalk and a brown top. The top isn't mushroom-shaped but looks more like a dried prune. It is reticulated, with lots of veins and undulating indentations on it, and has the most wonderful flavour.

Chanterelles look like loose cups on orange/cream stalks. Their tops are made of many lobes of flesh (looking a bit like a 1950s' hairdo), and underneath are lots of parallel gills. The gills are the best way of recognising a chanterelle. The cap is about 12cm in diameter and the whole mushroom, stem and all, is used. It is wonderful fried in butter with shallots.

III

Food
and
Cooking

Baking Bread

Bread-making has been an essential part of our lives for many centuries. It sustains and comforts us when we are hungry at all times of the day. Bread can be used for so many things, from sandwiches and bread puddings to thickening stews and casseroles.

Making your own bread has many benefits. The first is obvious: you know exactly what is going into your loaf. Reading the list of ingredients in a well-known white sliced loaf reveals that there are 12 ingredients, four of which are E-numbers. While these are not dangerous in themselves, one of them is a flour 'improver' – a substance that creates a stretchier dough so that, as the dough rises, it creates more air holes. Your loaf therefore looks bigger, which means the manufacturer is actually selling you air.

By making your own bread, you are in control of its salt and fat content. Baking it also makes the house smell wonderful, especially on a dreary winter's day. But best of all is the *flavour*: everyone I know loves homemade bread.

Today it has never been easier to make your own bread. Yes, you can use fresh and dried yeast, but fast-action dried yeast has almost halved the time it takes to make fresh bread. You can buy all the ingredients you need in the supermarket, so everything is readily available. You don't need much in the way of utensils, either; just a couple of strong baking sheets and a couple of loaf tins.

The recipes in this chapter are not suitable for bread-making machines – all are designed to be done by hand – but you can use a mixer with dough hooks if you have problems kneading the dough. After you have added the liquid, use the dough hooks to mix the dough for a few minutes until it is smooth, then to finish the kneading process you can continue with them or use your hands. No matter how you do it, however, the main aim is to enjoy both the making and the eating of homemade bread.

The secrets of successful bread-making
- It is essential to have a warm atmosphere in the place where you're making your bread.
- Always sieve your salt and flour together. Salt must not come in direct contact with the yeast; otherwise, it will kill it.
- Use enough liquid to make a moist dough which, when you are kneading it, becomes smooth and elastic in consistency.
- Knead well for at least 10 minutes.

Bread Shapes

I tend to make simple shapes: they cook more evenly and are easier to slice. But it is also enjoyable to experiment with dough and have some fun.

The tin loaf is obviously made in a loaf tin. This is usually a 450g tin, but you can get larger and smaller ones. The shape is the traditional rectangular, rounded-top loaf: easy to slice and good for sandwiches and toasters.

The split tin This is simply a tin loaf with a lengthways cut slicing about 1.5cm deep down the centre. The cut is done just after 25 minutes of proving time. Again, this loaf is easy to slice.

The bloomer To make this shape, the dough is rolled into a long, wide sausage and has three or four diagonal cuts (about 5mm deep) made into the top during proving, as with the split tin.

The cottage loaf is made of two dough balls – a small one on top of a large one – and resembles a large brioche.

To make this shape, cut a third of the dough and roll it into a ball, then do the same with the rest of the dough. Moisten the top of the larger piece of dough and put the smaller ball on top of the larger one. Use the floured handle of a wooden spoon to press down through the centre of both the layers of dough; this seals the two together.

I always have trouble with this loaf because it loses its shape during proving and becomes a big bread blob. But if you like the idea, have a go and just enjoy yourself; it will taste good anyway. Prove according to the recipe.

The plait Divide the dough and roll it into three thick sausages, each about 20cm long. Seal three of the ends together with a little water and press well. Plait the strands of dough fairly loosely and seal the open ends with water as before, pressing well to seal. Prove according to the recipe.

The hedgehog Roll the dough into a long, wide sausage and prove for 25 minutes. Cut into the dough diagonally along the top, making each stroke about 1cm deep, then cut in the other direction, criss-crossing the other cuts. The dough will have sticky-up points like a hedgehog.

Leave to prove for the rest of the time. Tweak the pointy bits up into sharper points just before baking.

Basic White Yeast Bread

If you want to have a go at making bread with ordinary yeast, it is still great fun.
The difference in preparation is that two proving periods are needed to
allow the bread to rise and soften.

Makes 3 large loaves

25g fresh or 15g dried yeast
900ml warm water
2 teaspoons sugar
4 level teaspoons salt
1.5kg strong white flour
2 tablespoons oil
  (sunflower, olive or rapeseed)

1. Crumble the fresh yeast into 100ml of the warm water, or if using dried yeast, add it to 200ml of the warm water. Whisk the dried yeast into the water with a fork. Stir the sugar into the yeast mixture, and leave in a warm place for 20 minutes, or until the mixture is very frothy and big and little bubbles are forming.

2. Sieve the salt and flour together into a large mixing bowl.

3. Make a well in the centre of the flour and pour in the yeast mixture, oil and the rest of the water.

4. Use a wooden spoon to combine the flour and liquid. If the mixture is too sticky, add a tablespoon of flour; similarly, if the mixture is too dry, add another 50ml of warm water.

5. Flour your hands and turn the dough out onto a clean, well-floured surface. Begin to knead the dough by pushing it slightly away from you with the heel of your hand, then bringing the far edge of the dough towards you and pressing it into the middle of the dough ball. Rotate the dough slightly, and repeat. Continue this fold-and-turn kneading for 10 minutes. This will ensure that you have a soft, light dough.

6. Put the dough in a floured mixing bowl, cover it with a tea towel and leave in a warm (not hot) place, away from any draughts.

7. After about 40 minutes, the dough should have doubled in size. Now it needs to be 'knocked back'. This simply means punching it down and kneading it for 3–4 minutes.

8. Shape the dough into whatever shape you choose, from individual rolls to large tin loaves. Place the shaped dough on a baking sheet or in the tins; just remember to grease whatever you use, even if it is non-stick.

9. Leave to prove for another 40 minutes, or until doubled in size again. Preheat the oven during this second proving to 220°C/gas mark 7.

10. Bake for 25 minutes, then turn down the heat to 200°C/gas mark 6 and cook for a further 15 minutes. The loaves should be deep golden in colour and if cooked in a tin, they should have shrunk away from the sides slightly. To test whether the bread is cooked in the centre, rap the base with your hand knuckles: it should make a hollow 'thud' noise. When testing your bread, remember to use oven gloves or a thick towel as it will be extremely hot.

11. Leave to cool on a wire rack for at least 30 minutes before slicing; otherwise the loaf will lose its shape.

Storage

The bread will stay fresh for 3–4 days if stored in an airtight tin.

Tip

Bread dough may be frozen after the first proving period. When you defrost it, allow it to thaw completely before shaping and proving the second time.

Variation

Use strong wholemeal and strong brown flour in this recipe if you wish, although wholemeal flour takes slightly more liquid than white or brown, so remember to have plenty of warm water in case you require it.

Simple White Loaf

This recipe uses fast-action dried yeast. You only need to prove the dough
a single time, so preparation time is almost halved.

Makes 2 large loaves

900g strong white flour
2 level teaspoons salt
1 x 7g sachet fast-action dried yeast
450–500ml warm water
1 tablespoon sunflower or rapeseed oil

Variation
Use wholemeal and brown flour in place
of the white if you wish, or mix white and
wholemeal or brown flours for a lighter taste
and texture. For this, I use 500g strong white
flour and 400g strong wholemeal or strong
brown flour.

1. Sieve the flour and salt together into a large
mixing bowl. Stir in the dried yeast.

2. Make a well in the centre of the flour and add
¾ of the water and all the oil. Mix well with a
wooden spoon. Add more water as necessary to
make a moist dough.

3. Use your hands to combine all the ingredients,
kneading to make a smooth dough. Continue
kneading on a floured surface for 10 minutes.

4. Shape the dough and place in greased tins or
on a baking sheet. Leave it in a warm place for
35–40 minutes, or until it has doubled in size.

5. During this proving time, preheat the oven to
220°C/gas mark 7.

6. After proving, bake immediately for 25–35
minutes. If the bread is cooking too quickly on
the top, turn down the heat after 20 minutes to
200°C/gas mark 6.

7. Cool on a rack for 30 minutes before slicing.

Milk Loaf
A very soft bread that makes wonderful toast.

Makes 1 large or 2 small loaves

500g strong white flour
1 level teaspoon salt
Half a 7g sachet fast-action dried yeast
280ml warm whole milk

1. Sieve the flour and salt together into a large bowl. Stir in the yeast.

2. Make a well in the centre of the flour and pour in ¾ of the milk. Stir with a wooden spoon to combine the ingredients, adding more milk as necessary.

3. Use your hands to combine all the ingredients fully and begin to knead the mixture into a smooth dough. You may find you can knead this amount of dough in the bowl, but if you prefer, knead on a lightly floured surface. Either way, knead for 10 minutes.

4. Either shape the dough into a long roll and place it on a greased baking sheet or put it into a greased loaf tin.

5. Leave to prove for 40–45 minutes, or until doubled in size.

6. During the proving time, preheat the oven to 220°C/gas mark 7.

7. Bake for 20 minutes, then turn down the heat down to 200°C/gas mark 6 and bake for 5–15 minutes longer.

8. Remove from the oven immediately and transfer to a cooling rack. Allow to cool for 30 minutes before slicing.

Dinner Rolls

The wonderful thing about rolls is that you can make them any shape or size.
This recipe is great for burger buns, sandwich rolls or small dinner rolls to
accompany a soup or starter course.

Makes 15–20 rolls

800g strong white flour
2 level teaspoons salt
1 x 7g sachet fast-action dried yeast
200ml warm milk
250ml warm water
1 tablespoon sunflower or rapeseed oil

1. Sieve the flour and salt together in a bowl. Stir in the yeast.

2. Combine the milk and water and pour into the flour. Add the oil.

3. Stir with a wooden spoon to combine all the ingredients and finish mixing with your hands.

4. Knead the dough for 10 minutes on a lightly floured surface.

5. Shape the dough into the required shapes and sizes of rolls and place on a greased baking sheet. To make sandwich or burger buns, roll the dough into small balls and press them flat on the baking sheet.

6. Leave to prove in a warm place until doubled in size – about 30 minutes. During this time preheat the oven to 220°C/gas mark 7.

7. To add a professional finish to your rolls, brush with a mixture of egg and milk: 1 beaten egg to 4 tablespoons milk. You could also sprinkle the tops with sesame or poppy seeds.

8. Bake for 15–20 minutes. Transfer to a wire rack to cool.

Mixed Seed Bread

The wonderful thing about making this loaf is that you can add your favourite seeds. I use a mixture of sesame, pumpkin and poppy, but there are onion, sunflower, linseed and many others. Just experiment with them and see which you prefer. I make this bread using half wholemeal and half white flour, as the flavour and softness is well-balanced.

Makes 2 medium-sized loaves

400g strong white flour
2 teaspoons salt
400g strong wholemeal flour
120g mixed seeds
1 sachet fast-action dried yeast
450–500ml warm water
1 tablespoon sunflower, olive or rapeseed oil

1. Sieve the white flour and salt together into a large mixing bowl. Stir in the wholemeal flour and the mixed seeds, reserving some of the seeds to sprinkle on top of the loaves. Make sure they are well-combined and that the seeds are distributed evenly throughout the mixture.

2. Stir in the yeast.

3. Make a well in the centre of the flour and pour in ¾ water and all of the oil. Mix together with a wooden spoon and add the rest of the water to make a soft but not too sticky dough. Use your hands to combine all the ingredients thoroughly.

4. Begin to knead the dough in the bowl, then lightly flour a surface, turn it out and knead it there for 10 minutes.

5. Shape the dough into 2 equal round cobs or loaves and place on a large greased baking sheet.

6. Cover with a tea towel and leave to prove in a warm place; it should have doubled in size after about 35–40 minutes. Brush the tops of the loaves with warm water and sprinkle them with the reserved seeds, pressing the seeds down very lightly into the dough.

7. While the bread is proving, preheat the oven to 220°C/gas mark 7.

8. Bake the bread for 20 minutes, then turn the temperature down to 200°C/gas mark 6 and bake for 10–15 minutes, or until the loaves are golden brown.

9. Transfer to a cooling rack and allow to cool for 30 minutes before slicing.

Old-fashioned Herb Loaf

This needs to be made with fresh or ordinary dried yeast. It is made in a very different way to the other loaves, as it uses a batter-type dough that is beaten rather than kneaded. Very light and open-textured, this is ideal for serving with pâté or soup. Use your favourite herbs in this recipe: for example, one teaspoon dried thyme, tarragon, parsley or marjoram. Dried herbs are best in this recipe because the moisture from fresh herbs affects the dough.

Makes 2 medium-sized loaves

1 egg, beaten
220ml warm milk
20g fresh or 15g dried yeast
3 teaspoons sugar
1 tablespoon sunflower, olive or rapeseed oil
350g strong white flour
1 teaspoon salt
1 teaspoon dried herbs of your choice
    (or a mixture of two)

1. Mix the egg with the warm milk, and blend 4 tablespoons of this mixture with the yeast to make a paste. Add the rest of the egg/milk mixture, the sugar and the oil.

2. Sieve the flour and salt together into a mixing bowl and stir in the herbs until well-combined.

3. Use a hand mixer to whisk the liquid into the flour. Beat for 3–4 minutes.

4. Grease 2 x 450g loaf tins and divide the doughy batter between them.

5. Leave in a warm place to rise for about 35–40 minutes.

6. During the proving time, preheat the oven to 220°C/gas mark 7.

7. When they are well-risen, bake the loaves for 25–30 minutes.

8. Remove from the tins as soon as they are baked and transfer to a cooling rack.

9. Cool for 30 minutes before slicing.

Fruit Tea Loaf

This sweetened bread is delicious with afternoon tea or toasted at breakfast.
The mixture can be made into individual teacakes as well as a loaf.

Makes 1 loaf

500g strong white flour
1 level teaspoon salt
1 sachet fast-action dried yeast
50g golden caster sugar
50g softened butter
350ml warm milk
1 egg, beaten
50g currants
50g sultanas
25g mixed candied peel, optional, or use extra
   sultanas or currants

Variation

To make the individual teacakes, roll out the dough into 10 balls and flatten them with your hand on a greased baking sheet. Leave to prove in a warm place for 35 minutes and bake for 20–25 minutes. Leave the heat at 220°C/gas mark 7 for the whole of the cooking time.

1. Sieve the flour and salt together and stir in the yeast and sugar.

2. Rub in the butter.

3. Combine the milk and the egg and pour it gradually into the flour mixture, stirring well with a wooden spoon.

4. Begin to knead the dough and gradually knead in the dried fruit.

5. When the fruit is fully combined, knead the dough for 8–10 minutes. Add a little more flour if the mixture is too sticky.

6. Grease 2 x 450g loaf tins and divide the dough into 2 equal sections. Place each section in the prepared tin and prove in a warm place for 35–40 minutes.

7. During the proving time preheat the oven to 220°C/gas mark 7.

8. When the dough has doubled in size, bake for 25–35 minutes, turning the heat down to 200°C/gas mark 6 after 20 minutes. The loaves should be deep golden in colour when baked.

9. Leave to cool on a wire rack for at least 30 minutes before slicing.

Irish Soda Bread

Soda bread is made without using yeast; the leavening ingredient is a combination of baking powder and either buttermilk or milk with a tablespoon of lemon juice mixed in. Irish soda bread was (and still is in some parts of Ireland) baked on a large griddle over an open, glowing fire – but this recipe can also be baked in the oven. This doesn't keep as well as other types of bread, but it is such a speedy recipe that you can have it made within 30 minutes.

Makes 1 large round loaf

250g strong white flour
1 level teaspoon salt
1 rounded teaspoon baking powder
200g strong wholemeal flour
280ml buttermilk or 280ml milk with
   1 tablespoon lemon juice stirred in

Variation
To vary the flavour and add a healthy dose of oats, add 100g medium rolled oats in place of 100g of either the wholemeal or the white flour. Add this to the mixture when you stir in the wholemeal flour.

1. Preheat the oven to 220C/gas mark 7. Grease a baking tray.

2. Sieve the white flour, salt and baking powder together into a bowl.

3. Stir in the wholemeal flour until combined with the other ingredients.

4. Add the milk or buttermilk and stir in. The mixture should be slightly sticky.

5. Bind the dough together with the hands but don't knead it. Form it into a round.

6. Place it on the prepared baking sheet and flatten slightly. Cut a deep slash (about 2cm) into the dough across the top in both directions. This divides the bread into 4 sections.

7. Bake for 20–25 minutes, or until well-risen and golden brown. Cool for 10 minutes before eating.

Making Butter

In the early part of the twentieth century, people in cities and towns bought their butter from grocers' shops, but country-dwellers still made their own. When I was small, we had a wonderful farm-produce stall at our local market and it sold dairy foods, eggs and preserves. The butter was tremendous.

It is only in the last five years that Paul and I have made our own butter. We were researching butter-making and trying to decide whether we should buy a butter churn when we started to think of other ways you could make the stuff. A butter churn simply stirs the cream so that the fat molecules stick together and separate from the buttermilk. Our milkman often delivers our milk in large 2-litre plastic bottles, and we were just about to throw one in the recycling bin when Paul took it from me and went away. Five minutes later he returned, jubilantly shouting 'BUTTER!'

He had used the plastic bottle to shake up some cream and make butter. The amount of space in the bottle was sufficient to 'churn' the cream and the vigorous shaking allowed the fat to stick together. It was as simple as that. We poured the liquid that was left behind into the dog's bowl and he lapped it up gratefully.

Left behind was creamy, yellow butter. We cut around the middle of the bottle and poured the butter into a sieve, rinsed it and tasted it on a piece of bread. It was salt-less so we added a little salt, chopping this into the butter, and tasted it again. It was delicious.

We have since learned that, if you want to keep your butter for any length of time, you must rinse the it well in very cold water to get rid of the dregs of the buttermilk; otherwise, this will turn sour and spoil the lot.

This modern method of butter-making takes up very little time, and you can make a week's worth (unless you use a lot!) in less than 30 minutes.

Quick and Easy Butter

Makes approximately 350–420g

1 litre of double cream; this *must* be at
   room temperature
1 x 2-litre plastic milk bottle, with lid
Salt to taste

Have ready some pots either made of pottery or
glass. **Do not use plastic, as the fat content
can dissolve it and contaminate the butter.**
If the pots don't have lids, make a cover with
greaseproof paper tied with string.

1. Rinse the milk bottle in tepid water. Pour in
the cream and secure the lid. The cream must
not be too cold – at least room temperature. If it
feels very cold, put the milk bottle under warm
(not hot) running water for a few seconds.

2. Shake the bottle vigorously. An up-and-down
motion is better than side-to-side. Keep going
until you hear a change in the contents. When the
butter appears, there is a 'thudding' sound as the
fat in the cream separates from the buttermilk.

3. Take off the lid and pour the buttermilk into
a jug.

4. Cut round the widest part of the bottle and
scoop out the butter. You'll need to put this into a
fine colander to rinse out the final buttermilk
dregs. This must be done, as the buttermilk will
cause butter to sour prematurely. Clean the butter
by using a slow, steady stream of cold water and cut
into the butter gently with a knife as you do so.

5. Add a teaspoon of salt, sprinkling it evenly
over the butter. Cut into the butter and keep
rinsing. Do this for 4–5 minutes. The salt will
be washed away in the liquid.

6. If you want unsalted butter, don't add any
more salt. If you like it salted, add a level
teaspoon of salt, put the butter on a clean
chopping board and use a knife to mix the salt
into the butter. More salt may be added in the
same way if you wish.

7. Press the butter into the prepared pots, cover
and store in the fridge. This can then be now
used for spreading, frying and baking.

Storage
This will keep for 2–3 weeks in the fridge.

Variation
To make a more spreadable butter, add 1
tablespoon sunflower or olive oil. After washing,
rinsing and salting the butter, put it into a large
bowl and beat in 1 tablespoon of oil. Don't
cream it like you would for a cake; just beat it in
gently; you don't want lots of air in the butter.
This spreads much easier and can be spread
straight from the fridge.

Flavoured Butters

These make excellent quick sauces for meats and desserts. Simply take your required quantity of butter out of the fridge for at least an hour before you want to add your flavours.

Brandy Butter

I have made this with both icing and soft brown sugar; the icing sugar makes it lighter and fluffy, but the brown sugar makes it richer and deeper in colour. We don't have this on our Christmas pudding because we prefer sauce, but a knob on a hot mince pie with a cup of coffee is sublime.

Makes about 5–10 portions, depending on how you wish to serve it

110g butter
40g icing or soft brown sugar
2 tablespoons brandy

1. Cream the butter and sugar together until light and fluffy.

2. Beat in the brandy.

3. Put in the fridge to chill for 30 minutes before serving.

Rum Butter

This is as equally delicious as Brandy Butter and just as gorgeous on mince pies and Christmas pudding.

Makes 5–10 servings

100g butter
40g soft brown sugar
A pinch of grated nutmeg
2 tablespoons rum

1. Cream the butter and sugar together until light and fluffy.

2. Beat in the rum and nutmeg.

3. Chill for 30 minutes before serving.

Buttercream for Cakes
This is the basic recipe you can use to fill or decorate cakes.

Sufficient to fill and decorate the top of a large cake or 12 cupcakes

150g butter, at room temperature
90g icing sugar

1. Cream the butter until light and fluffy.

2. Sieve in the icing sugar and beat in thoroughly.

3. Add your desired flavouring now and beat it in.

Other flavouring suggestions

- 50g melted chocolate
- ½ teaspoon vanilla extract
- ½ teaspoon almond extract
- 1 teaspoon coffee granules (mix into 1 tablespoon boiling water, cool, then beat into the buttercream)
- A few drops of peppermint oil and a drop of green food colouring
- Zest of 1 lemon and 1 teaspoon juice
- Zest of 1 orange and 2 teaspoons orange juice
- 1 tablespoon crème de cassis or framboise to make a delicious blackcurrant or raspberry flavour

Herb Butters

These are wonderful when used to top simple grilled or fried pork, lamb, beef or fish steaks. They also add flavour to plainly cooked vegetables.

Makes enough to serve 4 people

60g butter, at room temperature
2 teaspoons chopped parsley, dill, mint or tarragon
1 level teaspoon chopped sage, thyme, rosemary, basil or chervil
Pinch of salt (only if using unsalted butter)
Black pepper to taste

1. Put the butter in a bowl and mash with a fork until soft.

2. Work in the herbs, salt if you are using it, and black pepper. Your herb butter is now ready to use.

Serving suggestion
Roll the herb butter into a long sausage shape on some cling film, roll it up into a cylinder, then chill it in the fridge or put it in the freezer for 30 minutes. It can then be unrolled and cut into slices. I tend just to serve the butter in a bowl and let people spoon it onto their plates.

Anchovy Butter

Delicious served with steaks of all kinds. Try serving it with some king prawns grilled or barbecued on a skewer, then topped with this butter.

Makes about 8 servings

3 anchovies
120g butter
1 tablespoon lemon juice
A small garlic clove, grated

1. Mash the anchovies with a fork to make a paste.

2. Soften the butter and add the lemon juice, garlic and anchovies.

3. Beat well to combine all the ingredients.

Watercress Butter

I use this for making egg sandwiches, but it makes vegetable soups taste even more delicious.

Makes about 6 servings

1 bunch/about 40g fresh watercress, chopped
    and blanched for a minute in boiling water
100g butter
Salt and black pepper to taste

1. Use a food processor to purée the watercress, or grind it with a pestle and mortar.

2. Beat into the butter, then add salt and black pepper to taste and blend well.

Horseradish Butter

I use this for making tasty mashed potatoes with roasts and steaks.

Add to a kilo of mashed potatoes

50g butter
½ teaspoon grated horseradish

1. Blend both of the ingredients together by creaming as you would for a cake and add to the hot mashed potato.

Making Cheese

This is one of those skills that we in the modern world have forgotten about. Making cheese was one of the fundamental processes people had to do for themselves in the inner-city, back-to-back houses of Victorian Britain. The reason: they simply couldn't afford anything else.

The major routes out of the city were lined with shops, and few of them sold cheese. But people ate it all the same, and made it from the collected dregs of milk from a dozen houses. My own grandmother collected the milk from the bottoms of bottles to make her own cheese, and the process was very easy to complete. It still is – as this chapter is about to show you.

Types of milk

Cheese is nothing more than clotted milk protein. It has been around for many years – the earliest records predate the Egyptians – and then, as now, the first and most vital ingredient was milk. But exactly what kind of milk should you use to make cheese in the modern world?

Given the prevalence of diseases such as tuberculosis, I cannot bring myself to advise anyone to use raw milk. The same goes for goats and ewes milk. The very least you should aim for, in my opinion, is pasteurised cows milk. If you use sterilised milk, you will find that it takes longer for starters to work, but then this is no real tragedy. The big problem is the change in flavour.

The flavour of cheese is also dependent on the fat content of the milk that's used to make it. It so happens that fat molecules are trapped in a matrix as the cheese is produced, and fat brings flavour with it because it dissolves flavour molecules in the same way that water dissolves sugar.

If you're worried about your weight you can, of course, make cheese with skimmed or semi-skimmed milk, and it will have some flavour, but not much. However, making cottage cheese this way, with a tablespoon of crème fraîche, does result in a brilliant slimming cheese.

Unless you're watching your calories, however, take my advice and use full-fat milk to make your cheese: it is much tastier!

How to Set Protein

There are many stories about someone killing a calf and finding cheese in its stomach, but the truth is that when milk 'goes off', the protein sets naturally. The modern cheese-maker can use one of two main processes to set the proteins in milk. (Actually there are three, but we'll come back to that later.)

Acidity

When the bacteria present in milk multiply, the milk becomes sour and we reject it. However, if we wait until the acidity reaches pH 4.6, the protein casein will segregate from the liquid. Normally the smell and sight of this mixture causes us to heave and throw the lot away, yet it is only the sugary part of the liquid that is spoiled or 'off'; the separated protein is still quite fresh. So if you filter off the protein bit and wash it constantly until the last vestiges of 'bad milk' are gone, what is left behind is cheese.

There is no need to be squeamish about it; all you've done is allow bacteria to raise the acidity of the milk until the cheese is made. But you don't need 'off' milk to make cheese because you can use natural acids to make the protein set. The two most commonly used are vinegar and lemon juice. Interestingly, vinegar, when you wash it out of the milk, leaves less of a taint than lemon juice.

Diana uses vinegar to make cottage cheese or, with a little pressing, creamy Lancashire, and our daughter, Rebecca, makes a great cheesecake with cheese made from lemon juice.

Rennet

The second way of setting the protein in cheese is to use an enzyme. Obviously, calves drink a lot of milk; you would expect them to have an enzyme in their stomachs that will curdle milk, and so they do. It is called rennet, and this has been used for many hundreds of years to create cheese.

Enzymes work by causing a chemical reaction and are then released back into the solution to work again, so you only need a little rennet to curdle a lot of milk: on average, about one drop per 600ml will do the trick. Usually, cheese-makers use acidity and rennet combined by introducing some special bacteria into the milk, then adding rennet. This bacterial mix is usually referred to as a starter solution, and it keeps on working in the cheese to help it mature.

Anyone who doesn't like the idea of a calf being killed can buy vegetarian rennet. This is made from various plants, mainly ladies' bedstraw. It doesn't always work as quickly as animal rennet, so you have to be sure to experiment to find out the optimum amount.

The third way

The third way of making cheese is unique and interesting. Most people know that the protein in cheese is casein. However, there is another protein found in milk – the same one you find in eggs, known as albumen. Now, everyone knows that when you boil an egg, the white part, the albumen, sets solid. It isn't difficult to realise that if we boil milk, some of the albumen in it will set. Cheese made in this way is called ricotta.

Starters

Starters are frequently bought in powder form and mixed with milk. There are two main types: ones that withstand higher temperatures, called thermophyllic starters, and those that are used at lower temperatures, called mesophyllic starters.

You can also use homemade starters; double cream and yoghurt are used to make a really creamy cottage cheese. The recipes for cheeses will tell you which type of starter, if any, to use.

Runny and blue cheeses

According to his early biographer Eginhard, the Holy Roman Emperor Charlemagne (747–814) requisitioned several cartloads of Brie from a particular monastery, due simply to his fondness for it – a fondness that came close to bankrupting the monks in question. This information can be found in a report written some 1,300 years ago that relates how monks used to make this cheese. Brie was – and still is – achieved by adding a special starter; the cheese is 'consumed' by the bacteria, and the process turns it into a runny cheese.

Similarly, blue cheeses are made using a starter (or 'inoculum') called *Penicillium roqueforti*. This mould is added either to the milk or to the curds before pressing and causes the blueness and bitter flavour when the cheese is exposed to air. After piercing the cheese with sterile needles ('needling'), after around a fortnight the cheese will be transformed, showing the characteristic blue 'veins' running through it that give its name.

How to cheat

After a good deal of experimenting, I have found that, for the most part, the two cheese recipes in this chapter are all I need to make most kinds of cheese our family consumes. If I want a blue cheese, then just before the pressing stage I'll add a little blue cheese purchased from the shops. In a week I'll have a wonderfully flavoured cheese – no 'needling' required!

Basic Cheese-making Equipment

To make cottage cheese, you will need:
- A good thermometer
- A large pan
- A colander
- Salt
- Rennet, vinegar or lemon juice
- Muslin sheets
- Spoons and dishes
- Some way of hanging the muslin to drain the whey

To make harder cheeses, you'll need all of the above as well as:
- A cheese mould
- A cheese press or some weights

Keep it clean!

Cheese-making is a function of cleanliness. Imagine that you are handling the deadliest germs in the world – keep all of your equipment sterile and you shouldn't go far wrong. Also, don't mature your cheeses for long, and make sure that wherever you store them is spotless.

Temperature

Temperature is all-important in cheese-making. If a recipe says hold the temperature at 30°C for 15 minutes, you really have no room for manoeuvre. You need a good thermometer and you need to know your cooker in order to be able to manipulate 4.8 litres of milk in a large pan.

A confession

When I first made a cheese I didn't believe it only took a small amount of rennet, so I added drop after drop: probably over 25 in all. The cheese didn't set rock hard, but it had a very strange flavour, which was the rennet. Please don't add too many drops of rennet. Sometimes, on the box, you can find information as to how strong the batch is, so use this as a guide.

Basic Soft Cheese

With this simple cheese recipe you can make many others. If you make it ten times you may get ten different results, but this doesn't matter. You'll learn how milk behaves, how curds react to various treatments, and hopefully you'll have made some scones with the whey. (Diana told me to say that: there's a recipe later on!) This recipe is your starting point. It isn't complex and it doesn't take that long. It uses no starter and your finger instead of a thermometer, but it will make a good cheese. Improve it by mixing in some double cream at the end. Or add fruit, chives or garlic and turn it into something exotic.

Makes 300–400g of cheese

4.5 litres milk
Cool boiled water
4 drops of rennet (usually 2 drops per litre of milk)
Salt
Sterile bowl
Sterile knife
Several sterile muslin sheets (cheesecloths)
Sterile stockpot

1. Sterilise everything, and make sure that the muslin and all your utensils have been boiled. Wear an apron and wash your hands.

2. Put the milk in a large pan. Heat it until it feels warm to a clean finger, then turn off the heat.

3. Put a few tablespoons of cooled, boiled water in a cup, then add the rennet. Pour this into the milk and stir until it is completely mixed. You can't see it mixing, but just give it a lot of stirring.

4. Leave the mixture for 30 minutes. If the cheese has set, you should see a jelly-like appearance on the surface. If you put a knife into it you should see the milk curd break open,

like a small crack. The same happens if you put your finger in. This is called a 'clean break' and is fundamental to cheese-making. If the cheese hasn't set, leave it for another 30 minutes.

5. Once the cheese has set, use a sterile knife to cut the curds into cubes about 1cm square. When you do this you will see some of the whey come out of the solidified milk.

6. Remove as much whey as possible, because this goes off quickly and taints the cheese: pour the curds into a colander lined with 4 sheets of cheesecloth. Gather the corners together and squeeze out as much of the liquid as you can. Wash the cheese under cold water and repeat the process at least 4 or 5 times to remove all the whey.

7. Open the cheesecloth and add a heaped teaspoon of salt, mixing in with a spoon until it is evenly distributed. This action will 'draw' out more whey. Hang the cheesecloth on a hook and allow it to drain overnight.

8. What you have left is cottage cheese. Add a little cream and eat it like ordinary cottage cheese, or put it in a mould and press it to make a slightly firmer cheese.

Simple Hard Cheese

For this you need a thermophillic starter (see page 143), which will then make the cheese hard and creamy once it has been set in the mould after the cheese-making process.

Makes 300–400g of cheese

4.5 litres milk
200ml thermophillic starter
8 drops of rennet
Salt
Sterile bowl, knife, several muslin
    sheets (cheesecloths) and stockpot
Cheese mould
Cheese press or some heavy weights
Thermometer

1. Sterilise everything.

2. Put the milk into the stockpot and heat it to 32°C. Use your thermometer and try to maintain this temperature for 15 minutes.

3. Add 8 drops of rennet and wait for another 30 minutes for the curds to form. Look for a clean break and wait another 30 minutes if necessary.

4. Cut the curds into 1cm cubes and turn on the heat until the mix reaches 40°C. Turn off the heat and leave the pan to cool for 30 minutes. The curds will sit at the bottom of the pan, a process known as 'pitching'.

5. Ladle out the whey, disturbing the curds as little as possible. Then ladle the curds into the cheesecloth and bring the corners together so you can hang it overnight.

6. Once the curds have drained, open the cheesecloth and break up the curds, then add a level teaspoon of salt. Line a cheese mould – generally a plastic cup with holes in it to let the whey out – with a couple of muslin sheets. Place the curds in the mould and fold the muslin over them.

7. Put another piece of muslin, called the 'follower', inside the mould and push it down on top of the cheese. Either put the mould into a press, or place heavy weights on top. (Our first hard cheese was made using lots of tins balanced on top of the mould…) The idea of pressing is to get out as much whey as possible, and push the curds closely together. You need around 10kg of weights for this recipe, and sometimes twice as much with others. Some cheese presses give an indication of what force you are exerting.

8. Allow the cheese to mature. Simply take it out of the mould and leave the wrapping on for the first week, then remove it for the second. This way you get a creamy cheese that is really tasty and guaranteed microbe-free.

Tip
If, like me, you don't like mould growing over your cheese, leave it to mature for just a couple of weeks. I use an old fridge that no longer works as a place in which to mature my cheeses.

Making Sausage and Bacon

I t used to be commonplace for people to make their own sausages and bacon, especially when they kept their own pigs. What many people today don't realise, however, is that it isn't so long ago that people kept pigs in the city.

When I was a child in the 1960s, my friends and I used to help out at the abattoir where the local 'pig farmers' took their stock. I lived in Clayton, Manchester, whose industry included a wire works, a rubber plant, an abattoir, a jam factory and an aniline factory that coloured everything and everyone purple. There was a power station and a slag heap where we all collected coal; no one bought it because the power station boilers were so inefficient that the coal was never burned through.

This scene is hardly rural, but within a few doors from my house there was a chap who kept pigs in his garden, another man who had sheep that roamed on the grassy areas now covered by a housing estate, and almost everyone kept chickens.

We all swapped eggs or birds for lamb or pork and this barter economics worked for us. I well remember Mr Dennis's house. There you'd find a roll of pork soaking in brine, sausages in a kind of non-powered cool box (he didn't have a fridge) and dandelion leaves curing to dilute his 'baccy'. The day England won the World Cup, he made bacon sandwiches for the whole street.

Home-made meats today

Today, of course, you're not allowed to keep hens, pigs or sheep in the gardens of Clayton (or anywhere else in the UK that isn't granted an agricultural licence from the Department for Environment, Food and Rural Affairs; see page 66) and all the meat we eat is generally bought from the supermarket. In this chapter, however, you can at least learn how to make your own sausages and bacon – and discover just how delicious such home-produced meats can be.

Sausages

If you look on the side of a tin of chopped pork, or what is known as 'bacon grill', you will find the words 'other meats'. It is a loose term describing the pieces of flesh that, were you making the product for yourself, you might well throw away. The fact is that meat has always been expensive, so people have always found ways of making a little go a long way. This was as true in Grandma's day as today – but she had a few tricks up her sleeves that we would do well to learn.

I am going to make a statement that will make all butchers red with anger: *the best sausages are the ones made at home.* If you went to every butcher in the land and asked, 'Do you make your own seasoning from raw materials?' I would bet that over 99 percent of them would confess that it comes from a plastic packet made in a factory somewhere.

It might be a really excellent spice, but Grandma is more likely to have made her own – certainly before the Second World War, when most butchers sold sausage skins and every home had a hand grinder. Making sausages in the UK predates the Roman invasion; we have lived with them for a long time, although the person who realised you could stuff meat into a dead animal's intestine must have been an inventive cook indeed! The sausage itself goes at least as far back as 500BC.

It is interesting that the majority of air-dried sausages – chorizo and the like – come from hot, dry southern European countries like Italy and Spain. As you travel to the wetter north of Europe, the sausages are 'wet' and have to be cooked. A dried sausage will keep for a long time whereas the ordinary British banger will keep only keep a few weeks.

Skins or skinless?

Not all sausages have a skin. You can make up a mixture of sausage meat and simply roll it into shape and cook it in the normal way. The application of an egg white helps with the binding and you get a really excellent result.

Sausage skins nearly always come from an animal, although you can buy synthetic skins, but again, the raw material is animal-based. Truly vegetarian skins may possibly be available in the near future.

The most common skin is known as a hog skin and comes, naturally, from a pig. These are the easiest skins to use because they are quite strong and forgiving, and when you bite into them you get a pleasing resistance – what the Italians might call *al dente*. You can always tell a hog-skinned sausage by the slight curve; they are never straight.

When making sausages, you have to load the sausage skin onto a tube, which fits on the front of the grinder. As the sausage meat passes through the tube, it pulls the skin with it. You can make smaller, thinner sausages using sheep casings and you can make bigger sausages using beef casings.

Sausage skins are usually purchased from a specialist supplier, but if you ask your local butcher he will usually be glad to sell you some. They come packed in salt and have to be washed for at least 20 minutes to get the salt out. Once you've cleaned them, you'll find that the mass of skins is attached to a ring. Follow the skins along, separating them with your fingers, and after a while you'll find the end. Carefully open the end and trickle cold water into it to wash out the inside. This water also serves to lubricate the skin as it is pulled onto the stuffing tube.

When you've taken the number of skins you want, pack the rest in salt; they will keep for ages. If you buy sheep casings, be warned: they smell really bad but don't be put off: simply wash them and the smell goes away.

The hand grinder

There are many delivery systems for making sausages. By far the best one for novice sausage-makers is Grandma's hand grinder: the old-fashioned grinder turned by a crank handle. They come with sausage-stuffing attachments, usually three tubes of different thicknesses. The tubes fix onto the front of the grinder, but remember to remove the grinding plates so that you can more easily crank the mixture through. If you leave a little sausage skin hanging over the tube, the sausage meat will pull the skin over itself as it is forced out of the grinder – nothing could be simpler.

Sausage ingredients

A lot of people think that if they could make a 100-percent-meat sausage, it would be really tasty. Actually, you might as well just eat meat. It is important to understand that the ingredients in a sausage have a number of functions, each one as important as giving flavour.

Breadcrumbs

Breadcrumbs, or rusk, are added to the sausage to bulk out the meat, but they also have another function. When the sausage is cooking, the bread absorbs fat, thus increasing the flavour. A sausage should be between 15–20 percent breadcrumbs.

Water

This is the most vital ingredient. When a sausage cooks, it is the water content that cooks it. For this reason a sausage should be around 10–15 percent water. Your sausage meat should also have a definite wetness so that it flows easily through the grinder. It shouldn't be 'sloppy' in any way, but should have the consistency of thick but pliable porridge.

During the Second World War, the 'utility sausage' was dreamt up. It didn't contain much meat, but had an awful lot of water and breadcrumbs in a really strong skin. The result was a sort of tasty sausage that literally exploded in the pan, and it is these that led to the practice of pricking sausages to let the water escape. Modern sausages, thankfully, should not be pricked.

Fat

Another important part of the sausage is fat. This is sometimes added as diced fat, and sometimes just as the fat left on the meat. Of course, you're in control of what goes into your sausage when you make your own, but there should be some fat. About five percent is a good amount to use to enhance the flavour.

Salt

The word *sausage* actually comes from a Latin word meaning 'salted' which implies that this food is more about preserving meat. In a way it is, but we are concentrating on British bangers here, which don't last long and therefore need less salt.

In order to remain fresh on supermarket shelves, manufacturers add *a lot* of salt to sausages. Sometimes you'll find as much as a gram in a single large sausage and the flavour then has to be disguised by the addition of sugar.

You needn't be so cruel to your food. On the whole we make sausages from around a kilo of meat, which makes enough to eat at a couple of sittings (for a large family) and they don't have to last for weeks. You can freeze sausages, however; then they'll last for months.

On the whole, sausages should be three percent salt to remain fresh and edible for a couple of weeks. This translates to six level teaspoons of salt per kilo. I usually make low-salt sausages and use only three level teaspoons, and you can, if you wish (or if your doctor demands it), make no-salt sausages.

Meat

You can add any meat you like to a sausage. Usually, of course, it's pork, but beef, lamb and any combination of these three are possible. And since a sausage is simply food in a skin, you can also make seafood sausages, vegetarian sausages and even venison sausages if you like. On the whole, a really meaty sausage, full of flavour, is around 65 percent meat. Shop-bought ones by comparison are often less than 30 percent meat.

Other flavours

In the UK, every county (and sometimes every town) once had its own sausage style. Only a few of these are left today: Lincolnshire sausage, Cumberland and not much else. However, you now have the ability to make your own. The addition of sage, leek, chives, apple or sweet chilli sauce makes for a wonderful array of sausages.

Basic Sausage Recipe

Makes approx. 1.2–1.5kg sausages

1 large mixing bowl (a steel one stays cold),
   1 hand grinder, and 1 medium sausage tube
1kg pork (50% belly, skin removed, and
   50% leg)
250g breadcrumbs
Pepper and herbs to taste (optional)
30g salt
250ml very cold water
Hog casing: about 2.5 metres

1. First, sterilise all your equipment. The grinder, 'hides' meat, so you must clean it completely.

2. Cut the meat into small cubes. Pass them through the coarse plates of the grinder, then through the fine plates to make a great fine mince.

3. Mix the meat with the breadcrumbs and any other dry herbs and seasonings, if using. Dissolve the salt in the water, then add half the water and mix completely. The mixture should be easy to squidge between the fingers, but not floppy. Add more water to achieve this, if needed. Fry a little of your mixture to check the flavour and seasoning. Adjust both if necessary.

4. Load your skins on the tube, leaving a little to overhang. Remove the plates from the grinder and attach the loaded tube.

5. Put a small amount of sausage meat in the hopper of the mixer and, using your palm, press down while turning. The process is now a combination of loading and pushing down while turning the handle. The meat will come through at a reasonable pace. If you restrict the passage of the skins they'll fill more; let them run and they will fill less. At first, just allow the meat to flow without restriction. You'll have to move the filled sausages out of the way to make room for the rest (a hand grinder allows time to do this), so have a clean tray ready to 'catch' your sausages. If you run out of skins, simply cut more. Continue stuffing until all the filling has been used.

6. Wash your hands and keep them wet. Tie off the ends of the casings, then make links. The easiest way is simply to measure a hand's width of sausage, then twist it several times to make a link. Repeat all along the sausage. Cut through the links with scissors.

7. Rest the sausages in the fridge for a few hours before cooking in the usual way.

Variations
You can make almost any kind of sausage you like. Here are just a few flavour suggestions:
   • Somerset: add finely chopped apple and ice-cold apple juice instead of water
   • Pembrokeshire: add 50g chopped leeks
   • Cumberland: add 20g sage and 5g each black pepper and mace
   • Lincolnshire: add 50g chopped and rubbed sage

Making Bacon

Bacon is really only pork that has been salted to make it last longer. A simple bacon can be made from almost any cut of pork, so long as you remember that salt does not penetrate fat or skin very well.

Once you've made your own, you'll find that cheap, shop-bought bacon really isn't worth eating. Admittedly, at present you can't make bacon as cheaply as the cheapest you can buy from a shop, but you can make really good bacon – better than anything else in the world – for a third of the price of the most expensive stuff the supermarkets sell.

How salt preserves

In essence, salt preserves in two ways. Firstly, it is mildly poisonous, and this has an effect on any microbes present in the meat. Secondly, it pulls water from the meat, making it impossible for bacteria to grow because there isn't enough water available for them. Water is present, but the limited ability of microbes to get at it while saturated in salt makes the meat last longer.

The Cure

Curing meat was originally a way of keeping it through the winter. Now we eat bacon simply because we enjoy it; consequently there isn't the need to over-salt pork these days.

Experiment with making your own cures. Try adding lemon juice to the wet-cure recipe on the next page, for example, or pine needles to the salt recipe. Tea is another curing agent that makes great bacon.

You can also replace the sugar in the Best Bacon in the World recipe on page 154 with honey to make a brilliant ham that's perfect for slicing: simply wet-cure a piece of pork and when it's finished, drizzle it with honey, then bake the ham as normal. Simply delicious!

Wet-cure Bacon

This is simplicity itself. If you have a significantly thicker piece of pork, you'll need a bacon syringe, which is just like a huge doctor's hypodermic, to inject the brine directly into the centre of the meat.

Makes as much as you like!

1 large container such as a deep tray
Salt and water to make a brine solution:
   330g salt per 1 litre of water
A thin piece of pork, no more than
   2.5–5cm thick

1. Buy a cheap cut of pork and open it out by cutting through the strings. Remove the skin, taking much of the fat off, too.

2. Place the meat into the container: it has to be large enough to allow the meat to rest fully open. Cover with cold brine. You might need to weigh the meat down, but be sure turn it over every day.

3. After 3 days, drain off the old brine and replace it with new.

4. After a week, the bacon should be ready. Remove it from the brine, give a very quick rinse and pat dry.

5. Slice a small amount and cook it to see if it is salty enough. Too much salt can always be washed out at the cooking stage.

Dry-cure Bacon

Dry-curing is a simple but rather haphazard method for the home bacon-maker. Using this method you simply rub salt into the meat all around, wrap it in cling film, leave it for a day, then brush off what has become wet salt and reapply. Do this for 1 week. You will have taken a lot of water out of the meat in that time.

After this period give it a quick rinse, then leave it to stand in the fridge for a week. The saltiness will become more evenly distributed throughout the meat. You will have to cook and test a piece before serving to see if the bacon is too salty. If it is, soak it in water for 20 minutes and retest. I tend to slice the bacon, then soak the slices: it is much easier to achieve an even flavour this way.

Best Bacon in the World

This method will save your life and your wallet and turn you into the best bacon-maker there is. Choose your favourite cut of pork (I like belly) and get your butcher to slice it as though it were thick bacon. You are going to add cure to this bacon and overnight you will have a wonderful product. The bacon you buy from the shops can be up to three percent salt. This method makes one-percent-salt bacon, so it is really healthy stuff.

Known as green bacon, and being a sweet cure, this takes a little getting used to. Make sure you cook it in a seasoned pan so the sugar content doesn't caramelise and spoil. It's even better under the grill. If you like, you can use less sugar, or none at all, and you can treat the salt in the same way.

Makes as much as you like!

At least 1kg of your favourite cut of pork, sliced

For the cure
2 level teaspoons salt
2 teaspoons sugar

1. Spread the pork slices on a clean tray.

2. For every kilo of meat, add 20g of cure. Mix the salt and sugar well and sprinkle just on the meat, not the fat.

3. Pile up the slices on a plate, cover them with cling film and store in the fridge overnight.

4. The following morning you will have brilliant, healthy, low-salt bacon.

Making Stock

Good stock is the basis for all flavours, sauces, stews, soups and curries, and was a fundamental skill in our grandparents' kitchens. Whatever soup, casserole or meat sauce you're making, you will often need stock to help flavour your dish.

Making your own stock is economical, because you're using leftovers that would normally be discarded. Scraps of meat and gristle, poultry carcasses and meat bones, vegetable peelings and trimmings can all be used when making stock. Ask your butcher to chop up the larger bones or they'll never fit in your pan; the smaller the bones, the better the stock's flavour.

Supermarkets sometimes have their own butcher, but if not, buy a joint of meat with the bone in, such as shoulder of lamb, ham or pork shanks or hocks. Beef bones are harder to come by in the supermarket as they are so big, so a trip to a butcher is necessary. Pig's feet are ideal for making stock, but they're difficult to find. We buy ours from the big local outdoor market, but we have bought them in oriental supermarkets. If making fish stock, buy whole fish and use the heads, tails, skin and bones and cheaper cuts of fish such as coley or whiting. Don't use oily fish like mackerel or herring because the stock will be greasy. Only used smoked fish if that's the flavour of the dish you're preparing, like kedgeree. The giblets inside a turkey, chicken, or goose add depth to your stock's flavour, but if you don't have them, don't worry.

Stock-making equipment

Most stocks (except for fish) need long periods of cooking to produce the best flavour. Use a large, heavy-based pan with a tight-fitting lid. A pressure cooker will reduce the cooking time drastically. If using a pressure cooker, follow the manufacturer's guidelines for cooking this kind of food. Remember: the more you reduce the liquid in the stock, the more concentrated the flavour, so tasting at the various cooking stages is very important.

Storing your stock

If you plan to use your stock fairly quickly, then store it in the fridge. Chicken, meat and vegetable stocks keep for 5–6 days in lidded containers this way, fish stock for 3 days.

You can also prepare a large batch, then pour it cold into ice-cube trays; don't overfill. Two or three ice-cube trays may be needed, or a combination of trays and slightly larger containers. Label each type of stock, or you might end up using fish stock in a chicken soup! Add unthawed frozen stock cubes straight into dishes to enhance flavour.

Beef Stock

You'll get a much tastier stock if you roast the beef bones first. Because you won't
want to make this stock every day, it's worthwhile spending a bit of time when
you do make it in order to get the best-quality stock. It is time-consuming at first,
but once it's simmering, it only requires a quick check every 30 minutes
or so to see that it isn't boiling dry. This recipe makes plenty of stock –
approximately 1½–2 litres – so have plenty of containers or
ice-cube trays on hand, ready to hold it.
It is worthwhile getting marrowbones from a butcher and asking
him to chop them into manageable pieces. Another useful tip is to keep any
offcuts of beef you would normally throw away and freeze them for use when
making stock (defrost before using). Don't worry if they are fatty; this will add
to the flavour and will be skimmed off. This stock is very concentrated,
so you will not need to use much of it to flavour your dishes.

Approximately 2kg marrowbones

2 onions, quartered

2 celery stalks, with leaves, sliced into
5–6 pieces, with chopped leaves

2 large carrots, chopped into 4–5 large chunks

2.5–3 litres of cold water: sufficient to cover the
bones well

1 level teaspoon tomato purée

2 garlic cloves, peeled, optional

½ teaspoon dried mustard powder, optional

1 teaspoon dried parsley

½ teaspoon dried thyme

1 level teaspoon salt

Black pepper to taste

1. In a large roasting tin, arrange the bones and any other scraps of meat you have saved.

2. Add 1 of the onions, the celery and 1 carrot.

3. Add about 300ml water and roast at 200°C/gas mark 6 for about 40–50 minutes, or until brown, not blackened, as this will cause the stock to have a bitter taste.

4. Have a large saucepan ready to take the bones and roasted vegetables.

5. Put the contents of the roasting tin, including all the juices and bits on the bottom of the pan, into the saucepan and cover with water.

6. Add the other vegetables, tomato purée, garlic and mustard powder, if using, and sprinkle in the herbs and salt and pepper. Give a stir and put on the heat; bring slowly to the boil.

7. Once the stock is boiling, turn down the heat, partially cover the pan and simmer for 5 hours. Check the water levels off and on, topping up if it looks too low, but if it is simmering gently this shouldn't be necessary.

8. After the 5 hours of simmering time, bring to the boil and keep boiling for 10 minutes.

9. Remove from the heat and carefully drain the stock through a sieve into a large bowl or pan. Take care: the bones and liquid are very hot.

10. Return the liquid to the original pan and boil for 10 minutes, or until reduced to your taste. If you're satisfied with the taste after draining, don't bother with this stage.

11. Allow to cool, skim any settled fat off the top, then pour into prepared containers for storing (see page 155).

Chicken and Poultry Stock

This is much more straightforward to make than beef stock, and that's just as well, because you'll probably use this stock more often. Chicken stock can be used to enhance anything from soup to risotto, because its milder flavour blend more easily with a variety of ingredients.

Any chicken or turkey leftovers: skin, bones, giblets, cooked or raw
About 3 litres of hot water
½ teaspoon each of dried thyme, parsley, sage and tarragon
1 teaspoon salt
White or black pepper to taste
1 large onion, sliced thickly
1 carrot, unpeeled and cut into large chunks
2 stalks and leaves of celery, chopped roughly

1. Put the meat scraps and bones in a pan (break up the carcass if necessary) and cover with the hot water. Stir in the herbs and seasoning.

2. Bring slowly to the boil, then turn down the heat and simmer gently with the lid partially on, for 1½ hours.

3. Remove the lid and add the vegetables. Replace the lid and continue to simmer gently for a further 1½ hours, checking that the water level doesn't drop too rapidly. If it does, add a little more.

4. Check the flavour for seasoning and adjust if necessary. If the flavour isn't strong, bring to the boil to evaporate some of the liquid. This will take about 15 minutes of boiling.

5. Skim off any white foam if you wish, but this is only protein so it doesn't spoil the flavour. Strain the stock into a large, clean bowl or pan; use a sieve rather than a colander, because the latter has bigger holes and will allow bits of bone and debris through.

6. Allow to cool completely. Remove any fat that has settled on the top if you want to reduce the calorific value of your stock.

Fish Stock

When you're preparing fish, keep any trimmings and freeze them (unless previously frozen). This will allow you to avoid waste and bulk up the flavour of your fish stock. Don't forget to use shellfish trimmings such as shells and heads, but avoid any intestinal parts, as the stock may become bitter. Adding dry white wine really enhances the flavour of finished fish stock, but it may be omitted if you wish. It is hard to say how much fish you will need; I use just as much as will fit comfortably in 1½ litres of water with the other ingredients.

Fish trimmings and bits (see above)
1 leek, sliced roughly
1 carrot, quartered lengthways
2 celery sticks, chopped thickly
1.5 litres cold water
1 garlic clove (whole)
2 tablespoons fresh or
  2 teaspoons dried parsley
2 bay leaves
2 level teaspoons salt
Juice and zest of half a lemon
100ml dry white wine
Black pepper to taste

1. Put all the fish bits and vegetables in a large pan and cover with the water.

2. Bring slowly to the boil. Add the other ingredients, turn down the heat and simmer gently for 45 minutes.

3. Strain the liquor carefully into a large bowl using a fine strainer – there may be some small bones wishing to escape.

4. For extra-concentrated flavour, return the stock to the pan and boil for 10 minutes.

5. Cool completely before either freezing in small containers (see page 155) or storing in a lidded jar for up to 3 days in the fridge.

Vegetable Stock

Probably the easiest stock to make, so it's a good choice if you're in a hurry.
Like chicken stock, vegetable stock makes a versatile base for a wide variety
of dishes, including, of course, vegetarian ones.

20g butter
2 leeks, cut into 2cm pieces
2 onions, sliced
3 celery sticks, chopped into small pieces
3 carrots, chopped
2 bay leaves
2–3 sprigs fresh thyme or 1 teaspoon dried
1 teaspoon dried parsley
5–6 crushed black peppercorns
1 teaspoon salt
2 litres water

1. Melt the butter in a large pan and add all the vegetables. Keep on a low heat, cover and sweat the vegetables for 20 minutes.

2. Add the herbs, peppercorns and salt and stir in the water.

3. Bring to the boil, then simmer for 35–40 minutes.

4. Strain and use, or store in a lidded container or ice-cube trays. Freeze as soon as it is cold.

Soups

There are many reasons why I enjoy making soup. For a start, it generally only requires one pan to prepare and cook a soup. It is one of the easiest dishes to make from scratch, and provides a perfect opportunity to use up lots of bits and pieces you may have lurking in the refrigerator. They also generally freeze well, so you can easily double a batch, and freeze half of it for another time when you need something nourishing in a hurry.

Soup is very versatile, too. It makes a wonderfully comforting meal, and can be offered either as a light lunch or as a filling main course. You can make a very tasty soup from simple vegetables and, accompanied by crusty homemade bread or toast, this creates a meal that is satisfying not just because it tastes so good, but also because of the pride you'll feel after having made something so wholesome. If we're having a soup as a main meal, we sometimes make some thick chips to dip into it – delicious!

Soups can be thick and hearty with dumplings to serve as a main course, or delicate, thin and clear to serve as a starter course for a dinner party. Winter or summer, they go down well for lunch, dinner and supper (I really must think up a recipe for a 'breakfast soup'…), and in this chapter, I'm sure you will find at least one to suit your needs.

Celery Soup

This soup may be frozen after step 5, before adding the cream.
Stir in the cream as you are reheating the thawed soup.

Serves 4–6

50g butter
1 large onion, chopped
1 large potato, diced
5 sticks of celery, chopped
Salt and pepper to taste
1 litre vegetable stock (see page 160)
100ml milk
50ml double cream, at room temperature

Variation
To add extra flavour, crumble some strong-flavoured cheese on top of the soup just before serving.

1. Melt the butter in a large saucepan and fry the onions gently until soft.

2. Add the potato and celery and season to taste with salt and pepper. Cook for 4–5 minutes.

3. Stir in the stock and simmer gently for 20 minutes, or until the vegetables are soft.

4. Add the milk and cook for 2 more minutes. Remove from the heat.

5. Using a masher or a hand blender, mash or blend the soup until it reaches the desired texture. Some like it very smooth, but I like a bit of 'bite' to my soup.

6. Place back on a gentle heat and stir in the cream. Serve with crusty bread.

Celeriac Soup

I prefer celeriac to celery as a vegetable. It has a creamier, milder taste and makes wonderful vegetable mash as well as this soup.

Serves 4

50g butter
500g celeriac, scrubbed, peeled and cut into
   small cubes
1 large leek, chopped
2 carrots, sliced thinly
1 onion, chopped
1 medium potato, peeled and diced
Salt and pepper to taste
1 teaspoon dried thyme
1 tablespoon fresh chopped parsley
1.2 litres chicken or vegetable stock
   (see page 158 or 160)
2 tablespoons single cream
Paprika

1. Melt the butter in a saucepan over a low heat and add all the vegetables. Season with salt and pepper. Cover and allow to sweat for 8–10 minutes until the vegetables give off some of their liquid.

2. Add the herbs and the stock and bring to the boil. Turn down the heat as soon as it boils and simmer gently for 25–30 minutes, or until the vegetables are tender.

3. When cooked, blend it if you like a smooth soup, but reheat before serving.

4. Serve the soup with a swirl of cream and a sprinkle of paprika on top.

Serving suggestion
This goes well with warm homemade bread and a chunk of Cheddar.

Pea Soup

This version uses fresh peas and lettuce – a real homemade taste of summer.
Don't worry: you can use thawed frozen peas if you don't have fresh;
frozen actually taste very good in this recipe.

Serves 4

30g butter
Half a small onion, finely chopped
500g podded fresh peas or frozen (thawed)
800ml vegetable stock (see page 160)
1 head little gem lettuce, shredded
1 teaspoon sugar
Salt and pepper to taste
4 tablespoons single cream
Mint leaves for garnish

1. Heat the butter in a saucepan and fry the onion gently until soft.

2. Add the peas and 200ml of the stock. Simmer for 5 minutes if using fresh peas; if using frozen, simmer for just 2 minutes.

3. Add the lettuce, sugar and seasoning.

4. Cook for 10 minutes at a gentle simmer. Remove from the heat and stir in the cream.

5. Serve garnished with the mint leaves.

Tip
If you wish to thicken the soup after frying the onion, sprinkle on and stir in 1 level tablespoon of plain flour and continue with Step 2.

Parsnip Soup
The sweet parsnips and mild spiciness in this soup make it tasty and satisfying.

Serves 4–6

30g butter
1 large onion, chopped
1 garlic clove, grated or chopped
500g parsnips, peeled and diced
2 teaspoons honey
1 teaspoon mild curry powder
800ml vegetable stock (see page 160)
Salt and black pepper to taste
200ml milk
Paprika

1. Heat the butter in a saucepan and fry the onions for 2 minutes. Add the garlic and parsnips.

2. Drizzle the honey over the vegetables and cook gently for 8–10 minutes.

3. Stir in the curry powder and mix in about 100ml of stock.

4. Turn up the heat slightly and add the rest of the stock. Season with salt and pepper to taste. Bring to the boil. Turn down the heat to simmering and add the milk.

5. Simmer for 15 minutes, or until the parsnips are tender.

6. Blend to make a fairly smooth texture.

7. Serve garnished with a sprinkling of paprika.

Onion Soup

This isn't the French-style soup where the onions are caramelised; it is much creamier.
It still goes well with toasted French bread topped with some grated
cheese of your choice.

Serves 4–6

30g butter
600g onions, chopped finely
Salt and pepper to taste
1 litre chicken or vegetable stock
  (see page 158 or 160)
100ml single cream

1. Heat the butter in a saucepan and fry the onions until soft but not brown.

2. Season to taste with salt and pepper and stir in the stock.

3. Bring to the boil, stirring continuously, then simmer for 30 minutes.

4. Stir in the cream and serve.

Variation
If you prefer a slightly thicker soup, after softening the onions sprinkle 1 tablespoon of plain flour over them and stir well. Add the stock immediately, stirring continuously.

Cream of Artichoke Soup

Serves 4

30g butter
1 onion, sliced thinly
2 sticks of celery, chopped
500g Jerusalem artichokes
1 litre chicken or vegetable stock
  (see page 158 or 160)
2 tablespoons chopped fresh parsley or
  1 level teaspoon dried
Salt and pepper to taste
150ml single cream
A few parsley sprigs for garnish

1. Heat the butter in a saucepan and fry the onion and celery gently until soft.

2. Add the artichokes and cook until the vegetables soften; this takes about 5 minutes. Don't allow them to brown.

3. Stir in the stock and the parsley and bring to the boil.

4. Season to taste and turn down the heat to simmering. Cook for 20 minutes, then remove from the heat.

5. Liquidise or blend until smooth.

6. Return to a gentle heat and stir in the cream. Don't allow the soup to boil at this stage.

7. Serve garnished with the parsley sprigs.

Tip
When preparing artichokes, drop them in a bowl of water containing the juice of 1 lemon. This prevents them from going brown.

Country Vegetable Soup

I don't really know why this is called 'country vegetable'. Maybe it is because the vegetables are left whole in the soup. Obviously if you want a smooth soup you can always blend it after cooking, but somehow I think it makes for a more interesting eating experience if you can taste the individual vegetable pieces.

Serves 6

30g butter
1 large or 2 small onions, chopped
3 large or 4 small carrots, sliced into discs
1 leek, chopped
2 sticks celery, chopped
2 potatoes, diced
1.2 litres vegetable stock (see page 160)
3 tablespoons frozen broad beans
  (or fresh if you have them)
3 tablespoons frozen peas
  (no need to defrost)
2 tablespoons freshly chopped parsley
2 sprigs of thyme
A handful of spinach leaves or a small bunch
  of watercress
Salt and pepper to taste

1. Heat the butter in a large saucepan and fry the onion, carrots, leeks and celery gently for 5 minutes.

2. Turn down the heat, add the potatoes, cover and allow the vegetables to cook and release their juices and flavours – about 15–20 minutes more.

3. Pour in the stock and add the frozen vegetables, herbs and spinach or watercress.

4. Season to taste and bring to the boil.

5. Turn down the heat to simmering and cook for 20–25 minutes, or until the vegetables are cooked but still chunky.

Serving suggestion
This is delicious served with a hunk of homemade bread (see pages 124–34).

Carrot and Tomato Soup

My aunt made this when her tomato plants went wild during hot summers.
I always preferred it to tomato-only soup due to its sweeter taste. We used to drink
it out of large mugs, dipping fingers of buttered bread into it.

Serves 4

25g butter
1 medium onion, chopped
2 garlic cloves, chopped
1 tablespoon tomato purée
200g carrots, diced finely
500g ripe tomatoes (skin them if you like,
 but I don't bother), chopped
1 dessert apple, peeled and chopped
2 sprigs fresh thyme or ½ teaspoon dried
1 level teaspoon dried marjoram
½ teaspoon dried rosemary or 1 sprig of fresh
1 litre vegetable stock (see page 160)
Salt and black pepper to taste
4 tablespoons double cream, optional

1. Heat the butter in a saucepan and fry the onion with the garlic for 3–4 minutes on a gentle heat. Stir in the tomato purée.

2. Add the carrots, tomatoes, apple and herbs and a little of the stock. Cook gently for 5 minutes, or until the stock has almost disappeared.

3. Add the rest of the stock and season with salt and pepper to taste.

4. Cook for 35–40 minutes, or until the carrots are soft.

5. Remove any herb stalks and blend or liquidise the soup. I sometimes simply use a potato masher as I like a bit of texture.

6. Reheat if necessary (but do not boil), then serve in mugs or bowls with a swirl of cream if you wish.

Oxtail Soup

Cooking this piece of meat makes one of the most appetising smells you will ever come across. If you can, ask your butcher to joint the oxtail for you.

Serves 6–8

2 tablespoons sunflower oil
1 oxtail, cut into small joints
   (about 8 pieces), washed and dried
2 large onions, chopped
1 rasher of streaky bacon, chopped
2 sticks of celery, chopped
3 carrots, diced
2 sprigs of thyme, 1 bunch of parsley
   and a sprig of rosemary, tied into a
   bouquet garni with some string, or
   put into a small muslin bag and tied
2 litres beef stock (see page 156)
Salt and black pepper to taste
2 tablespoons plain flour
5 tablespoons port, cream sherry or Madeira

1. In a large pan, heat the oil over a high heat and brown the oxtail all over, a few pieces at a time. Remove the oxtail from the pan and set aside on a plate.

2. Over a gentle heat, fry the onions and bacon in the same pan and cook for 2–3 minutes.

3. Add the celery and carrots and cook for a further 5 minutes, stirring continuously.

4. Add the meat to the pan with the bouquet garni and pour in the stock.

5. Season to taste and bring to the boil.

6. Turn down the heat to simmering and cover the pan. Cook slowly for at least 2½ hours, or until the meat is falling away from the bones.

7. Strain the meat through a fine colander or sieve, making sure all the stock pours into a pan or bowl. Allow to cool slightly and discard the vegetables and herbs.

8. Take all the meat from the bones and chop up any large pieces.

9. Skim away any fat from the stock and pour it into a pan.

10. Add the meat and heat gently. Mix the flour with a little cold water to make a thick paste and add a tablespoon of the heating soup. When the soup is boiling, stir in the flour paste and whisk in.

11. Reduce the heat and cook for 4 minutes. Check and adjust the seasoning, if necessary, and stir in the port, sherry or Madeira. Serve immediately.

Pea and Bacon Soup

This recipe was originally called 'London Particular' and was linked to the
dense, pea-souper fogs that lingered over London during the winter months.
But as horrific as the fogs could be, the soup was heartening and wholesome.
It was originally made with cured hock of pork or pig's trotters.
This is an easier but just as tasty version.
When you plan to make this soup, remember to soak your dried peas
the night before in cold water. Dried peas give the best results, as they cook
more evenly and in less time than fresh or frozen ones.

Serves 6

1 tablespoon oil
6 large rashers of streaky bacon, chopped
1 large onion, chopped
1 large carrot, chopped
½ level teaspoon celery salt
200g dried green peas
200g dried split yellow peas
2 litres stock: chicken or vegetable
   (see pages 158 or 160)
Salt and pepper to taste

1. Heat the oil in a saucepan and fry the bacon for 3 minutes. Add the onions and cook over a medium heat until the bacon is done and the onions are soft. This will take about 10 minutes.

2. Add the carrot and sprinkle in the celery salt.

3. Drain the soaking peas and add them to the bacon and vegetables.

4. Pour in the stock and stir. Bring to the boil, then reduce the heat and season to taste. Simmer for about 1 hour, or until the peas are tender.

5. Blend either fully or partially smooth, according to your taste, and serve with some extra fried crispy bacon pieces.

Scotch Broth

This soup can be made with whatever vegetables are in season, so long as you use barley, some dried peas and the cheapest cut of lamb or, even better, mutton. Remember to soak your peas in cold water the night before.

Serves 4–6

700g any cheap cut of lamb or mutton, excess fat removed; if the meat has some bones, use 100g more when making the soup
1.5 litres water
Salt and pepper to taste
  (I prefer white here because of the kick it gives)
25g butter
1 medium onion, chopped
1 leek, sliced thinly
2–3 carrots, diced
1 small turnip, chopped
130g pearl barley
1 tablespoon freshly chopped parsley
2 sprigs of thyme
150g dried peas, soaked overnight
A handful of shredded cabbage

1. Place the meat in the water along with some salt and pepper and bring to the boil. Once boiling, reduce the heat to a gentle simmer. Cover and cook for 2½–3 hours, or until the meat is tender. Skim off any fat from the surface.

2. When the meat is cooked, lift it out and pour the stock into another vessel for later. Remove any bones and chop up the meat into small chunks, about 1cm in size.

3. Melt the butter in the pan used for cooking the meat and fry the onion, leek, carrots and turnip gently for 5 minutes.

4. Add the barley, herbs and drained peas and pour in the reserved stock.

5. Bring to the boil, then reduce the heat and simmer for 35 minutes. Stir in the cabbage and cook for 25 minutes more, or until the peas are tender.

6. Add a little more water if the soup is too thick during the cooking time.
This is delicious served with soda bread (see page 134).

Cooking with Pastry

As a nation, we British have always been passionate about pastry. We love to use it in so many ways – from an individual pasty to a raised pork pie. Every British region and historic era has its own signature pastry dish.

This type of cookery is also so varied and such great fun. Children particularly love making pies and playing with pastry. Many times my dad came home to a very grey-looking 'jam pie', and I remember once preparing him a 'salt pie', which he bit into and very thoughtfully and discreetly spat out so I didn't see. (I would not advocate making such a pie if I were you!)

So many things, from desserts to huge, family-sized meat pies and tiny party snacks, can be tucked into or under a crust that you never need get 'fed up' with pastry. Keeping some shortcrust and puff pastry in the freezer is always a good idea because you can whip up a cheese-and-onion pie in 30 minutes or so.

Just like soups, pies are also a useful way of making ingredients go further: you need less meat per person to make a pie than a casserole. They are very filling as well, which makes them excellent as cold-weather meals.

Making pastry of any kind is always worth doing, because it gives you a sense of achievement – and you know exactly what goes in it. It is also cheaper and you can make more than you need at any one time and freeze it for when time is short.

A handy tip

The old saying 'Cold hands and a warm heart' describes the type of person who is good at making pastry. I have never met anyone with a cold heart and warm hands (!), but if yours do happen to be warm, simply cool them under running water and you will be able to make the best pastry in the world.

Shortcrust Pastry

This is the quickest and easiest type of pastry you can make. Why not make double and freeze half? Similarly, when a recipe calls for half a quantity of the pastry, use half and freeze the other – or make something else with it, such as jam tarts.

Makes 300g of pastry

300g plain flour
½ level teaspoon salt
65g butter, cut into small pieces
65g lard, cut into small pieces
2 tablespoons cold water

1. Sift the flour and salt into a bowl; lift the sieve as high up as possible so that the flour gets a really good airing.

2. Add both the fats and begin to rub the fat into the flour. If you find halfway through that the fat softens too much, put the bowl into the fridge for 10 minutes.

3. Keep rubbing in until the mixture looks like breadcrumbs. (This stage may be done in the food processor.) Keep it light and if your hands get hot, run your wrists under cold water, dry them and keep going.

4. Add 1 tablespoon of water and mix in with a knife; the pastry should start to form clumps. Add the other tablespoon of water and keep mixing in with the knife.

5. Bring the pastry together with your hands as lightly and quickly as possible. Don't be tempted to knead it as it will end up tough and inedible.

6. When the dough forms a smooth ball, wrap it in cling film and put it in the fridge to cool for at least 30 minutes before use.

Variation
Use half wholemeal and half white flour in this recipe if you wish.

Tips for successful shortcrust pastry
• Keep all ingredients as cool as possible.
• Cut the fat into small pieces and put in the fridge again to cool.
• Roll out the pastry quickly and to the thickness you desire. Too much rolling makes pastry heavy.
• Make sure the fat is very cold – straight from the fridge – and that the water is ice-cold.

Rough Puff Pastry

This is the quickest and easiest recipe I know, and the result is
always light and flaky pastry.

*Makes enough to cover 1 large pie, make 6 large
apple turnovers or 12 sausage rolls*

225g plain flour
½ teaspoon salt
180g butter, straight from the fridge
80–100ml cold water

Tip
Be very gentle with this pastry when rolling
so as not to allow any of the air to escape.

1. Sift the flour and salt into a bowl.

2. Add the butter in a whole block and cut it up
into the flour with a knife until the pieces are
about 1cm in size. Alternatively, put the butter
in the freezer for 1 hour, remove and grate, then
stir it into the flour.

3. Stir in the water and bring the mixture
together with the knife. Only use your hands at
the very last minute to make a soft dough.

4. Dust your work surface with flour and roll
out the pastry into a rectangle about 3 times as
long as it is wide.

5. Fold the top third over to the centre, then the
bottom third over the top and seal the edges by
pinching them together.

6. Turn the pastry so one sealed edge is facing
you and roll it out into another rectangle. Fold
and seal in the same way.

7. Do this twice more, then leave the pastry to
rest for 30 minutes before using in your recipe.

Hot-water Crust Pastry

This type of pastry is traditionally used to make a raised crusted pie,
such as the pork pie on page 184.

Makes 1 raised crusted pie

500g plain flour
1 level teaspoon salt
220ml boiling water
220g lard

1. Sieve the flour and salt together into a mixing bowl and make a well in the centre.

2. Pour the boiling water into a heatproof jug and add the lard. Allow it to dissolve into the water before stirring it into the flour with a wooden spoon.

3. Bring the pastry together with your hands to form a smooth, pliable dough. Cool before using.

Savoury Pies

Steak and Oyster Pie

Oysters used to be so plentiful in the 1600s that even the poorest families could eat them most days. They were put in beef pies to make the meat go further – not the reason they are used today, unfortunately, when oysters are much more of a luxury. They are used in this pie to add a depth of flavour.

Serves 6

2 tablespoon oil
25g butter
1 onion, sliced thinly
1kg best braising steak, cut into
    small 1.5cm cubes
300ml beef stock
250ml brown ale
1 teaspoon dried thyme
150g button mushrooms
1 tablespoon plain flour
Salt and pepper to taste
1 dozen oysters, shelled
1 quantity puff or a half quantity shortcrust
    pastry (see pages 175 and 174)
1 egg beaten with 2 tablespoons milk

1. Heat the oil and butter in a large pan and fry the onions gently for 3 minutes. Add the meat and fry until the meat browns slightly.

2. Stir in the stock and add the ale. Bring to the boil, stirring continuously, and lower the heat to simmering.

3. Add the thyme. Cover and cook for 1½ hours, or until the beef is tender.

4. Add the mushrooms and cook for 10 minutes.

5. Thicken the sauce with the flour by mixing it with 2 tablespoons of cold water to make a paste, then stir this into the meat mixture. Bring to the boil and cook at boiling until the sauce thickens. Season to taste.

6. Transfer everything in the pan to a large pie dish and press the oysters into the meat mixture.

7. Preheat the oven to 200°C/gas mark 6.

8. Roll your choice of pastry out to fit the pie dish with an overhang of about 5mm. Brush the top of the pastry with the egg-and-milk mixture and make a slit in the centre of the pastry to allow the steam to escape.

9. Bake for 35–40 minutes, or until the pastry is golden brown (and well-risen if using rough puff).

Serving suggestion
Serve with creamed potatoes and a mixture of carrots and turnips, steamed or boiled together for 5 minutes, chopped with a knob of butter and salt and plenty of white pepper.

Fidget Pie

Nobody really knows why this delicious pie has such a strange name. It is a traditional Shropshire farmer's pie, and although it has gammon in the list of ingredients, in lean times it would be made simply with vegetables.

Serves 4

450g potatoes, sliced thinly
400g gammon, cut into small cubes
2 onions, sliced thinly
2 Bramley apples, peeled and sliced thinly
2 teaspoons brown sugar
½ teaspoon dried or 2 sprigs fresh thyme leaves
280ml vegetable or chicken stock (see page 160 or 158)
Salt and pepper to taste
200g shortcrust pastry

Serving suggestion
Serve with a green vegetable and/or sweetcorn.

1. Preheat the oven to 180°C/gas mark 4. Grease a deep pie dish with plenty of butter.

2. Put a layer of potatoes in the base of the pie dish, cover with a layer of gammon, then one of onion and apple. Sprinkle with a teaspoon of the brown sugar and repeat the layers until the dish is full; finish with the last teaspoon of sugar.

3. Top with the thyme and press the filling down well. Pour over sufficient stock just to show through the filling and season with salt and pepper to taste.

4. Roll out the pastry to make a thick crust – about 5mm thick – and cover the filling, allowing the lid to overhang slightly around the edge. Press the pastry down gently around the rim of the pie filling. Cut a slit in the top for the steam to escape.

5. Bake for 20 minutes, then turn down the heat to 170°C/gas mark 3 and continue to cook for 45–50 minutes. If the pastry is browning too much after about 20 minutes, cover the pie loosely with foil.

Liver and Onion Pie

Many people I know say they dislike liver; they often remember the bitter-flavoured
dish that was served up for school dinners. However, when I serve them this pie
made with tender lambs liver, most (I won't say all) change their minds,
and many now cook liver for themselves.

Serves 4

30ml oil
4 medium onions, sliced
700g lambs liver, cut into thin slices
30g plain flour
Salt and pepper to taste
½ teaspoon dried or a sprig of fresh rosemary
400ml water or beef stock (see page 156)
300g shortcrust pastry

Serving suggestion
Serve with this wonderfully easy-to-prepare
cabbage: shred sufficient Savoy cabbage to
serve 4 people. Boil or steam the cabbage for
3–4 minutes and, when just cooked, remove it
from the heat and drain. Chop 3 rashers of
streaky bacon into little strips and fry until
crispy. Add the drained cabbage to the pan
and fry for a few minutes in the bacon juices.
Serve immediately with the pie.

1. Preheat the oven to 190°C/gas mark 5.

2. Heat the oil in a saucepan and fry the onions
gently until soft. Spoon half into a pie dish.

3. Toss the liver into the flour and coat all over,
then season with salt and pepper.

4. Add half of the liver to onions in the dish,
then spoon over the rest of the onions and the
rest of the liver.

5. Sprinkle with the rosemary.

6. Warm the stock until just hot and stir it into
the liver and onions.

7. Roll out the pastry to fit the top of the pie
and cover the filling.

8. Cut a slit in the centre of the pastry to allow
steam to escape and bake it for 20 minutes.
Turn down the heat to 170°C/gas mark 3 and
bake for 50–60 minutes. Cover the pastry
loosely with foil if it is browning too quickly.

Pigeon Pie

This is a very rustic yet elegant pie, and this recipe is very easy to make. You can obviously shoot your own birds – only ones living in the countryside, though! – or buy them from butcher's shops or farmers markets.

Serves 4

5 prepared pigeons
300g best braising steak, cut into
  small chunks
25g freshly chopped parsley
½ teaspoon dried thyme
Salt and pepper to taste
2 teaspoons cornflour (optional)
250g shortcrust pastry

1. Keep the pigeon breast meat to one side in a cool place and put the rest of the carcass in sufficient water to cover. Bring to the boil, then simmer for 1½ hours. This will make your pigeon stock.

2. Preheat the oven to 180°C/gas mark 4.

3. Butter a deep pie dish and place the braising steak chunks in the bottom.

4. Cut each pigeon breast in half and lay these on top of the beef.

5. Sprinkle the herbs over the meat and season well with salt and pepper.

6. Pour over sufficient of the prepared pigeon stock to cover the meat by 2cm.

7. Cover with foil and stand the dish on a baking sheet. Place in the oven and cook for 1½ hours. Remove the dish from the oven and raise the heat to 200°C/gas mark 6.

8. Thicken the gravy if you wish with 2 teaspoons cornflour mixed with a little cold water to make a thin paste. Stir well into the meat gravy.

9. Roll out the pastry to fit the top, cover the dish and cut a slit in the centre of the pastry to allow steam to escape. Bake for 30 minutes, or until the pastry is golden.

Serving suggestion
I like to serve this rich pie with crispy homemade chips so that they may be dipped in the gorgeous gravy.

Mutton and Turnip Pie

This pie was traditionally served to a hunting party, so it was often made on a large scale. Lamb can be used instead of mutton, but use the meat from the shoulder. The fragrant taste of the turnips enriches the flavour of the mutton.

Serves 6

2 tablespoons oil
1kg mutton or lamb, cut into 2cm cubes
2 large onions, chopped
450g turnips, peeled and sliced thickly
1 level teaspoon dried or 1 teaspoon
   freshly chopped rosemary
1 tablespoon chopped parsley
Salt and pepper to taste
300ml warm beef stock (see page 156)
   or water
1 tablespoon plain flour
225g rough puff pastry

1. Heat the oil in a large lidded saucepan and fry the meat and onions together for 4–5 minutes, turning everything so that the meat fries evenly.

2. Add the turnips and cook for 3 more minutes.

3. Add the herbs and season to taste.

4. Pour in the stock or water and stir. Allow to simmer, then cover with the lid and cook at simmering for 1½ hours. Check the liquid levels and add a little more if necessary.

5. Add the flour to 2 tablespoons water and stir it into the meat mixture. Bring to the boil, stirring constantly, then turn down to simmering. Cook at simmering for a further 15 minutes.

6. Preheat the oven to 200°C/gas mark 6.

7. Pour the pie filling into a deep pie dish and roll out the pastry to fit the top. Allow the filling to cool for 10 minutes or the pastry won't rise; instead, it will become soggy. Cover the meat with the pastry, making a slit in the centre for the steam to escape.

8. Bake for 35–40 minutes, or until the pastry has risen and is golden and flaky. Serve immediately with boiled new potatoes and garden peas.

Deep-filled Cheese and Onion Pie

I adore cheese and onion pie – you can serve it hot or cold.
This version uses potato to add body to the filling.

Makes a large pie to serve 8

1 quantity of shortcrust pastry
200g red Leicester cheese, grated
200g mature Cheddar, grated
1 large onion, very finely chopped
1 medium potato, peeled, cubed
   and boiled for 3–4 minutes
   until just cooked
1 egg
½ teaspoon ground black pepper
1 level teaspoon mustard powder

1. Preheat the oven to 190°C/gas mark 5.

2. Butter a large, deep pie dish and roll out just over half of the pastry to line it.

3. In a bowl combine the cheeses with the onion. Mix until fully combined, then stir in the potato.

4. Beat the egg and whisk in the pepper and mustard. Stir into the cheese mixture.

5. Pile the cheese into the pastry and roll out the lid. Dampen the edges with water and lay the lid on top of the pie. Crimp or squeeze the edges together. Brush the top with egg and milk if you like a shiny finish.

6. Bake the pie for 35–45 minutes, or until the top is deep golden in colour.

7. Allow the pie to rest for 10 minutes before serving it with baked beans or a salad.

Herbed Salmon with Creamy Mustard Sauce

This is a an economic way of serving salmon that makes an excellent dinner-party dish.

Serves 6

80g butter
1 tablespoon each chopped fresh dill and parsley
1 tablespoon lemon juice
Salt and black pepper to taste
300g shortcrust pastry
2 thick salmon fillets, each about 400–450g
1 egg beaten with 3 tablespoons of milk, to glaze

For the sauce
50g butter
2–3 shallots, chopped finely
2 teaspoons chopped fresh tarragon or ½
  teaspoon dried
1 tablespoon chopped fresh parsley
1 teaspoon chopped dill
1 rounded teaspoon Dijon mustard
2–3 teaspoons lemon juice
2 egg yolks
280ml double cream
Salt and pepper to taste

1. Preheat the oven to 200°C/gas mark 6.

2. In a bowl, combine the butter, herbs and lemon juice and season with a little salt and pepper – not too much as you will need to season the salmon lightly.

3. Roll out the pastry until it is a rectangle large enough to fit the salmon fillets lengthways, with extra to spare, and also widthways with an extra 3–4cm to allow it to be sealed.

4. Lay one of the fillets down the centre of the pastry and spread the entire surface of the fish with the butter-and-herb mixture. Lay the other fillet on top to make a 'fish sandwich'. Season with a little salt and pepper.

5. Wrap the fish in the pastry, sealing the centre fold with a little cold water and folding securely. Seal the top and bottom edges in the same way.

6. Lay the salmon parcel seal-side down on a greased baking sheet. Brush well with the egg and milk mixture. Make 3 slits in the pastry down the centre to allow the steam to escape.

7. Bake for 30–40 minutes, or until golden brown.

8. While the salmon is baking, make the sauce. Heat the butter in a saucepan and fry the shallots gently until soft; add the herbs. Stir in the mustard and lemon juice.

9. Whisk the egg yolks and cream together, then pour into the herb-and-mustard mixture. Season to taste. Stir well on a low heat until the mixture is the desired thickness. Make sure it is hot when serving.

10. Serve in slices with the hot sauce.

Serving suggestion
Pair this with a mixed salad, or boiled new potatoes and whole green beans.

Pork Pies

These are good for parties or buffet suppers. You need slightly thicker
pastry to withstand the longer cooking time, so when you roll out the pastry
make sure it is at least 1cm thick.

Makes 8–9 individual pies

600g shortcrust pastry (double the quantity
  in the basic recipe)
1kg minced pork
2 level teaspoons salt
White pepper to taste

Variations
Add one of the following to the meat:

• ½ teaspoon sage
• A little grated nutmeg
• 1 teaspoon mustard powder
• ½ teaspoon celery salt

1. Preheat the oven to 175°C/gas mark 3.
Grease a muffin tin.

2. Roll out the pastry to at least 1cm thick.
Cut saucer-size rounds and press each into a
hole in the muffin tin, allowing a little pastry
to overhang the edges.

3. Put the meat in a bowl with the salt and
pepper and stir everything well.

4. Press the meat down firmly into the pastry
case and top with a lid.

5. Seal down the edges firmly and brush with an
egg and milk glaze if you wish.

6. Place the tin on a baking sheet so as to catch
any drips from the meat and make it easier to
get in and out of the oven.

7. Bake for 1 hour, then test the centre with a
knife; it is cooked if it comes out clean. If not,
cook for 15 minutes more.

8. Leave to cool in the tin, preferably overnight,
and the juices will firm up. The pies will keep
covered in the fridge for 3–4 days.

Sweet Pies

Pastry can be used in so many ways to serve as a pudding or teatime treat, and such desserts generally keep well in an airtight container. So why not have a baking session and make several different pastries that will see your family through the week? Then there will always be some tasty treat in the tin when your sweet tooth gets the better of you – and, best of all, you won't have spent a fortune.

Yorkshire Curd Tarts

Living in Leeds made me hooked on really good curd tarts. They are a very satisfying sweet pastry, and if you like cheesecake, you will love these.
The recipe for cheese tarts goes back to the thirteenth century, when soft, young cheese was pounded together with eggs, spices and honey to make a pastry filling. You can use your own sieved cottage cheese (see page 145) instead.

Serves 8

225g shortcrust pastry (see page 174)

For the filling
450g curd cheese
80g soft brown sugar
3 eggs
The tip of a teaspoon of allspice
Grated zest and juice of 1 lemon
40g melted butter
2 tablespoons double cream
80g currants
A little grated nutmeg for the top, optional

1. Roll out the pastry to line a greased 20cm fluted loose-bottomed flan tin. Chill in the fridge while you prepare the filling.

2. Preheat the oven to 190°C/gas mark 5.

3. Put the cheese in a bowl and stir in the sugar. Beat in the eggs, spice and lemon zest and juice. Stir in the butter and cream. Stir in the currants.

4. Pour the filling into the chilled pastry case and top with a sprinkling of nutmeg. Bake for 35–40 minutes, or until the filling is set and the pastry is golden.

5. Allow to cool for about 20 minutes in the tin. Lift out of the tin before serving.

Cornflake Tart

This is a recipe my mum used to make. We discovered it at school, and I loved it
so much I got her to make it for us and it became a family favourite. Mum used
to put the cornflakes in a plastic bag and crush them with the end of a rolling pin.
Just make sure they don't end up like crumbs!

Serves 6

225g shortcrust pastry

For the filling
5–6 tablespoons of your jam of choice
60g butter
60g golden caster sugar
2 tablespoons golden syrup
180g cornflakes, lightly crushed

1. Preheat the oven to 200°C/gas mark 6.
Grease a 20cm loose-bottomed flan tin.

2. Roll out the pastry to fit the tin and chill it for
15 minutes. Bake the pastry 'blind' by lining the
pastry with some baking paper and placing some
baking beans on top, then baking for 25 minutes.

3. Spread the base of the flan with the jam.

4. In a saucepan melt the butter with the sugar
and golden syrup.

5. When everything is mixed and melted
together, stir in the cornflakes and spread the
mixture carefully over the jam.

6. Bake for 5 minutes only and leave to cool
completely before slicing.
Serve with custard or cream.

Custard Tarts

My all-time favourite pastries. A creamy custard tart is delicious as a dessert or as an afternoon teatime treat. You can make them individually, but I prefer to make a large one – then you don't eat as much pastry. Well, that's *my* excuse!

Serves 6

225g shortcrust pastry
2 eggs
150ml milk
50ml single cream
50g golden caster sugar
Pinch of nutmeg for the top

1. Preheat the oven to 200°C/gas mark 6. Grease a 20cm flan tin.

2. Roll out the pastry fairly thinly and line the flan tin. Prick the pastry with a fork in several places on the base and chill for 20 minutes in the fridge.

3. Bake the pastry 'blind' by lining the pastry with some baking paper and placing some baking beans on top, then baking it for 15 minutes. Remove the pastry and reduce the heat to 180°C/gas mark 4.

4. Break the eggs into a bowl and stir, don't whisk, the milk, cream and sugar into them.

5. Pour the filling into the pastry case, sprinkle with a little nutmeg and bake for 20–25 minutes until set.

Lemon Meringue Pie

My friend's mum always made her lemon meringue pie from a packet, and my mum used to say it was just as easy making one from scratch with fresh lemons – and it tasted much better! Use as deep a flan tin as you can get for this recipe.

Serves 6–8

120g shortcrust pastry (see page 174)

For the filling
50g cornflour
300ml water
180g caster sugar
Grated zest and juice of 2 lemons
2 egg yolks
15g butter

For the meringue
2 egg whites
75g caster sugar

1. Preheat the oven to 200°C/gas mark 6. Grease a 20cm loose-bottomed flan tin.

2. Roll out the pastry and line the tin, then bake it 'blind' by lining the pastry with some baking paper and placing some baking beans on top, then baking it for 15 minutes. Remove the beans and baking paper and bake for a further 5–8 minutes, or until the pastry is golden brown.

3. Turn the oven down to 150°C/gas mark 2 and allow the pastry shell to cool in the tin while you make the filling.

4. Mix the cornflour with enough water to make a thin paste.

5. Put the rest of the water, sugar and lemon zest in a pan and heat to boiling.

6. Mix in the cornflour paste and simmer briskly for 2 minutes.

7. Remove from the heat and stir in the lemon juice. Add the egg yolks one at a time and beat well with a wooden spoon. Stir in the butter.

8. Pour the mixture into the pastry shell and smooth over the surface. I find this easier to do with the back of a metal spoon.

9. To make the meringue, use a clean, grease-free bowl; use one of the lemon rinds to rid the bowl of any grease by rubbing the it over the base and sides of the bowl, then pat dry with a sheet of kitchen roll. Whisk the egg whites in the bowl until they form stiff peaks. Whisk in half of the sugar and fold in the rest with a metal spoon.

10. Spread the meringue evenly over the lemon filling. Cook for about 20 minutes. Turn off the heat and leave the pie in the oven for 5 more minutes to make sure the meringue is set and slightly golden in colour. Serve cold.

Jam Roly Poly

This is a true winter comforter, and it *has* to be served with creamy custard.
The crust is made of the easiest pastry to make: suet crust. For really light pastry, keep the
kneading and rolling of it to a minimum.

Serves 6

Your jam of choice

For the pastry
200g self-raising flour
A pinch of salt
100g vegetarian suet
Water to mix to a soft dough

To make the pastry
1. Sieve the flour and salt together into a bowl and stir in the suet.

2. Add 2 tablespoons of water and stir in. Continue adding a little water to make a soft dough – one that you will be able to roll out lightly.

3. Use your hands to gather the mixture into a ball.

4. Knead very lightly until smooth.

To make the Roly Poly
1. Preheat the oven to 200°C/gas mark 6

2. Roll out the pastry to about 4mm thick and 25cm square.

3. Spread with sufficient jam to cover the surface of the pastry, leaving the edges clear or it will ooze out.

4. Dampen the edges and roll up.

5. Place on a greased baking sheet and bake for 30–40 minutes. Serve hot with custard.

Grandma's Main Meals

Food really does evoke memories. We often miss many of the dishes our parents and grandparents made for us, and we all have favourite dishes we looked forward to coming home to as children – the aromas as you walked through the door after school heralded the excitement of the meal ahead.

Casseroles, fricassées and stews were part of most people's upbringing, so here are some famous (and some not so famous but nonetheless tasty) recipes I hope will bring back wonderful foody memories.

Lemon Chicken Casserole

Chicken and lemon go so well together, and because you use chicken pieces, this dish doesn't take long to cook.

Serves 4

50g butter
1 chicken, 1.2kg–1.8kg, cut into 4 sections, or 2 leg and 2 breast portions weighing a similar amount
Juice of 2 lemons
300ml chicken stock (see page 158)
1 tablespoon plain flour
1 tablespoon chopped parsley
½ teaspoon chopped mint
1 teaspoon chopped chives
Salt and pepper to taste

1. Preheat the oven to 170°C/gas mark 3.

2. Heat the butter in a large pan and fry the chicken all over for a few minutes, until 'sealed'. Add the lemon juice and half of the stock and bring the liquid to the boil.

3. Transfer the chicken to an ovenproof casserole. Mix the rest of the stock with the flour and pour this into the casserole. Add all the juices from the pan.

4. Stir in the herbs and season to taste. Cover and cook in the oven for 1 hour.

5. Serve with boiled potatoes and a green vegetable.

Farmhouse Chicken

I call this 'farmhouse' simply because, when I was a child, it was made for us by some friends of my parents' who lived on a farm in Saddleworth. They also had a restaurant, and every time we went there for meals, I would ask for this.

Serves 4

50g butter or sunflower oil, for browning
4 rashers streaky bacon
4 chicken pieces, or a chicken cut into 4 joints, weighing approximately 1.8kg
120g pork sausage meat
1 onion, sliced
½ teaspoon dried sage
½ teaspoon dried marjoram
200g canned chopped tomatoes
1 tablespoon plain flour
200ml chicken stock (see page 158)
Salt and pepper to taste
120g fresh or frozen peas
100g fresh or frozen broad beans

1. Preheat the oven to 170°C/gas mark 3.

2. Heat the butter or oil in a frying pan and fry the bacon for a few minutes. Brown the chicken pieces all over in the pan along with the bacon, then place it all in a large casserole dish.

3. Form the sausage meat into small balls and fry in the same pan. Place the balls between the chicken pieces.

4. Fry the onions in the same pan and layer these over the meat.

5. Sprinkle in the herbs and add the tomatoes.

6. Mix the flour with a little of the stock and pour over the chicken. Stir in the rest of the stock. Season to taste.

7. Cover and cook for 1 hour. Stir in the peas and broad beans and cook for 30 minutes more.

Serving suggestion
Serve with creamed or diced and fried potatoes.

Chicken Casserole with Red Cabbage

If you wonder what to do with red cabbage other then bottling it in vinegar, try this delicious way to cook chicken. I think this dish is good enough to serve at a dinner party, and the chestnuts give it an autumnal touch.

Serves 4

50g butter
1 onion, sliced thinly
4 large chicken portions, or 4 drumsticks and 4 thighs
450g red cabbage, shredded
12 cooked chestnuts
½ teaspoon dried marjoram
130ml red wine
Salt and pepper to taste

1. Preheat the oven to 180°C/gas mark 4.

2. Melt the butter in a large frying pan and fry the onions gently for a few minutes.

3. Add the chicken portions and brown them all over. Place in a casserole dish.

4. Add the cabbage to the frying pan to mop up the juices, then spread this over the chicken.

5. Add the chestnuts and marjoram and pour over the wine. Season to taste.

6. Cover and cook for 45–50 minutes and serve with baked potatoes and buttered carrots.

Boiled Beef in Brown Ale

Putting this dish together may seem like a long process, but it is actually very easy and isn't too time-consuming. It is, however, the most delicious way of cooking cheaper cuts of beef. The flavour is amazing and the meat melts in your mouth.

Serves 6

1.5kg stewing beef (or a piece of brisket)
500g onions, peeled and sliced thickly
1 litre brown ale

For the marinade
100ml red-wine vinegar
2 tablespoons black treacle
3 cloves
1 teaspoon each of dried thyme, sage,
  marjoram and rosemary
1 teaspoon turmeric
½ teaspoon mace
Ground black pepper and salt to taste
1 sprig of fresh parsley

1. Put all the marinade ingredients except the parsley in a jug and whisk them together.

2. Put the meat and onions in a large lidded pan and pour in the marinade. Leave covered for 5 hours, spooning the marinade over the meat at least 2–3 times.

3. Pour in the ale and bring to the boil. If you want to be assured of a thicker sauce, add a tablespoon of flour to the pan when adding the brown ale and stir in well so that no lumps form.

4. Reduce the heat to a slow simmer, check the seasoning and adjust if necessary, then cover and cook for 3 hours. Make sure it is cooking slowly.

5. Slice the meat and put it back in the sauce, making sure everything is piping hot to serve.

Serving suggestion
This is delicious served with boiled new potatoes and a sweet chutney.

Meat and Potato Hash with Onions in Vinegar

This is one of my mum's recipes. She would make it on a cold winter's day, and the smell of it cooking when I came home from school was so comforting and homely. We always had sliced onions in malt vinegar with it, and any leftover onions went into a wonderful cheese sandwich the next day.

Serves 4

1 tablespoon oil
400g onions, sliced
500g stewing steak, cut into small chunks
500ml beef stock (see page 156)
1 tablespoon flour
500g potatoes, peeled and cut into chunks
4 medium carrots, chopped into discs
Salt and white pepper to taste

1. Heat the oil in a saucepan and fry the onions gently until they are soft.

2. Add the meat and fry until it all changes colour. Pour in most of the stock, leaving a couple of tablespoons to mix with the flour.

3. Simmer the meat for 1¼ hours, then add the stock mixed with the flour. Stir until it thickens, adding a bit more water if it is too thick.

4. Add the potatoes and carrots and season with salt and pepper.

5. Simmer for a further 20 minutes, or until the potatoes are cooked.

To make the onions in vinegar

Slice 1 large or 2 small onions thinly and put in a lidded jar. Season with salt and white pepper and pour over sufficient malt vinegar just to cover. Screw the lid on and give a it a shake. If you do this before cooking the meat for the hash, the onions will be ready to serve with the meal.

Beef Stew with Dumplings

This is a traditional dish of beef and dumplings, but the dumplings are particularly tasty due to the addition of mustard and thyme.

Serves 4

25g butter
1 tablespoon sunflower oil
1kg braising steak, shin or skirt, trimmed of
   excess fat and cut into small chunks
2 celery sticks, chopped
3 carrots, chopped
10 small shallots, peeled
2 tablespoons plain flour
500ml beef stock (see page 156)
Salt and pepper to taste
1 teaspoon dried thyme
1 teaspoon dried or 1 tablespoon fresh
   chopped parsley
100g mushrooms

For the dumplings
100g self-raising flour
½ teaspoon dry mustard powder
White pepper to taste
½ teaspoon salt
½ teaspoon dried thyme
50g vegetarian or beef suet
Enough water to make a sticky, rollable dough

1. Preheat the oven to 180°C/gas mark 4.

2. Melt the butter and oil together in a large frying pan and brown the meat all over. Transfer to a casserole dish. Add the celery and carrots to the casserole around the meat.

3. In the same frying pan, brown the shallots, then add them to the casserole.

4. Turn down the heat and sprinkle the flour over the fat in the pan and stir in. Gradually stir in the stock, then pour it over the meat and vegetables. Season to taste.

5. Add the herbs, cover, and cook in the oven for 2 hours.

6. Add the mushrooms, cover and continue to cook for 20 minutes.

7. Make the dumplings while the mushrooms cook. Sieve the flour, mustard powder, pepper and salt together into a mixing bowl. Stir in the thyme.

8. Stir in the suet, then add the water a teaspoon at a time until the dough is sticky but you can roll it into balls – this will be about 8 teaspoons.

9. Roll small amounts of the dough into 12 small balls. Place the dumplings in the casserole evenly between the other ingredients. Put the lid back on and place in the oven. Turn up the heat to 190°C/gas mark 5 and cook for 20–25 minutes, or until the dumplings are risen and fluffy.

Serving suggestion
Serve with hunks of fresh bread or boiled potatoes.

Beef and Bean Pan Stew

This is a tasty and quick one-pot meal for those days when you want something hearty but speedy. It is also easy on the pocket.

Serves 4

1 tablespoon sunflower oil
1 large onion, chopped
500g minced beef
2 garlic cloves, chopped
2 tablespoons tomato purée
2 celery sticks, chopped
250ml beef stock (see page 156)
100g broad beans, fresh or frozen
50g whole green beans, fresh or frozen
200g canned haricot beans
A dash of Worcestershire sauce
Salt and pepper to taste

1. Heat the oil in a large saucepan and fry the onion gently until soft.

2. Add the meat, garlic and tomato purée and fry until brown.

3. Add the celery and stock and stir well. Cover and cook for 30 minutes on a gentle heat.

4. Stir in the broad beans and green beans and cook for 15 minutes.

5. Add the haricot beans and the Worcestershire sauce and season to taste with salt and pepper. Cook for 15 minutes.

6. Serve with boiled brown rice or new potatoes.

Silverside of Beef in Red Wine

This is another deliciously succulent way to cook beef. It is easy to prepare and makes an ideal dinner-party dish.

Serves 6

1 tablespoon sunflower oil
Approximately 1.5kg joint of silverside beef
6 rashers streaky bacon, chopped
1 large onion, sliced thickly
3 garlic cloves, chopped
4 carrots, cut chunkily
250ml red wine
300ml beef stock (see page 156)
3 sprigs of thyme
Salt and pepper to taste

1. Preheat the oven to 160°C/gas mark 2.

2. Heat the oil in a frying pan and brown the meat all over to seal. Place in a large casserole dish.

3. Add the bacon to the frying pan and fry gently for 2 minutes, then add the onions and garlic. Fry for 5 minutes, then place in the casserole around the meat.

4. Add the carrots to the meat dish and pour in the wine and stock. Place the sprigs of thyme around the meat and season to taste.

5. Cover the dish and cook in the oven for 1 hour, then turn down the oven to 140°C/ gas mark ½ and continue to cook for 3 hours. Pour the juices over the meat from time to time so that the top doesn't dry out.

6. Lift out the meat and slice it, then put it back in the casserole with the sauce. Heat in the oven for 5 minutes if the sauce has cooled while you were slicing the meat.

7. Serve with new potatoes and cauliflower cheese (see page 208).

Lancashire Hotpot

This was traditionally made in a bread oven and left to cook all day after the bread was made. It was usually made with mutton, but this is often difficult to get hold of, so use neck of lamb cut into cutlets or any cheaper cut of lamb.

Serves 6

1.5kg lamb, cut into cutlets
Salt and pepper to taste
2 large onions, sliced thickly
150g mushrooms
50g lamb kidneys, chopped
1.2kg potatoes, peeled and sliced thickly
600ml beef or lamb stock (see page 156)
30g butter

1. Preheat the oven to 180°C/gas mark 4. Butter an ovenproof casserole dish.

2. Season the lamb with salt and pepper, then put a layer of the lamb in the casserole dish. Add a layer of onions.

3. Add another layer of cutlets, mushrooms and the kidneys, then some more onions and a layer of potatoes.

4. Pour in the stock.

5. Layer like this and finish with a layer of overlapping potatoes.

6. Dot with butter and cover. Place in the oven and cook for 2 hours, then remove the lid and cook for another hour.

Serving suggestion
I like to serve this with peas, carrot and swede, boiled or steamed together and chopped with a little butter and plenty of white pepper.

Scouse

This traditional dish hails from Liverpool. Again, it uses cheaper cuts of meat
because it is cooked for a long time on a low heat.

Serves 6

1 tablespoon sunflower oil
500g neck of lamb, cut into large cubes, any
  large bits of fat removed
500g stewing beef, cut into large cubes
3 onions, sliced thickly
1kg potatoes, peeled and sliced
450g carrots, peeled if you wish and cut into
  thick discs
3–4 sprigs thyme
600ml beef stock (see page 156)
Salt and pepper to taste

1. Preheat the oven to 170°C/gas mark 3.

2. Heat the oil in a pan and fry the meat to seal
it. Transfer to a large ovenproof casserole dish.

3. Fry the onions for 3–4 minutes in the same
pan, then add them to the meat.

4. Chop up one potato's worth of slices into
small pieces and add them to the meat.

5. Mix in the carrots so that they are evenly
spread throughout the dish.

6. Add the thyme and pour in the stock.

7. Press the potatoes into the meat mixture and
leave some on the top.

8. Season to taste and cover with a lid or foil.
Put in the oven and cook for 4 hours.

Hash of Beef or Lamb

This isn't the normal potato-type hash, but an old farmhouse-style dish using butter beans or any other dried beans that may be available. It is a filling way of using up leftover cooked meat from a joint.

Serves 4

220g dried butter beans, soaked in
  cold water overnight
50g butter
2 onions, sliced
100g mushrooms, halved if they are large
10–12 slices of cooked beef or lamb
30g plain flour
580ml beef stock (see page 156)
1 level teaspoon dried thyme
½ teaspoon dried rosemary
Salt and pepper to taste
300g tomatoes, chopped
1 teaspoon brown sugar
  or 1 tablespoon honey

1. Preheat the oven to 180°C/gas mark 4.

2. Drain the soaking water from the beans, then place them in a saucepan filled with sufficient fresh cold water to cover.

3. Bring to the boil, then turn down the heat and simmer for 30 minutes, or until soft but not falling apart.

4. Meanwhile, heat the butter in a saucepan and fry the onions gently until cooked. Place them in an ovenproof casserole.

5. Fry the mushrooms in the same pan for a few minutes, then place on top of the onions.

6. Place the slices of meat over the vegetables; cut the meat up if the slices are large.

7. If there is very little fat remaining in the pan after frying the vegetables, add a little more. Sprinkle over the flour and stir well.

8. Add the stock gradually and stir in the herbs. Bring to the boil and stir until the sauce thickens.

9. Drain the beans when cooked and add them to the casserole. Pour in the sauce and season with salt and pepper if necessary.

10. Top the whole dish with the chopped tomatoes and sprinkle with the sugar or drizzle with the honey.

10. Cook for 35–40 minutes, uncovered.

Serving suggestion
Serve with crusty bread or pasta, but this is very filling on its own so don't cook too much to go with it!

Pork with Baked Beans

Beans and pulses are so useful for making hearty meals, and they're very good for you as well. Using them also means that you don't need as much meat in the dish to give satisfying results. Fresh tomatoes were used in the original recipe, but I use a can of plum tomatoes instead.

Serves 6

450g dried haricot beans, soaked in
  plenty of cold water overnight
2 tablespoons sunflower oil
500g pork steak, cut into cubes
2 rashers streaky bacon, chopped
500ml beef or vegetable stock
  (see page 156 or 160)
1 garlic clove, chopped
½ level teaspoon dried oregano
½ level teaspoon dried thyme
1 level dessertspoon brown sugar
400g canned plum tomatoes
Salt and pepper to taste

1. Preheat the oven 160°C/gas mark 2.

2. Drain the beans of the steeping water and boil them in fresh water for 10 minutes.

3. Heat the oil in a pan and fry the pork and bacon until the meat changes colour. Place in a lidded ovenproof casserole.

4. When the beans are ready, drain them and stir them into the pork mixture.

5. Heat the stock in the frying pan. Add the garlic, herbs, sugar and canned tomatoes. Chop the tomatoes into small pieces as they heat in the stock, or do this separately before adding to the pan. Bring everything to the boil, then pour it over the meat-and-bean mixture and season to taste.

6. Cover the casserole and cook in the oven for 3 hours. Stir and cook for another 40–50 minutes.

Serving suggestion
This is good served with baked potatoes or boiled rice.

Pork Sausage and Apple Casserole

Sausages, especially if you make them yourself or buy good ones, make an excellent casserole as they are not fatty – just tasty. Apple goes so well with all kinds of pork, and sausages are no exception.

Serves 4

2 tablespoons sunflower oil
8 thick pork sausages
2 Bramley apples, peeled and diced
1 large onion, sliced thinly
2 celery sticks, chopped
1 tablespoon plain flour
400ml dry cider
4 or 5 chopped fresh sage leaves
Salt and pepper to taste

1. Preheat the oven to 180°C/gas mark 4.

2. Heat the oil in a frying pan and fry the sausages until they are brown all over. Add the apples and cook them with the sausages for 3–4 minutes. Transfer the sausages and apples to an ovenproof casserole dish.

3. Fry the onions in the same pan as the sausages, removing any excess fat from the pan. Add the celery and cook until the onions are soft.

4. Sprinkle in the flour and stir it into the oil left in the onion mixture.

5. Gradually stir in the cider. Add the sage and season with salt and pepper as necessary.

6. Pour the cider mixture over the sausages. Cover the casserole and cook for 30–40 minutes, or until the apples are cooked and beginning to 'fall' into the sauce. Serve with potato wedges and a green vegetable.

Rabbit Fricassée

Rabbit is a very useful and tasty meat and I don't understand why it isn't used more often in Britain today – it used be so popular. It is eaten very widely in France instead of chicken. It is very versatile and can be used in so many dishes: pies, casseroles or roasts. This is a traditional way of serving rabbit, and it is probably my favourite.

Serves 4

1 large rabbit, jointed
Salt and pepper to taste
1 onion, chopped
1 turnip, diced
2 carrots, chopped
½ teaspoon dried or 1 tablespoon freshly chopped parsley
½ teaspoon dried or 2 sprigs fresh thyme
1 bay leaf

For the sauce
30g butter
30g flour
175ml of the rabbit stock
2 tablespoons dry sherry
50ml double cream
Salt and pepper to taste

For the croutons
2 slices wholemeal bread, cut into cubes
2 tablespoons olive oil

1. Put the rabbit into a large pan and pour over sufficient water to cover. Season with salt and pepper, then bring to the boil and simmer for 10 minutes.

2. Add the vegetables and herbs and simmer for 35–40 minutes, or until the rabbit is tender.

3. Pour 175ml of the stock into a jug and place the meat and vegetables in an ovenproof casserole dish.

4. Take all the meat from the bones and discard the latter. Add the meat to the dish and keep it warm in the oven – at about 160°C/gas mark 3.

5. Make the sauce by melting the butter in a pan and stirring in the flour. Add the rabbit stock gradually over a low heat until it is all combined.

6. Bring to the boil, stirring continuously. Cook for 3–4 minutes, then remove from the heat.

7. Stir in the sherry and cream then pour the sauce over the rabbit and vegetables.
Keep the casserole in the oven while you fry the bread cubes in the oil until crispy.

8. Serve the dish with the croutons and some boiled potatoes and steamed or boiled green cabbage.

Fish Pie

I love fish pie – you can make it with whatever fish takes your fancy. Mine just has to have prawns and mussels in it, although these aren't traditional. A good combination of smoked and plain fish is what gives the pie its well-loved flavour.

Serves 6

450g fresh haddock, pollack or cod
220g smoked haddock
100ml milk
100ml white wine
100ml water
1 thick lemon slice
1 bay leaf
Salt and black pepper to taste
25g butter
25g plain flour
Juice of half a lemon
1 tablespoon chopped fresh parsley
100g shelled prawns
50g shelled mussels

For the topping
500g potatoes, boiled and mashed
    with 30g butter

Serving suggestion
Serve with peas or broccoli or a fresh
green salad.

1. Preheat the oven to 190°C/gas mark 5. Butter a deep ovenproof casserole dish.

2. Put the fish, but not the prawns or mussels, in a pan with the milk, wine, water lemon slice and bay leaf and season with salt and pepper.

3. Heat to simmering, then cook gently for 10 minutes. Put the fish on a plate and flake it.

4. Bring the cooking liquor to the boil and boil for 2 minutes. Remove from the heat.

5. In a separate pan, melt the butter over a low heat and stir in the flour.

6. Gradually add the hot liquid from the fish and stir in constantly, raising the heat so that the sauce boils and thickens. If you like a very thick sauce, reduce the amount of liquid you use.

7. Reduce the heat and add the lemon juice and parsley. Stir in the prawns and mussels and season with salt and pepper if necessary. Remove from the heat and carefully stir in the flaked fish.

8. Spoon the mixture into the prepared casserole dish and top with the mashed potato.

9. Dot the mash with small knobs of butter and bake for 20–30 minutes, or until the top is golden brown.

Mussels in Tomato Sauce

Mussels were a main source of protein for the poor people of the eighteenth century and they are still relatively inexpensive. This tomato-based sauce is an English version of *moules meunière*.

Serves 3–4 as light lunch or supper dish

30ml sunflower or rapeseed oil
1 onion, chopped finely
2 garlic cloves, chopped or grated
2 teaspoons honey
2 tablespoons tomato purée
1 tablespoon chopped fresh parsley
100ml dry cider
400g chopped tomatoes, fresh or canned
Salt and pepper to taste
1.5kg mussels, scrubbed; discard any that have broken shells or do not close when tapped

1. Heat the oil in a large pan and fry the onions with the garlic for 4–5 minutes until soft.

2. Add the honey, tomato purée and parsley.

3. Stir in the cider and fresh or canned tomatoes. Season to taste.

4. Bring to the boil and add the mussels all in one go. Cover and cook on a high heat for 5 minutes. Shake the pan gently to allow the mussels to open, but not too vigorously or the shells will break.

5. Serve the mussels and sauce in shallow soup dishes.

Serving suggestion
Pair this with some fresh bread to mop up the tomato sauce.

Haddock Mornay

This was a recipe I made when I first started high school. It became a firm favourite with my mum and she passed it on to many of her friends. You can make it with any type of fish. Personally, I'm not keen on the cheese and salmon combination, but most other white fish work well.

Serves 4

300ml milk
1 tablespoon fresh parsley, chopped
1 very small onion, quartered
1 bay leaf
4 crushed black peppercorns
1kg haddock fillets, cut into 4 portions, all bones removed
25g cornflour
A large knob butter
1 teaspoon English mustard powder
3 tablespoon double cream
150g grated medium–strong Cheddar
Salt to taste

1. Butter an ovenproof dish.

2. Put the milk in a saucepan. Add the parsley, onion, bay leaf, crushed peppercorns and the fish. Poach it gently for 10 minutes.

3. Lift the fish carefully out of the liquid and place it in the prepared dish.

4. Bring the liquid to the boil. Meanwhile, mix the cornflour with a little milk to make a thin paste and stir this into the fish liquid. Stir constantly and add the butter and mustard powder. Simmer for 3 minutes, then remove from the heat. Stir in the double cream.

5. Add half of the cheese, stir well, then season the sauce.

6. Pour the cheese sauce over the fish and sprinkle on the rest of the cheese.

7. Place the dish under a hot grill until the top browns.

Serving suggestion
I love to eat this with new potatoes and whole green beans.

Asparagus with Lightly Boiled Eggs

This is one of my all-time favourite lunches. When we have some new asparagus growing,
I would have this every day. Now that we have our own chickens it's almost
a free lunch. Well, that's what it seems like…

Serves as many as you like!

4 asparagus spears per person
1 egg per person
A knob of butter
1 thinly sliced piece of wholemeal bread per
   person, toasted, buttered and cut
   into quarters
Salt and white pepper to taste

1. Steam the asparagus for 3–5 minutes, depending on size.

2. Boil the eggs for 2½–3 minutes, then take a small amount of shell away from the flatter end and plunge them in cold water for a few seconds. You will now be able to peel off the shell fairly easily.

3. Place your cooked asparagus on a small plate and put a knob of butter on each serving.

4. Place the egg on top and slice it open so that the yolk trickles over the asparagus. Serve with the toast.

Cauliflower Cheese

This is a satisfying supper dish or an excellent accompaniment to roast dinners.
Some people like to serve the cauliflower whole, but I prefer to have smaller florets
because the cheese sauce covers it better.

Serves 2–4

1 medium cauliflower, broken into florets
600ml milk
25g butter
Salt and black pepper to taste
1 level teaspoon English mustard
2 tablespoons cornflour mixed with
   3 tablespoons cold milk to make a paste
120g Cheddar

1. Put the cauliflower in a saucepan and pour in the milk. Cook gently for about 20 minutes, or until the cauliflower is tender.

2. Remove from the heat and lift out the cauliflower, leaving all the milk still in the pan. Put the cauliflower in a buttered ovenproof dish. Season with salt and pepper.

3. Stir the mustard into the warm milk and put back on the heat. Bring to the boil and stir in the cornflour paste. Turn down the heat and simmer gently for 2 minutes. Remove from the heat.

4. Stir in most of the cheese, apart from a sprinkling for the top. Check the seasoning, remembering that you have already seasoned the cauliflower.

5. Pour the sauce evenly over the cauliflower. Sprinkle the rest of the cheese over the top and place under a hot grill until the top browns and bubbles. Serve immediately.

Pease Pudding

This is best served with cooked bacon or gammon, but I also like
to serve it with sausages.

Serves 4–6

450g dried split peas
60g butter
1 egg, beaten
Salt and black pepper to taste

1. Cover the dried peas with cold water, leaving a free depth of 3cm because they will swell. Leave to soak overnight, or do this early in the morning for an evening meal. They need to soak at least 7–8 hours.

2. Drain the peas and put them in a saucepan with enough fresh, cold water to just cover them. Bring to the boil.

3. Turn down the heat and simmer for 1 hour. Preheat the oven to 180°C/gas mark 4.

4. Drain the peas and put them back in the pan. Mash them with the butter and egg, season with salt and black pepper and mix well together.

5. Transfer the peas to a buttered pudding basin and cover with foil. Stand the basin on a baking tray and bake in the oven for 25–30 minutes.

6. Serve in wedges.

Budget Meals

I nevitably there are times of the month or the week when money is short, but you still want to eat well. Don't worry: using less-expensive ingredients such as pulses and basic seasonal vegetables means you can spend less but still have a satisfying, healthy diet. It's a tried-and-tested tradition, really: during the Second World War people made some clever, tasty dishes with very few ingredients, budgeting very carefully on each meal.

Today, we have a much wider range of ingredients, so when what we call our 'ballyann' weeks roll around, this means that we can still eat well. Sometimes we find that we actually eat better when preparing a budget meal, probably because we've planned our shopping more precisely and have taken greater care during the preparation and cooking of what our money has allowed us to buy.

Tricks of the trade

When you prepare food on a budget, you soon learn a few useful tricks to make meals stretch, yet still taste delicious. For example, minced beef and pork, which form the basis for this first selection of recipes, are very useful when you're watching pennies. They're so versatile and can be cooked with many other flavours to add variety (and taste) to the meat. I use minced beef in many budget dishes because it goes further but always tastes good. And the suet pastry crust used in the recipe opposite is very easy and economical to make, yet is light and soft inside – and because it contains a little butter, it tastes wonderful.

Minced Beef and Pork

Potato and Meat Pie

This dish has more vegetables in it than meat, but there's enough of the latter to flavour the filling.

Serves 4–5

1 tablespoon sunflower oil
2 large onions, chopped finely
400g minced beef
1 litre beef stock (see page 156)
2 carrots, peeled and diced
½ teaspoon dried thyme or a sprig of fresh
800g potatoes, peeled and cut into large chunks
1 level tablespoon plain flour
Salt and pepper to taste

For the pastry crust
225g self-raising flour
1 level teaspoon salt
100g suet
25g butter, chilled and grated
About 150ml water

1. Heat the oil in a lidded pan large enough to take the potatoes later and fry the onion for 3-4 minutes. Add the meat. Fry the meat until it changes colour.

2. Stir in half the stock and bring to the boil. Turn the heat down to simmering and add the carrots and the thyme. Cover and cook for 30 minutes.

3. Add the potatoes and the rest of the stock and cook for a further 15 minutes.

4. Make the pasty while the potatoes cook. Sieve the flour and salt together in a mixing bowl. Stir in the suet and butter. Add enough water to make a soft, pliable dough and knead this for 1–2 minutes, or until smooth.

5. Back to the pie filling: mix the flour with 2 tablespoons cold water; stir this into the filling. Season to taste. Turn up the heat to cook the flour, stirring carefully, for about 3 minutes. Don't break up the potatoes too much.

6. Preheat the oven to 190°C/gas mark 5. Remove the filling from the heat and pour it into 1 large pie dish. Place the dish on a large baking sheet to help lift it in and out of the oven.

7. Dampen the edges of the dish and roll out the pastry to fit; it should be about 1cm thick as it will rise while cooking. Cut 3 slits in the centre.

8. Bake in the oven for 30–35 minutes.

9. Serve immediately with a green vegetable or some pickled red cabbage.

Cottage Pie

This was a recipe my grandma usually made with leftover vegetables from the roast
we had the day before. She used 225g minced beef, but I use slightly more meat
in this recipe and have added a clove of garlic.

Serves 4

1 tablespoon oil
1 onion, chopped
350g minced beef
1 garlic clove
2 tablespoons tomato purée
½ teaspoon dried marjoram
150ml beef stock
2 carrots, peeled and chopped
1 small turnip, peeled and chopped
50g frozen peas
50g frozen green beans
2 teaspoons plain flour (or gravy powder)
    mixed with 4 teaspoons cold water
    to make a paste

For the potato topping
800g potatoes, peeled and
    cut into small chunks
Salt and pepper to taste
30g butter
1 small leek, chopped
50g mature Cheddar, grated

Serving suggestion
I usually serve this with a sliced tomato
and pickled onions, but a green salad
would be good.

1. Heat the oil in saucepan and fry the
onion gently for 4–5 minutes.

2. Add the meat, garlic, tomato purée and
marjoram. Fry until the meat changes colour.

3. Add the stock, carrots and turnip and
simmer for 10 minutes.

4. Add the peas and beans and simmer for
30 minutes.

5. Stir in the flour paste and continue stirring
until it the gravy thickens. Cook for 3
minutes more, then pour into a deep pie dish.

6. To make the potato topping, boil the
potatoes until tender, drain, and season well
with salt and pepper. Leave in the pan.

7. Preheat the oven to 190°C/gas mark 5.
In a frying pan, melt the butter and fry the
leeks until soft, but don't brown them.

8. Stir the leeks into the potatoes and mash
them together. Spread the potato mixture
over the meat and sprinkle the cheese on top.

9. Bake for 20–25 minutes, until the cheese
has melted. To brown the top, either raise
the heat to 220°C/gas mark 7 and cook for
5 more minutes, or place under a hot grill.

Savoury Rissoles

These were the 'burgers' of the time when my mum was small. They were often made with leftover roast meat minced finely with vegetables, seasoned, then mixed with breadcrumbs and egg. They are still formed into patties like a burger and fried in oil. I serve them with a bread roll, salad and relish.

Makes 8 rissoles

5 spring onions, chopped finely
1 small red pepper, chopped finely
Oil for shallow-frying
400g minced pork
50g breadcrumbs for mixing with the meat, plus 30g for coating
1 tablespoon tomato purée
1 garlic clove, grated
1 tablespoon chopped fresh parsley
2 teaspoons Worcestershire sauce
1 large egg, beaten
Salt and pepper to taste
2 tablespoons milk

Variations
• Spice up the rissoles by adding ½ teaspoon ground cumin and ½ teaspoon chilli flakes to the main mixture.
• For an oriental flavour, add ½ teaspoon five-spice powder and 1 tablespoon soy sauce.

1. If you wish, you can fry the onions and pepper in the oil for a few minutes to soften them; otherwise leave them raw.

2. Combine the meat, vegetables, breadcrumbs for mixing, tomato purée, garlic, parsley and Worcestershire sauce in a large bowl. Mix well with your hands so all the flavours are evenly distributed.

3. Stir in three-quarters of the beaten egg and season with salt and pepper. Mix well to combine.

4. Put the rest of the egg into a shallow dish with the milk and stir. Put the breadcrumbs for coating into another shallow dish.

5. Form the meat mixture into 8 flat patties. Heat some oil in a frying pan. Dip each patty in the egg /milk mixture, then in the breadcrumbs and shallow-fry for about 5 minutes each side. Don't have the heat too high as the rissoles will be cooked on the outside and raw in the middle.

6. Cook 2–3 at a time; when done, keep them warm in the oven while you fry the others.

Spaghetti Bolognese Sauce

This isn't really a recipe my grandma used to make; however, my aunt went to Italy on holiday in the 1950s and enjoyed eating this so much that she made it for all the family. It became a firm favourite with us – just as it still is in most families.

This version uses a mixture of pork and beef mince. The secret is to cook it slowly for longer to allow the flavours to develop. You don't have to serve it with spaghetti; any pasta will work well. I know that my boys always found spaghetti too messy – mainly because they were far too hungry to wrap it round their forks properly – so I serve it at home with pasta shapes.

Serves 4

1 tablespoon olive oil
1 large onion, finely chopped
200g minced beef
200g minced pork
2 garlic cloves, grated
4 tablespoons tomato purée
5 tablespoons water
1 x 400g can plum tomatoes
1 level teaspoon oregano
Salt and pepper to taste

1. Heat the oil in a saucepan and fry the onion until soft.

2. Stir in the 2 meats, garlic and tomato purée. Cook everything on a medium heat until the meat has changed colour. Add the water and stir into the meat.

3. Stir in the tomatoes and oregano, then season to taste.

4. Cover and simmer gently for 1½ hours.

5. Serve with your pasta choice and some grated Parmesan.

Tip
I have also served this with baked potatoes and it has served 6 people – so long as there is plenty of grated cheese (Cheddar or Parmesan).

Vegetables and Pulses

Never mind the meat: vegetables and pulses make excellent, reasonably priced and tasty meals in their own right.

Red Lentil and Vegetable Curry

This makes a filling meal with some boiled rice – or, as we prefer, some chapatis.

Serves 4

25g butter
1 tablespoon sunflower oil
1 large onion, chopped
1 red or green pepper, chopped
1 courgette, sliced into discs
1 carrot, sliced into discs
5–6 cauliflower florets
50g frozen green beans
1 medium potato, peeled and diced
3 garlic cloves
2 level tablespoons mild madras curry powder
1 teaspoon turmeric
1 teaspoon ground cumin
4 tablespoons water
550ml vegetable stock (see page 160)
150g red lentils
1 handful of baby spinach leaves
Salt to taste

1. In a lidded saucepan melt the butter and oil together over a very low heat and add all the vegetables except the spinach.

2. Stir in the garlic, curry powder, turmeric and cumin. Add the water, cover and allow the vegetables to sweat for 15 minutes. This process extracts all the flavours and juices from the vegetables and softens them slightly.

3. Add the stock and stir in the lentils; season to taste. Raise the heat and bring to the boil. Turn down the heat as soon as it is boiling and cover and simmer gently for 25 minutes, or until the vegetables are tender.

4. Add the spinach and cook for 5 more minutes. Serve with rice or chapatis.

Vegetable Stew with Cheese Dumplings

Serves 4

30g butter
1 onion, chopped
4 carrots, chopped
1 green pepper, chopped
8 broccoli florets
600ml tomato juice
½ teaspoon thyme
100g green lentils
100g frozen peas
1 tablespoon chopped fresh parsley
Salt and pepper to taste

For the dumplings
120g self-raising flour
A pinch salt
½ teaspoon mustard powder
Black pepper to taste
55g vegetarian suet
30g mature Cheddar cheese
Sufficient water to make a soft dough

1. In a large saucepan, heat the butter and fry the onion for a few minutes, then add the rest of the vegetables except the peas. Cook for 5 minutes.

2. Stir in the tomato juice, thyme and lentils. Bring to the boil, then cover and simmer for 15 minutes. Stir in the peas and fresh parsley and simmer for 15 minutes more. Season with salt and pepper to taste.

3. Make the dumplings by sieving the flour, salt, mustard powder and black pepper together into a mixing bowl.

4. Stir in the suet and cheese and add enough water to make a soft dough.

5. Bring the dough together with your hands.

6. Create little dough balls using a little flour to prevent it from sticking. Make 12, as they cook quickly and there are 3 per person.

7. Ensure the stew is simmering and drop the dumplings into the liquid, evenly spaced so that they cook thoroughly. Replace the lid

8. Cook for 15–20 minutes, by which time the dumplings should be well-risen and fluffy.

9. Serve in bowls with some extra grated cheese if you wish.

Leek and Potato Bake

Serves 4–5

300ml milk
1 level tablespoon cornflour mixed with
2 tablespoons milk
½ teaspoon mustard or mustard powder
Salt and pepper to taste
3 large potatoes, peeled and sliced
    into 5mm slices
2 large leeks, sliced thinly
A knob of butter
Grated cheese for topping

1. Make a white sauce by heating the milk in a microwave or saucepan until hot and pouring it over the cornflour mixture. Stir in the mustard and seasoning and return to the pan. Bring to the boil, stirring all the time with a wooden spoon, then turn down the heat and simmer for 2 minutes.

2. In a separate saucepan, boil the potatoes for 4 minutes. Drain. Butter an ovenproof dish.

3. In a frying pan, sauté the leeks in a knob of butter until tender. Preheat the oven to 200°C/gas mark 6.

4. Spoon a layer of leeks into the prepared ovenproof dish, then add a layer of potato. Repeat this process, finishing with a thick layer of potato. Season with black pepper.

5. Pour on the white sauce and top with grated cheese.

6. Bake in the preheated oven for 20–25 minutes, or until the top begins to brown.

Serving
Serve on its own with some crusty bread or with some crispy bacon.

Mushroom Risotto

In our grandmothers' day, mushrooms were used frequently in pies and casseroles to make meat go further, but I think they are delicious without meat. This is a very economical recipe, yet it would make a delicious dinner-party dish.

Serves 4

1 tablespoon oil
1 onion, chopped
2 garlic cloves, grated
2 tablespoons tomato purée
250g mushrooms, sliced
230g Arborio rice
600ml vegetable or chicken stock
  (see page 160 or 158)
Salt and black pepper to taste

1. Heat the oil in a saucepan and fry the onions until just soft.

2. Stir in the garlic and tomato purée, then add the mushrooms. Fry until tender.

3. Remove a couple of tablespoons of the mushrooms and set aside to add later.

4. Add the rice and fry with the other ingredients for a few minutes.

5. Stir in a quarter of the stock and boil until it has been absorbed. Do the same with another quarter and so on until it has been absorbed but the rice is still juicy. It should not be dry, so add more stock if necessary. Check the seasoning and add a little salt and pepper if necessary.

6. Stir in the extra mushrooms and serve immediately with some grated cheese if you wish.

Variation
Add 80ml of dry white wine to the stock for a richer flavour.

Bubble and Squeak with Pork Sausages

Yes, you can use leftover potato and greens, but I make them especially for this dish if I don't have any. This is a more interesting sausage-and-mash recipe. If you make our own sausage it can be a very reasonably priced meal. Either way, it's very tasty.

Serves 4

500g mashed potatoes
200g cooked cabbage, sprouts or other green,
  leafy vegetable
Salt and pepper to taste
15g butter
1 tablespoon oil
1 spring onion, chopped finely
Cooked pork sausages, to serve

1. Mix the potato and cabbage together in a bowl and season with salt and pepper.

2. Heat the butter and oil in a frying pan and fry the spring onion gently until soft.

3. Add the potato and cabbage mixture to the frying pan with the onion and press it down to form a flat, round cake.

4. Turn up the heat and fry for 6–8 minutes until golden brown. Turn over carefully and fry for another 6–8 minutes. Serve with grilled or roasted pork sausages.

Variation
Make individual cakes and top each with a poached egg.

Something for Dessert

As our grandmothers knew, cooking on a budget doesn't mean forgoing all sweet treats. Here are some dessert recipes that taste delicious – without breaking the bank.

Gooseberry Brown Betty

This pudding uses breadcrumbs and sugar as a topping rather than flour, sugar and butter. You can make it with most fruit that can be stewed. Choosing fruit in season makes it a very economical dessert indeed.

Serves 4

450g gooseberries
4 tablespoons water
30g golden granulated sugar
225g fresh wholemeal breadcrumbs
50g soft brown sugar
2 tablespoons apple juice

1. Preheat the oven to 170°C/gas mark 3.

2. In a large saucepan, stew the gooseberries in the water and sugar until they are just soft.

3. Combine the breadcrumbs with the brown sugar.

4. When the fruit is cooked, place it in a buttered ovenproof dish and sprinkle it with the breadcrumbs mixture.

5. Drizzle the apple juice over the top.

6. Bake for 30–40 minutes, or until the top is golden brown and firm. Serve with custard or cream.

Eve's Pudding

This is such a change from jam or syrup sponge. It is also very cheap to make because you don't need a large sponge to give four people a good portion each.

Serves 4

2 Bramley apples, peeled, cored and sliced
2 tablespoons caster sugar
4 tablespoons apple juice

For the sponge
100g butter
100g caster sugar
100g self-raising flour
1 egg
2 tablespoons milk

1. In a large saucepan, cook the apples and sugar in the apple juice for 10 minutes until soft. Place in a buttered ovenproof dish.

2. Preheat the oven to 180°C/gas mark 4.

3. Make the sponge by creaming the butter and sugar together in a mixing bowl. Add a tablespoon of the flour and beat in the egg.

4. Sieve in the rest of the flour and fold into the creamed mixture. Stir in the milk.

5. Spoon over the apples and smooth out the top. Make a well in the centre to stop it rising unevenly.

6. Bake for 20–25 minutes until well-risen and golden in colour. Serve with custard.

Vanilla Ice Cream

A purse-loving yet satisfying ice cream that can be made with
or without an ice-cream maker.

Serves 6–8 portions

4 egg yolks
120g caster sugar
500ml milk
100ml double cream
1 teaspoon vanilla extract

1. Whisk the eggs and sugar together in a bowl until light and creamy.

2. Heat the milk, cream and vanilla in a pan until hot; don't allow it to boil.

3. Pour the milk over the egg and sugar mixture and whisk until smooth.

4. Transfer the custard back to the pan and heat gently, stirring all the time until it thickens – about 12–15 minutes.

5. Remove from the heat and whisk for 1 minute, then pour into the freezeable container.

6. Cover and freeze for 1 hour, then take out and beat the ice cream; this will break down any large ice crystals. Put back in the freezer and repeat this after another hour.

7. Leave then to freeze completely for at least 4 more hours.

8. Take the ice cream out of the freezer 10 minutes before serving, or 5 minutes if it is a very warm day.

Scones

Whenever money is a bit tight, I always make some scones for
a treat. They cost very little and are quick and easy to make.

Makes 8–12 scones

1 tablespoon lemon juice
380ml milk
450g self-raising flour
2 tablespoons golden caster sugar
60g butter, chopped into small pieces

Variations
Add 50g raisins, halved glacé cherries or
sultanas to the mixture for fruit scones.

1. Preheat the oven to 200°C/gas mark 6.
Grease 2 baking sheets.

2. Mix the lemon juice in the milk and stir, leave
for 5 minutes while you weigh out the ingredients.
This acidified milk helps lighten the scones.

3. Sieve the flour into a bowl and stir in the sugar.

4. Add the butter and rub it into the flour until
the mixture looks like breadcrumbs.

5. Mix in the milk with quick, light strokes until
well-combined.

6. Bring the mixture together with your hands.
Knead as lightly and as little as possible until the
dough is workable.

7. Roll out half of the dough to about 2.5cm
thick and cut it into rounds.

8. Place on a baking sheet. Do the same with
the other half of the dough. Rolling in two
batches like this stops the dough from getting
tough after being re-rolled.

9. Bake for 20 minutes, or until well-risen and
golden brown.

10. Cool for 15 minutes, then enjoy with butter
or cream and jam.

Christmas Food

In this modern era, celebratory meals can take many forms. Yet whether you celebrate it or not, Christmas really *does* come at the right time of the year, just at that point when we all need a boost and a reason to feast. As our grandparents knew, winter is a time when eating well is extremely important to our health and general well-being. And as we all know today, few things in life are more satisfying and enjoyable than making a wonderful meal on a special occasion for your family and friends.

The recipes in this section provide plenty of holiday 'food for thought', from starters and snack foods right through to dessert. Some are traditional English dishes, made in the way my grandparents would have recognised; others have been adapted to suit modern methods and ingredients, but all of them have been developed lovingly over the years to provide maximum flavour and enjoyment – without too much preparation time or expense.

Whether you're partial to pâte or stuffing, turkey or goose, pork pie or ham, or simply fancy a taste of some home-made cranberry sauce, you'll find everything you need here to prepare a sumptuous Christmas feast for your family. There are also plenty of vegetable options and gravies to accompany the main courses – and naturally, I haven't forgotten the mince pies!

Christmas Pâtés

Pâté can be made and served as a starter with some melba toast or as a snack with crackers. Making homemade pâté is so much easier if you have a food processor because you can use it to mince your own meat and blend all the ingredients together. If you don't have a food processor, just ask your butcher to mince the pork shoulder, liver or bacon for you.

Quick Chicken Liver Pâté

Serves 6

350g chicken livers
30g butter
1 garlic clove, grated
4 tablespoons double cream
1 tablespoon lemon juice
½ teaspoon English mustard
Salt and black pepper

1. Fry the chicken livers gently in the butter. Add the garlic. Cook until the livers are no longer pink, then blend or process them until they are as smoothly textured as you prefer.

2. Add all the other ingredients and whizz for a few seconds to blend well.

3. Transfer to a serving dish and chill for 2 hours before serving.

Pork Pâté

Serves 8

450g pork shoulder, with the fat left on
300g pork liver
250g streaky bacon, chopped
2 garlic cloves, grated
1 teaspoon black pepper
1 teaspoon salt
30ml brandy
½ teaspoon dried thyme
3 bay leaves
10 whole black peppercorns

1. Mince the pork, liver and bacon together in a food processor until the mixture resembles large crumbs.

2. Add all the other ingredients except the bay leaves and whole peppercorns and whizz together for a few seconds. If you're not using a processor, combine everything in a bowl using a large spoon, mashing well.

3. Cover the bowl and leave in a cool place for 2 hours to allow all the flavours to develop.

4. Preheat the oven to 150°C/gas mark 2. Pack the pâté into a loaf tin, making sure you press the mixture down firmly.

5. Press the whole peppercorns into the top of the pâté and put the bay leaves down the centre.

6. Place the tin in a roasting tin and pour in enough warm water to come halfway up the pâté tin.

7. Cook for 1 hour 40 minutes. Remove from the roasting pan and allow to cool completely.

8. Cover the pâté with greaseproof paper and use weights to press it down; it must be left for 24 hours like this. The pâté will then be ready to slice.

Stilton and Port Pâté

Serves 4

50g butter
4 spring onions, finely chopped
4 tablespoons of port
Grated zest of 1 lemon
200g Stilton (blue or white)
Black pepper to taste

1. Melt the butter in a small pan and fry the onions very gently until soft.

2. Add the port and simmer for 4 minutes.

3. Remove from the heat and add all the other ingredients.

4. Put the mixture into a food processor and blend until smooth, or mash with a fork.

5. Place in a serving dish and chill for 1 hour before serving.

The Main Event

Our Christmas meal usually revolves around a turkey, mainly because I generally have many hungry mouths to feed and it contrasts well with the other things I like to cook, such as a ham (see page 232) and a large raised pork pie (see page 233).

As a child, however, we were more familiar with goose taking 'centre stage', and this once-popular festive bird is now making a comeback – which is why I've included a good recipe for goose as well on page 230. Whether you opt for a turkey or a goose, however, don't feel daunted by the prospect; it's much easier than you might think. Cooking a large bird doesn't have to bring you out in a cold sweat, although admittedly for our first four or five Christmases, I was always understandably anxious until our turkey was cooked and cooling.

Whatever you decide to have as your showcase dish, remember to choose something that will contrast well with the other foods you will cook to go with it.

How will I know when it is cooked?

The foolproof way to make sure your turkey is cooked is to test it with a skewer in the deepest part of the breast and leg. If the juices run clear, it is done, but if there is a hint of pink, it must continue cooking. If you use a meat thermometer then the temperature of the deepest part of the breast should read 77°C.
A rough guide to cooking times is:

- Turkeys under 6.5kg: 20 minutes per 450g, plus 20 minutes extra
- Turkeys over 6.5kg: 15 minutes per 450g, plus 15 minutes extra

---

Roast Turkey

I've found that it is better to cook the bird on Christmas Eve, when the oven is free and I can give it more time without worrying about other things. It is also much easier to carve the next day, and we like having it cold while everything else is piping hot. If you prefer it warm, of course, then it must be cooked on the day. Always remember that the turkey is heavy and hot, so be fully kitted out with oven gloves when lifting it out of the oven.

Serves 6

1 turkey, at your desired weight
100g butter
12 rashers of streaky bacon

1. Take your turkey out of the fridge at least 2 hours before it needs to go in the oven and keep it covered. If you put a cold turkey or any meat in a hot oven, the meat will be less tender. I never stuff our turkey because this alters the cooking time, and stuffings and accompaniments can be made just as deliciously without being inside a bird.

2. Preheat the oven to 180°C/gas mark 4.

3. Massage the butter under the skin of the breast into the flesh on both sides of the breastbone.

4. Cover the breast and legs with good-quality streaky bacon. I use 4 rashers for each side of the breast, 2 for each leg, and in addition to keeping the turkey moist, this works to season the bird.

5. Put the turkey into a large roasting tin and surround it with 3cm tepid water.

6. Cover with a tent of foil and place in the oven.

7. Cook until all the juices run clear (see box, opposite). About 30 minutes before the cooking time is up, remove the foil to crisp up the bacon.

8. When cooked, remove from the oven. Lift the turkey out of the roasting tin and place it on a large plate.

9. Put all the juices in a large pan, ready to make the gravy.

Roast Goose

We used to have goose every other year when I was a child, and it is a wonderfully rich meat – not a bit greasy if cooked properly. The best thing about cooking a goose is the fat that comes from the bird. It makes *the best* roast potatoes you have ever tasted (see page 241)! Cooking the goose on a trivet allows the fat to cook slowly out of the meat and drip into the bottom of pan. The cooking time for a goose is 15 minutes per 450g, plus 15 minutes extra.

---

1 goose at your chosen weight
Salt

1. Preheat the oven to 200°C/gas mark 6.

2. Dry the skin of the bird well with kitchen paper, then place the goose on a trivet in a large roasting tin and prick the skin all over to allow the fat to drain out.

3. Season with a little salt and cover with a tent of foil.

4. Put the goose in the oven and cook it for the allotted time. About 40 minutes before the end of cooking, turn up the heat to 220°C/ gas mark 7 and uncover the bird; this will crisp up the skin.

5. Remove from the oven and plunge a skewer into the deepest part of the breast to check that the juices run clear.

6. When cooked, remove the goose from the tin and set it on a large plate. Pour the fat into a bowl to use for the roast potatoes on page 241.

Stock and Gravy

No Christmas bird would be complete without gravy to go with it, and to make gravy, you also need a good stock.

Giblet Stock

While your goose is cooking, use the giblets from it to make a stock for the gravy. I also use some of the stock to make my sage-and-onion stuffing. Put any unused stock either in the fridge for 2–3 days or freeze it as soon as it is cool for up to 3 months.

1. Season the giblets with salt and pepper to taste, and place them in a pan with sufficient water to cover fully.
2. Bring to the boil. Turn down the heat and simmer for 2 hours. Check the water level occasionally and add a little more if it gets too low.

Gravy

This is usually my last job before sitting down to the meal. Many people don't think you should use prepared gravy powder, but I do, and everyone loves my gravy. You can use seasoned flour if you prefer.

4 level teaspoons of flour or gravy powder
 per 300ml stock
Red wine, port or brandy (optional)
Salt and pepper to taste

1. Mix the flour or gravy powder with a little cold water to make a thin paste.

2. Bring the stock you are using to the boil, then turn down the heat and stir in the paste. Add a little red wine, port or brandy for extra flavour if you wish and check and adjust the seasoning if necessary.

3. Simmer for 4 minutes, then serve immediately.

Making a Christmas Ham

I've found that the best way to cook a large ham is to boil it first, then
roast it after adding the flavourings and coatings of your choice.
The meat is more tender and juicier this way.

1 ham, approximately 1–1.3kg
Honey, marmalade or syrup of your choice,
   for coating
15 cloves

1. Boil your ham in a pan large enough to hold it and enough water to cover.

2. Bring to the boil slowly, then turn down the heat, cover and simmer for 20 minutes per 500g.

3. Preheat the oven to 190°C/ gas mark 5.

4. Take the ham out of the water and remove as much skin or fat as you wish. Coat with honey, marmalade, syrup and press in about 15 cloves.

5. Place the ham on a trivet in a roasting pan and put it in the oven. Turn down the heat to 180°C/gas mark 4. Roast for 10 minutes per 500g, until the outside of the ham is golden brown.

6. Leave to cool before slicing.

Raised Pork Pie

This uses hot-water-crust pastry and was traditionally made during the Christmas period and kept in a cool place to serve to guests if they dropped in over the busy festive days. But we make them all year round because there is nothing like homemade pork pie. You know exactly what has gone into it and can flavour it to suit your tastes.

Makes about 8–10 portions

1 quantity of hot-water-crust pastry
    (see page 176)
500g minced pork
500g pork shoulder, cut into 1cm pieces
    with a little of the fat kept on
2 level teaspoons salt
White pepper to taste

Variations
To vary the flavour, add any of the following to the meat:

- ½ teaspoon sage
- A little grated nutmeg
- 1 teaspoon mustard powder
- ½ teaspoon celery salt

Storage
The pork pie will keep fresh, covered in the fridge, for 3–4 days.

1. Preheat the oven to 175°C/gas mark 3. Grease a 20cm round loose-bottomed or springform tin.

2. Roll out the hot-water-crust pastry when it is cool and use it to line the tin. It should be rolled out slightly thicker than other pastry because it has to be cooked for longer.

3. Combine the two meats with the salt and pepper and stir everything well.

4. Press the meat down firmly into the pastry case and top with a lid.

5. Seal down the edges firmly and brush with an egg-and-milk glaze if you wish.

6. Place the tin on a baking sheet so as to catch any drips from the meat and make it easier to get in and out of the oven.

7. Bake for 1½ hours, then test the centre with a knife. It is cooked if it comes out clean; if not, cook for 15 minutes more.

8. Leave to cool in the tin, preferably overnight. The juices will firm up and then the pie will be ready to slice.

Stuffings, Sauces and Accompaniments

Because I don't stuff the turkey, we always have an array of different sauces and stuffings. If you have plenty prepared, then people can choose their favourites.

Forcemeat Balls

Forcemeat is what you would put in the carcass of the bird, and in our grandparents' day it was sliced with the meat to make it go further. Today I make these simply because they're so tasty and are good to have with any leftovers.

Makes 10–12

150g good-quality sausage meat
2 rashers streaky bacon, chopped finely
80g breadcrumbs
1 teaspoon chopped parsley
½ teaspoon dried sage
Grated zest of 1 lemon
Salt and pepper
1 egg, beaten

1. Preheat the oven to 180°C/gas mark 4.

2. Put the first 7 ingredients in a bowl and combine well with your hands. Mix in the egg until the mixture forms a ball.

3. Roll small portions into balls and place them on an oiled baking sheet.

4. Cook for 25–30 minutes until crispy.

Sage and Onion Stuffing

This goes very well with both turkey and goose – all poultry, in fact, as well as pork.

Serves 6

25g butter
2 small or 1 large onion(s), finely chopped
4 tablespoons poultry stock (see page 158)
2 tablespoons fresh sage leaves,
   chopped finely, or 1 tablespoon dried
Salt and pepper
120g fresh breadcrumbs

1. Preheat the oven to 180°C/gas mark 4. Heat the butter in a saucepan and fry the onions gently until soft, but not brown.

3. Stir in the stock; use more or less to make a softer or stiffer stuffing. Add the sage and season with salt and pepper.

4. Add the breadcrumbs. Remove from the heat. Transfer to an ovenproof dish and press down.

5. Bake for 10 minutes. Serve hot with the meat.

Lemon and Parsley Stuffing

This fresh-tasting stuffing that also goes well with goose or turkey,
but if you're cooking fish, it makes an excellent crust for the top.
Fresh parsley is best for this recipe if you can get it.

Serves 6

120g fresh breadcrumbs
2 tablespoons fresh parsley
Zest and juice of 1 lemon
Salt and pepper to taste
30g butter, melted

1. Preheat the oven to 180°C/gas mark 4.

2. In a bowl combine the breadcrumbs, parsley, lemon juice and zest and season to taste.

3. Pour the melted butter over the mixture and stir well so that everything is well-coated.

4. Transfer to an ovenproof dish and press down well. Heat for a few minutes just before serving.

Chestnut Stuffing

This is a very rich and tasty accompaniment to a Christmas dinner.

Serves 6

300g chestnuts, slit round
   the widest part
2 chicken livers
2 teaspoons fresh parsley,
   finely chopped
Salt and pepper to taste
100g butter, melted

1. Preheat the oven to 180°C/gas mark 4.

2. Put the chestnuts in a pan with sufficient water to cover them and simmer for 25–30 minutes until tender.

3. When cooked, cool for a few minutes, then remove the shells.

4. Pound the nuts in a mortar with a pestle or use a food processor. You can grind them to as coarse a texture as you like.

5. Chop the chicken livers finely and mix into the chestnuts. Add the parsley and season to taste.

6. Pour the melted butter over the mixture and mix well.

7. Put into an ovenproof dish and bake for 10–15 minutes, or until the top has browned. Serve hot with the turkey or goose.

Bread Sauce

Bread has been used to thicken sauces, soups and stews for centuries, and this accompaniment to Christmas dinner stems from medieval times. The secret of a well-flavoured bread sauce is not to over-boil or otherwise heat the sauce too much.

Serves 6

280ml milk
Half a very small onion,
   chopped finely
1 bay leaf
4 cloves
Salt and pepper to taste
60g white breadcrumbs
50g butter
1 tablespoon single cream
A little grated nutmeg for serving

Tip
Use more or fewer breadcrumbs, depending on how thick you like your sauce.

1. Put the milk in a small saucepan. Add the onions, bay leaf, cloves and seasoning and bring to just boiling, then turn down the heat and simmer for 5 minutes.

2. Turn off the heat, pour into a bowl and leave for 30 minutes to allow all the flavours to infuse the milk.

3. Put the breadcrumbs in an ovenproof serving dish.

4. Strain the milk back into the pan and add the butter. Heat until the butter melts and the milk is hot. Stir in the cream and pour this mixture over the breadcrumbs.

5. Finish with a little grated nutmeg sprinkled on top.

Apple Sauce

This sauce is a traditional accompaniment to roast goose, although we eat it with pork and poultry. I tend to make too much, but it keeps for three to four days in the fridge and freezes well.

Serves 6

2 Bramley apples, peeled, cored and diced
5 tablespoons apple juice
25g caster sugar
Juice of half a lemon
A pinch of ground cinnamon
A knob of butter

1. Cook the apples in a saucepan with the apple juice, sugar and lemon juice.

2. Bring to the boil, then simmer for 15 minutes, or until the apples 'fall' into the juice. Mash with a fork.

3. Stir in the cinnamon and beat in the butter. Serve warm or cold with the meal.

Cranberry Sauce

This is a must for serving with our turkey. We all love it!

Serves 6

200ml water
300g caster sugar
450g cranberries, washed and
   trimmed of stalks
80ml fresh orange juice
2 tablespoons ruby port (optional)

Storage
This will keep in a sealed jar for a week in the fridge.

1. Put the water and sugar into a pan and heat gently, stirring until the sugar dissolves.

2. Add the cranberries and bring to the boil.

3. Turn down the heat and simmer for 10–15 minutes, or until the cranberries burst and begin to tenderise.

4. Stir in the orange juice and simmer for 3-4 minutes.

5. Remove from the heat and stir in the port, if using.

Cumberland Sauce

This sauce is based on redcurrant jelly, but it tastes even better.
We enjoy it with turkey and cold ham.

Serves 6

300g redcurrant jelly (see page 273)
100ml ruby port
Zest and juice of 1 lemon
Zest and juice of half an orange
2 teaspoons Worcestershire sauce
A pinch of cayenne pepper

1. Put the jelly in a pan over a low heat until it has melted, then bring it to the boil and add the port. Turn down the heat and simmer quite rapidly for 10–15 minutes, or until the liquid has reduced by about a half.

2. Turn the heat right down and add the fruit juice, Worcestershire sauce and cayenne pepper.

3. Stir well and serve cold with the Christmas meats.

Christmas Vegetables

It would be wonderful to make elaborate vegetable dishes on Christmas day, but my family and I prefer simple, delicious-tasting vegetables that are as fresh as possible – and this is what our grandparents would have eaten in any case.

However, I do cheat with one vegetable, and that's sweetcorn. You can't buy good-quality corn in December and frozen doesn't have much flavour, but I've found that a good-quality tinned version really does taste very good indeed. It also has the benefit of only needing to be heated just prior to serving.

Other than that, I serve mostly roasted root vegetables: parsnip, swede, turnips, carrots and (obviously) potatoes – the veg that was available in Grandma's day. I usually cook some potatoes with the other vegetables, but also roast some very crispy ones separately – these never go out of fashion, and you will find my favourite recipe for them on page 241, along with one for creamy mashed potatoes with a bit of a bite.

I also serve peas, green beans, cauliflower and/or broccoli, sprouts and, as mentioned, the tinned sweetcorn. If this sounds like a lot, just remember that it caters for most people's tastes, which means that everyone can have three or four different vegetables at least. After all, it's Christmas!

Steamy efficiency

If you steam vegetables, they can all be cooked in the same tower of pans – an economical method of which Grandma most certainly would have approved. Start with sprouts and cauliflower/ broccoli, as they take the longest to cook. Give them about 4 minutes, then add the green beans and peas in another layer on the steamer. Cook everything for another 4–5 minutes and they should all be ready to be seasoned and placed in serving dishes with a knob of butter.

Roasted Vegetables

Serves 6

5 tablespoons sunflower or olive oil
3–4 medium carrots, scrubbed and
  cut into 3cm pieces
3–4 medium parsnips, peeled and cut
  into thick batons
1 small swede, peeled and cut into
  large chunks
3 small turnips, peeled and cut
  into large chunks
Salt and black pepper to taste
  1 teaspoon dried thyme

1. Preheat the oven to 200°C/gas mark 6.

2. Put 3 tablespoons of the oil into the bottom of a large roasting tin.

3. Arrange the prepared vegetables in the oil. Use your hands to make sure they are well-coated.

4. Drizzle the rest of the oil over them evenly and season with salt and pepper to taste.

5. Sprinkle with the thyme.

6. Roast for 40–45 minutes in the oven, or until the vegetables are tender and beginning to brown.

7. Place some kitchen paper in a large, warm serving dish and transfer the vegetables to the dish. Remove the kitchen paper before serving.

Easy Roast Potatoes

Serves 6

9 medium potatoes, peeled and quartered
60g lard, duck or goose fat
Salt and black pepper to taste
1 teaspoon of rosemary

1. Preheat the oven to 220°C/gas mark 7.

2. Boil the potatoes for 7–10 minutes in salted water that just covers them.

3. Just before they have finished boiling, put the fat into a roasting tin and put the tin in the oven to heat.

4. Drain the potatoes and put them back in the pan. Shake them gently over a low heat – this dries the potatoes and roughs the edges so that they will crisp up better in the oven.

5. Season with salt in the pan.

6. Carefully lift the hot roasting tin out of the oven and transfer the potatoes to the oil. Arrange evenly in the oil and turn so that they are well-covered.

7. Sprinkle with the rosemary and black pepper to taste, then roast in the oven for about 30 minutes, or until they are golden and crispy.

8. Have a warm dish ready with a piece of kitchen paper to catch any unwanted dribbles of fat. When the potatoes are ready, transfer them to the dish and remove the paper just before serving.

The cream of mashed potatoes

Creamy mashed potatoes are a traditional Christmas treat; when boiling the potatoes for the crispy roasts, prepare extra for mashing. When boiled, leave the ones for mashing in a warm place while you put your roasting potatoes in the oven. Put the mashing potatoes in a pan over a very gentle heat and mash them with 2 tablespoons of double cream and a large knob of butter. Season with salt and white pepper to taste. These can be put in a lidded ovenproof casserole and warmed just before serving. A teaspoon of Dijon mustard added with the cream will give it a savoury kick.

And Now for Dessert

In Grandma's day, the yuletide feast would have been rounded off by a traditional Christmas pudding that had been prepared weeks in advance and left to mature, giving it plenty of fruity flavour. Traditional it may well be, but not everyone likes Christmas pudding in our household, and I've learned that this is true of many people. Having an alternative dessert is always a good idea, so in addition to the Christmas pudding, I've included a chocolate version on page 244 that should satisfy any non-traditionalists in the family. And don't worry: I haven't forgotten the brandy sauce!

You'll also find out how to make a delicious Bûche de Noël, or Yule Log on page 246. But first, what would Christmas be without some good old-fashioned mince pies?

Mincemeat

Mince pies are a must at Christmas time, and they taste even better if you make your own mincemeat, just as your grandparents did. However, this recipe makes use of vegetarian suet, and is so easy to make that you will wonder why you've never tried it before (I certainly did!). Make it at least four weeks before Christmas to allow all the flavours to develop.

Makes about 4 x 450g jars

2 large Bramley apples, peeled and diced
225g vegetarian suet
300g soft brown sugar
400g sultanas
400g raisins
300g currants
110g glacé cherries; half of them cut in half
½ level teaspoon cinnamon
½ level teaspoon mixed spice (or a full teaspoon if you like it spicy)
Zest and juice of 1 lemon
5–7 tablespoons brandy, depending on your taste

1. Cook the apples on a very low heat until they begin to fall apart. Leave to get cool completely.

2. Mix together all the other ingredients in a large bowl. Mix well so that all the fruit is covered in brandy.

3. Stir the cooled apples into the other ingredients and mix thoroughly.

4. Spoon into sterilised screwtop jars (see page 300). Label and date.

Storage
This should keep for up to 4 months unopened.

Traditional Christmas Pudding

The only difficult thing about this recipe is the list of ingredients: you have to be very organised when making it! I weigh everything out first, then tick off the ingredients as I go. Next I arrange them in the order in which they are mixed. Everything else is easy. This can be made 4–6 weeks before Christmas.

Serves 6–8

50g self-raising flour
½ teaspoon each cinnamon and mixed spice
A pinch of grated nutmeg
110g vegetarian suet
175g soft brown sugar
110g breadcrumbs
350g dried fruit: a mixture of sultanas, raisins, currants, halved glacé cherries and candied peel

50g chopped almonds
1 peeled and grated carrot
1 Bramley apple, peeled and diced
Zest and juice of 1 lemon and 1 orange
2 large eggs
1 tablespoon dark treacle
150ml dark ale
3 tablespoons rum or brandy

1. Sift the flour and spices together into a large mixing bowl.

2. Stir in the suet, sugar and breadcrumbs, then the fruit, nuts, carrot, apple and both zests and juices.

3. Beat the eggs in a jug with the treacle, ale and rum or brandy. Mix well.

4. Stir the egg mixture into the dry ingredients and mix well for 4–5 minutes.

5. Cover, leave to settle and allow the flavours to develop for 4–5 hours. This can be left overnight if you wish as the cooking time is 7 hours.

6. Butter a 1.2-litre pudding basin and pour the mixture into the basin, packing it down so that there are no air bubbles. Cover the top of the pudding with a close-fitting disc of baking parchment, then add a double layer of greaseproof paper. Tie securely with string.

7. Place the pudding in a steamer over a pan of simmering water and steam for 6½–7 hours. Tick off the hours as they go by and keep an eye on the water level. Top up if necessary.

8. When the cooking time is up, leave to cool for 2 hours, then remove the wrappings.

9. When completely cool, wrap the pudding in a layer of greaseproof paper and a layer of foil and store in an airtight container.

10. To reheat before eating, steam for 2 hours, or put in the microwave for 4–6 minutes, depending on the power of your oven. Serve with your choice of sauce.

Double Chocolate Pudding

The Christmas pudding-eaters will hope for a helping of this. It goes really well with the brandy sauce I make for the Christmas pud, but it does have its own special sauce. I cook it in the microwave because it takes minutes rather than hours to steam.

Makes 6 portions

For the sauce
100g dark chocolate, broken into small pieces
4 tablespoons double cream
15g butter

For the pudding
180g butter
180g caster sugar
180g self-raising flour
3 eggs, beaten
3 tablespoons milk
60g cocoa powder
60g dark chocolate, broken into pieces

1. Butter a 1.2-litre pudding basin (microwaveable if cooking in the microwave).

2. Make the sauce by melting the chocolate, cream and butter together in a heatproof bowl set over a pan of hot water, or in the microwave.

3. Stir well and pour the sauce into the prepared pudding basin.

4. To make the pudding, cream the butter and sugar together in a mixing bowl until light and fluffy.

5. Add a tablespoon of flour and beat in the eggs gradually. Beat in the milk.

6. Sieve the flour and cocoa together into the creamed mixture and fold in gently.

7. Stir in the chocolate pieces and pour the mixture over the sauce.

8. If you are steaming the pudding, cover it with a layer of greaseproof paper and a layer of foil. Tie securely with string. Place in a steamer over a pan of boiling water and steam for 2¼–2½ hours. Alternatively, cover with cling film and cook on high in the microwave for 5–8 minutes, depending on the power of your oven.

9. Serve turned out on a plate.

Brandy Sauce

This is our favourite. It is a rich, creamy sauce that can be as boozy as you wish to make it. Make it with rum if you prefer.

Serves 6

340ml evaporated milk, made up to
   600ml with regular milk
2 rounded tablespoon cornflour
2 tablespoons sugar
4 tablespoons brandy

1. Mix 4 tablespoons of the milk mixture with the cornflour to make a thin paste.

2. Heat the rest of the milk in the pan to simmering, then stir in the cornflour mixture very briskly with a balloon whisk.

3. Stir in the sugar and bring to the boil, stirring constantly.

4. Turn down the heat and simmer for 3 minutes. Stir in the brandy and pour into a serving jug.

Tip
This can all be done in the microwave in the same way, but heat the milk in a bowl, stirring occasionally rather than constantly when bringing it to the boil.

The Christmas Log or Bûche de Noël

Most recipes ask for a Swiss roll to be made for the cake part of this Christmas or Yule Log, and you can make a chocolate version of a Swiss roll if you wish. But I cheat and make the sponge in a 450g loaf tin, then shave bits off the edges to make a log shape. Once decorated, it looks the same as one made with a Swiss roll and is just as delicious.

The filling and coating is a chocoholic's dream: made completely from ganache, which is the centre of most chocolate truffles and is basically cream and chocolate combined. You don't have to be an expert with a piping bag, either; just use a fork to make the log look like rough bark – be creative and have fun!

For the cake
150g butter, at room temperature, plus extra for greasing
150g self-raising flour
30g cocoa powder
150g caster sugar
2 eggs
4 tablespoons milk

For the filling
2 tablespoons black-cherry jam

For the ganache
300g dark chocolate
300ml double cream

Storage
This will keep fresh in an airtight container in a cool place for 3–4 days – *if* it lasts that long!

First, make the cake

1. Preheat the oven to 180°C/gas mark 4. Butter and line a 450g loaf tin.

2. Sieve the flour and cocoa together into a bowl and add all the other ingredients.

3. Using a hand mixer, whisk the ingredients together for 5 minutes.

4. Spoon the mixture into the prepared tin and bake for 30–35 minutes until well-risen and springy to the touch.

5. Cool for 10 minutes in the tin, then transfer to a wire rack to cool completely.

Now make the ganache

1. Break up the chocolate into small pieces and put them in a bowl over a pan of hot, simmering water.

2. When the chocolate has melted, add the cream and stir gently to combine. Lift the bowl away from the hot water and set aside to cool.

Finally, assemble the log

1. Trim the sponge so that it is a basic round, cylinder shape. Cut it in half lengthways.

2. Spread a couple of tablespoons of the ganache mixture over the surface of one half of the sponge and spread the jam on the other half.

3. Sandwich the two halves together and place them on a serving plate or a gold-coloured cake board.

4. Use a piping bag to pipe the rest of the filling/coating over the length of the log, around the sides and over the ends so that all the cake is covered.

5. Use a fork dipped in hot water to make bark-like lines in the chocolate coating.

6. Dust with icing sugar and add a sprig of holly for a real old-fashioned festive touch.

Cakes and Puddings

Family Cakes

I love baking cakes. There is something special about creating a spongy, sweet treat that is very comforting and fills you with pride. The best-tasting cakes are always made with butter and fresh eggs, and I tend to use golden caster sugar because it has more flavour than white sugar. Because it is unrefined, it is also better for you.

Techniques for cake preparation

Creaming is the process of combining butter, sugar and air to produce a light-textured cake. Always make sure the butter is at room temperature. Use either a wooden or silicone spoon to beat the butter until soft, then add the sugar. Continue to beat the butter and sugar together until the mixture becomes lighter in colour and fluffy in texture.

Rubbing in is most commonly used in making shortbreads and some fruit loaves. The flour is sifted into a mixing bowl and the butter is added in small pieces, rubbed into the flour using the fingertips. The mixture should resemble breadcrumbs.

Folding in combines flour and the creamed mixture in a way that retains as much air as possible. Sifted flour is gradually added to creamed butter and sugar. Using a large metal spoon, cut into the mixture in one sweeping action, turning it over to combine. Mix the flour into the butter-sugar cream this way until it has all been incorporated.

Tips for successful cake-making
- Preheat the oven to the correct temperature.
- Read the recipe thoroughly and prepare and weigh all the ingredients before you begin.
- Measure all ingredients accurately.
- Prepare any required tins or baking sheets before you start.
- Times given for cooking are approximate and will depend on your oven, so always bear this in mind when baking your own cakes.
- When a cake is baked, transfer it to a cooling tray or wire rack. This allows air to circulate around the cake, cooling it more quickly and evenly.

Dundee Cake

The most famous part of this cake is its top, decorated with almonds, yet the orange and lemon juice and zest are the essential ingredients. This was reputedly a favourite of Winston Churchill's, served with afternoon tea. Apparently he got quite cross if it was unavailable!

Makes 10–12 generous portions

200g butter
200g soft brown sugar
250g plain flour, sifted
5 eggs
200g sultanas
125g currants
80g glacé cherries, rinsed of syrup and dried
50g mixed chopped peel, optional
30g ground almonds
Juice and zest of 1 lemon and half an orange
30g whole almonds

1. Grease and line a 23cm round cake tin with baking parchment. Preheat the oven to 150°C/gas mark 2.

2. Cream the butter and the sugar together until light and fluffy.

3. Add a tablespoon of the flour and gradually beat in the eggs.

4. Put all the dried fruit together in a bowl and sprinkle with 2 tablespoons of flour and the ground almonds. Mix well with a large spoon.

5. Fold the flour into the creamed sugar and egg batter and stir in the fruit mixture. Add the juices and zests and stir.

6. Spoon the mixture into the prepared tin and press down lightly to make sure it has no air bubbles in the base. Smooth out the top and make a shallow dip in the centre.

7. Arrange the almonds on the top of the cake in concentric circles.

8. Bake for 1½–2 hours. Check the cake after 40 minutes; if it is beginning to brown too quickly, cover it with a piece of foil. Make sure this doesn't actually touch the cake, however.

9. After 1½ hours, test the centre of the cake with a metal skewer. If it comes out clean, the cake is baked; if any mixture is still clinging to the skewer, it needs extra cooking time, so let it bake for 10 minutes more and check again.

10. Put the cake, still in the tin, on a cooling rack for 15 minutes. Lift it out of the tin and let it cool for 20 minutes before removing the paper.

11. Allow the cake to cool completely before wrapping it in greaseproof paper and foil and storing it in an airtight container.

Storage

This cake is best if allowed to mature for 3 days before eating. It will keep for at least 3 weeks, so long as it is wrapped up well and kept in the airtight container.

Madeira Cake

This cake doesn't, as I always assumed, come from Madeira, but is so-called because it was originally made to serve morning visitors in 'posh' households accompanied by a glass of Madeira wine. It really is worth trying, although I must admit I cannot drink alcohol in the morning – otherwise I would be asleep by lunchtime!
You must use butter and really fresh eggs in this cake; if you don't, it lacks taste.
If using unsalted butter, add a pinch of salt to the flour when sieving.

Makes 6–8 portions

180g butter
180g golden caster sugar
220g self-raising flour, sieved
4 small eggs, beaten
Zest of 1 lemon

Storage
This will keep fresh for at least 7 days in an airtight tin.

1. Grease and line an 18cm round cake tin with baking parchment. Preheat the oven to 170°C/gas mark 3.

2. Cream the butter and sugar until the mixture is pale and fluffy.

3. Add 2 tablespoons of the flour and then gradually beat in the eggs.

4. Fold the flour into the mixture along with the lemon zest, then spoon the mixture into the tin.

5. Bake for 45 minutes, then reduce the temperature to 150°C/gas mark 2 and bake for a 45 minutes more. Test the centre of the cake with a metal skewer. If it comes out clean, the cake is baked; if any mixture is still clinging to the skewer, then it needs extra cooking time, so let it bake for 5–10 minutes more and check again.

6. Cool for 10 minutes in the tin before removing to a wire rack. Leave the paper on for 10 more minutes before removing.

7. When completely cool, store in an airtight tin.

Gran's Rich Chocolate Cake

This was always made as a New Year treat in Gran's house; then it became a tradition my aunt carried on, making it for our family on New Year's Eve. Just like all the revelling, it was usually finished by the next morning. I loved it!

Serves 10–12

220ml milk
50g plain chocolate, broken into pieces
175g butter
250g soft brown sugar
230g self-raising flour sieved together with
 1 tablespoon cocoa powder
3 eggs
1 tablespoon black treacle

For the icing
400g caster sugar
120ml milk
80g butter
1 dessertspoon golden syrup
1 heaped dessertspoon cocoa powder
50g plain chocolate

1. Grease and line 3 x 18cm sandwich tins with a disc of baking parchment. Preheat the oven to 180°C/gas mark 4.

2. Heat the milk and the chocolate together gently in a pan or a microwave until the chocolate has melted. Remove from the heat immediately and leave to cool.

3. Cream the butter and sugar together until the mixture is pale and fluffy.

4. Add a tablespoon of the flour/cocoa mixture and beat in the eggs gradually.

5. Stir in the treacle. Fold in the rest of the flour.

6. Stir in the cooled milk and chocolate mixture. The mixture will be more like a thick batter.

7. Divide the mixture among the 3 cake tins and bake for 25–30 minutes. When baked, the cakes should be soft and spring back when pressed.

8. Allow to cool for 10 minutes in the tins, then remove to wire racks to cool completely.

9. While the cakes cool, make the icing. Put all the ingredients together in a pan and heat gently, stirring all the time with a wooden spoon.

10. When the sugar has dissolved completely, bring to the boil and continue to boil until the mixture thickens to a spreadable paste – or reaches 115°C using a jam thermometer. Leave to cool for 15 minutes. Use this to sandwich the cakes together and cover the top.

Serving suggestion
You can also decorate this with curls of milk or white chocolate or glacé cherries for an extra festive touch.

Farmhouse Fruit Cake

This is a delicious, lightly spiced fruit cake for those who don't like too much fruit.
I like to sprinkle some demerara sugar on top just before baking, as it creates a crunchy
topping. Or you can sprinkle it over the top just after the cake comes out of the oven.

Makes 8–10 portions

180g butter
180g golden caster sugar
220g self-raising flour
2 medium eggs
½ level teaspoon cinnamon
A pinch nutmeg
Zest of 1 lemon
25g currants
50g raisins
25g sultanas
4 tablespoons milk
1 dessertspoon demerara sugar,
    for sprinkling

1. Grease and line an 18cm round cake tin with baking parchment. Preheat the oven to 180°C/gas mark 4.

2. Cream the butter and sugar together until very light and fluffy.

3. Add a tablespoon of the flour and beat in the eggs.

4. Sieve the flour and spices together into the creamed mixture and begin to fold in.

5. Add the lemon zest and dried fruit and fold in.

6. Stir in the milk, then spoon the mixture into the prepared tin. Sprinkle a little sugar over the top at this stage for a crispy topping.

7. Bake for 1–1¼ hours, or until deep golden in colour.

8. Cool in the tin for 10 minutes, then transfer to a cooling rack and cool completely before slicing.

Parkin

This is a truly autumnal cake and we love to eat it on Bonfire Night along with other treacly confections. It is quick and easy, and you can make parkin using only treacle, but I find it too strong a flavour and use half golden syrup and half treacle. You still get the traditional dark colour and rich flavour without that 'bitter edge'. Parkin develops a stickiness if left for 24 hours before eating and the flavour is better than when it's fresh, so make this the day before you want to eat it.

Makes 12 squares

1 level teaspoon ground ginger
130g self-raising flour
50g butter
2 tablespoons black treacle
2 tablespoons golden syrup
50g brown sugar
1 egg
2 tablespoons milk
130g fine oatmeal

Serving suggestion
Try eating a piece with some Stilton or strong Cheddar. Sensational!

1. Grease a 15cm square cake tin and preheat the oven to 170°C/gas mark 3.

2. Sieve the ginger with the flour into a large mixing bowl and stir in the oatmeal.

3. Put the butter, treacle, syrup and sugar together in a pan over a very low heat. As soon as the butter has melted, remove from the heat, stir well and beat in the egg.

4. Pour the buttery mixture into the flour and mix vigorously with a wooden spoon.

5. Add the milk and beat again. It should be a soft, easily poured mixture. If not, add another tablespoon of milk.

6. Pour the mixture into the tin and bake for 50–55 minutes. It should be firm to the touch in the centre when cooked; if not, bake for 5 more minutes and check again.

7. Allow to cool in the tin on a wire rack. After 10 minutes of cooling, cut the cake into 12 equal squares.

8. When cool, lift the squares out of the cake tin and transfer to an airtight storage tin.

Spiced Apple Cake

My gran had relatives in Australia. Every year they came to visit, and it was very exciting because Aunt Marjorie was an excellent cook, which meant Gran had a few days off from cooking. My aunt made this cake for us and it is a winner with spice-lovers.

Makes 10 portions

130g butter
130g brown sugar
80g stewed Bramley apples, puréed
180g self-raising flour
½ level teaspoon ground cinnamon
½ level teaspoon ground nutmeg
80g raisins

1. Grease and line an 18cm round cake tin and preheat the oven to 150°C/gas mark 2.

2. Cream the butter and sugar together until fluffy. Stir in the apples.

3. Sift the flour and spices together into the mixture and fold in with a wooden spoon. If the mixture is too stiff, add a tablespoon of milk.

4. Stir in the raisins.

5. Spoon the mixture into the prepared tin and bake for 1 hour.

6. Allow to stand in the tin for 10 minutes before transferring to a wire rack to cool.

Crunchy Topped Marmalade Cake

This has a crunchy topping made with cornflakes and a tangy taste from the marmalade. You can use thin- or thick-shredded marmalade, depending on your taste, or even use shredless. This recipes makes a large cake, but it will keep for up to 2 weeks in an airtight container.

Makes 12 large pieces

180g butter
8 tablespoons golden syrup
2 eggs, beaten
10 tablespoons marmalade
350g self-raising flour
1 level teaspoon ground cinnamon
150ml milk
50g cornflakes, crushed

1. Grease and line a 20cm square cake tin. Preheat the oven to 180°C/gas mark 4.

2. Cream the butter with 6 tablespoons of the golden syrup.

3. Beat in the eggs.

4. Stir in 5 tablespoons of the marmalade.

5. Sift the flour and cinnamon together into the mixture and fold in with a metal spoon.

6. Stir in sufficient milk to make a stiff consistency so that it will hold the topping.

7. Spoon the mixture into the prepared tin.

8. Combine the cornflakes, the rest of the syrup and the marmalade and spread carefully over the top of the cake.

9. Bake for 50–60 minutes, or until well-risen.

10. Cool in the tin for 15 minutes before transferring to a wire rack.

11. Leave to cool for 2 hours before cutting.

Cider Cake

This traditional cake dates back to the late nineteenth century, but I have given it a twist by adding some Bramley apples at the base. You can use dry or sweet cider; I prefer sweet because the dry can be rather powerful! Try both and see which you prefer.

Makes 12 pieces

130g butter
130g golden caster sugar
230g self-raising flour
2 medium eggs
½ teaspoon ground cinnamon
A pinch nutmeg
200ml cider
1 Bramley apple, peeled, cored and sliced;
    keep in water containing a little lemon
    juice to keep the apple white
Demerara sugar, for topping

Variation
You can make this cake without the apple at the bottom if you prefer. Everything else remains the same.

1. Grease a 20 x 13cm rectangular cake tin. Preheat the oven to170°C/gas mark 3.

2. Cream the butter and sugar together until pale and fluffy.

3. Add a tablespoon of flour and beat in the eggs.

4. Sieve the flour and spices together into a separate bowl, then fold half into the creamed mixture.

5. Pour the cider into the mixture, stirring well.

6. Stir in the rest of the flour.

7. Place the apple slices at the bottom of the tin.

8. Pour the mixture over the apples into the tin and bake for 40 minutes, or until firm but springy.

9. Leave to cool for 30 minutes before removing from the tin. Cool completely on a wire rack. Sprinkle with a little demerara sugar.

Lemon Swiss Roll

The secret of a light Swiss roll is whisking and double-sifting your flour.
First, sift your flour onto a plate, then sift it again into the bowl at the correct time.
Use an electric hand whisk to make this – it helps create the lightness,
yet the sponge remains more rollable. Also for ease of rolling, line the Swiss roll tin with
baking parchment. Use sufficient to be able to hold onto it and lift the cake out of the tin.

Makes 8 portions

4 medium eggs
120g golden caster sugar
150g plain flour, sifted
25g ground almonds
5–6 tablespoons lemon curd
   (see page 276)

Storage
This will keep for 2–3 days in an airtight tin,
but it is best eaten within 24 hours.

1. Grease and line 33 x 23cm rectangular Swiss roll tin. Preheat the oven to 190°C/gas mark 5.

2. Whisk the eggs and sugar together until thick and pale.

3. Sift the flour into the eggs and sugar and fold it in lightly with a metal spoon.

4. Fold in the ground almonds.

5. Pour the mixture into the prepared tin and bake for 12–15 minutes. The sponge should be golden in colour and springy to the touch.

6. Leave to cool in the tin.

7. Lift the cake out of the tin and spread the surface with the lemon curd. Roll up the cake carefully, gently pulling it away the baking parchment. Sprinkle with a little extra caster sugar.

Madeleines

These little coconut cakes were a great favourite of mine when I was growing up.
In fact, I adore any coconut cake or biscuit. I have one big problem now, which is
that none of my family likes coconut, so I feel disinclined to make my beloved
madeleines just for me. I know I would eat them all!
Dariole moulds are traditionally used to make these, but I just use my non-stick
bun tins; they aren't the same shape, but it doesn't make much difference to the taste.

Makes 10 cakes

120g butter
120g golden caster sugar
120g self-raising flour, sifted
2 large eggs
4 tablespoons raspberry or strawberry jam;
  this is best sieved to remove large bits of
  fruit and seeds
50–60g desiccated coconut
10 glacé cherries

1. Grease 10 large bun-tin holes. Non-stick
ones are best, as it is annoying if sponge sticks
and spoils the shape of your cake. Preheat the
oven to 180°C/gas mark 4.

2. Cream the butter and sugar together until
light and fluffy.

3. Add a tablespoon of sifted flour and beat in
the eggs.

4. Sift the flour into the creamed mixture and
fold in with a metal spoon.

5. Spoon the mixture into the bun holes – don't
fill more than two-thirds full.

6. Bake for about 15 minutes until well-risen
and springy.

7. Leave to cool for 5 minutes in the tin, then
transfer them to a wire rack to cool completely.

8. Brush the cakes all over with jam, then roll in
the coconut – it's messy but fun!

9. Finish with a cherry on top.

Puddings

Everybody loves a comforting pudding now and then. They make a dull day much brighter and, when served with custard or cream, what could satisfy you more? As I've got older and the children have grown, I have become more adventurous in my pudding-making, but I still get asked for fruit crumbles or steamed sponges more than any others. Thus the recipes that follows are designed for when you want something that tastes familiarly wonderful.

Fruit Crumble

This is usually associated with apples, but it can be made with many types of fruit or combinations of different ones. Cooking beforehand isn't always necessary, but I usually partially cook the fruit with 30g sugar or 2 tablespoons of honey and 3–4 tablespoons of water. You won't need much sugar, as the topping is rather sweet. Use a little extra sugar if cooking rhubarb or gooseberries, though, as they can be very tart. Try peach or apricot, plum, strawberry, stoned cherry, blackberry and raspberry or dried fruit soaked in juice or water.

Serves 6

500g fruit
250g plain flour
50g porridge oats
180g butter, at room temperature
180g unrefined caster sugar

1. Preheat the oven to 200°C/gas mark 6.

2. Place the fruit in an ovenproof dish.

3. Sift the flour into a bowl, then stir in the oats.

4. Rub in the butter, then stir in the sugar.

5. Sprinkle the topping over the fruit and bake the crumble for about 30 minutes, or until the top is golden brown.

6. Serve with custard, cream or ice cream.

Traditional Rice Pudding

We had this at least once a week when I was a child because it was my dad's favourite. It is very easy to prepare, and if you boil your rice with a little water or some of the milk for 5 minutes, this reduces the cooking time in the oven. If you wish you can put it in the oven using uncooked rice, but this adds an extra hour to the baking time.

Serves 4–5

55g short-grain/pudding rice
1 tablespoon butter
1 x 410g can evaporated milk, made up
  to 580ml with water
75g golden caster sugar
Grated nutmeg for the top

Variation
Use 580ml of ordinary whole milk if you prefer.

1. Preheat the oven to 170°C/gas mark 3.

2. Put the rice in a pan and add enough water just to cover. Bring to the boil and cook for 5 minutes. Drain well and put it in an ovenproof dish. Add the butter and pour in the milk.

3. Stir in the sugar and sprinkle with a little nutmeg.

4. Bake in the oven for 1½ hours, stirring at intervals to distribute the rice.

5. Serve with your favourite preserve, or simply on its own.

Syrup Pudding

This is an old favourite and it never fails the 'mmm' test. You can steam it in the traditional way, but it's made in no time at all in a microwave.

Serves 4

4 tablespoons golden syrup
100g self-raising flour
50g vegetarian suet
50g golden caster sugar
2 eggs
1 teaspoon vanilla extract
4 tablespoons milk

Variations
Substitute any one of these for the syrup:

- 3 tablespoons orange marmalade
- 3–4 tablespoons jam
- 4 tablespoons lemon curd
- 3 tablespoons honey

1. Butter a 1.2-litre pudding basin and put the golden syrup in the bottom of it.

2. Sift the flour into a mixing bowl and stir in the suet and sugar.

3. Beat the eggs and vanilla into the milk, then stir this into the flour mixture with a fork. Work the liquid in briskly.

4. Spoon into the basin and cover with cling film. Pierce the film in the centre with the point of a knife.

5. Cook in the microwave at full power for 4–4½ minutes. The pudding should reach the cling film; this indicates that it's ready. Remove from the oven and allow it to stand for 2 minutes before removing the film.

6. Turn out onto a plate if you wish and serve with custard or cream.

Bread and Butter Pudding
The basic but always delicious custard-based pudding.

Serves 4

4 slices well-buttered white bread,
 crusts removed
280ml milk
2 teaspoons vanilla extract
Zest of 1 lemon
3 eggs, beaten
50g golden caster sugar
Grated nutmeg

1. Butter an ovenproof dish and preheat the oven to 180°C/gas mark 4.

2. Cut each slice of bread into 4 triangles and arrange in layers, butter-side up, in the dish.

3. Whisk the milk, vanilla and lemon zest into the eggs and stir in the sugar. Pour over the bread.

4. Sprinkle with a little grated nutmeg.

5. Bake in the oven for 30–40 minutes, or until risen and crusty on the top.

6. Serve hot with cream or cold with ice cream.

Variation
Marmalade Bread and Butter Pudding can be made using the same ingredients, but, after buttering the bread, spread with marmalade and sprinkle with 80g currants before pouring on the custard.

Old-fashioned Queen of Puddings

I tend to make this pudding with stale cake crumbs, but it should be made with breadcrumbs as in this recipe. Try it both ways and see which you prefer. It is a delightful dessert that can be eaten hot or cold.

Serves 4

4 eggs
560ml milk
30g caster sugar
120g fresh breadcrumbs or stale cake crumbs
    (I usually grate mine using the fine side,
    but they can be made very quickly in a
    food processor)
75g caster sugar,
    for the meringue
4 tablespoons of your favourite jam

1. Preheat the oven to 170°C/gas mark 3. Butter an ovenproof dish.

2. Separate 3 of the eggs and keep the egg whites for the meringue. Add the other whole egg to the yolks.

3. Whisk the eggs and milk together with the 30g caster sugar.

4. Stir the breadcrumbs into the egg-and-milk mixture and pour into the prepared dish.

5. Leave for 20 minutes to allow the breadcrumbs to soak up the custard, then bake for 35–40 minutes until firm and risen.

6. Meanwhile, whisk the egg whites until they form firm peaks. Fold in the 75g caster sugar.

7. When the custard has finished cooking, spread with the jam and spread with the meringue.

8. Turn the oven down to 150°C/gas mark ½–1 and put the pudding back in the oven for 20 minutes until the meringue is golden and set.

Apple Amber

This would have been made with dried eggs during the war. How lucky we are to have fresh eggs to make it with – and if you have your own chickens, even better!

Serves 4

2 Bramley apples, peeled, cored and sliced
2 tablespoons caster sugar
4 tablespoons water
50g fresh breadcrumbs
3 eggs
130ml milk
2 tablespoons double cream

1. Preheat the oven to 170°C/gas mark 3.

2. Stew the apples with the 2 tablespoons of the sugar and the water for 8–10 minutes until they begin to 'fall'.

3. Add the breadcrumbs.

4. Whisk the eggs and milk together and stir into the apple mixture.

5. Transfer the mixture to a buttered ovenproof dish.

6. Bake for 35–40 minutes until firm.

Serving suggestion
This is best eaten immediately with cream or vanilla ice cream.

Preserves of All Kinds

Preserving fruit and vegetables for the lean winter months was something our ancestors did without hesitation. Today, we are blessed with plenty of sugar to help us in this process – unlike our forebears, who had only vinegar and salt.

Making your own chutney, jams and marmalade is a great pleasure and doesn't take up as much tine as you'd think. These recipes don't make loads and loads of the same preserve; I like to make a variety, and having only a small amount of cupboard space makes preparing a large quantity impossible for me. The only preserve that does take a long time to make is a jelly: you have to strain the juice from the fruit without pushing it through, or else your jelly will spoil. But it is worthwhile making, because the flavour, particularly the blackcurrant, makes wonderful tarts.

Jams and jellies

Whenever you make preserves of any kind, always make sure you have enough sterile jars with secure screwtops on hand because you never really know exactly what your jam yield will be. It always depends on the juice content of the fruit.

Most jam and jellies will keep for at least a year unopened, but always check them from time to time to see they still look fresh and haven't shrunk away from the sides. Should this occur, it means that the seal was not secure, and the preserve has lost liquid content and may have been contaminated.

When you are boiling your jam, some fruits cause a foamy scum on the top. You can get rid of this either by adding a knob of butter to the boiling jam, or else by skimming it off the surface with a large metal spoon.

Jam-making Essentials

Besides fruit and sugar, two essential ingredients make jam- and preserve-making successful, and work together to produce a set preserve. The first is pectin, a gel-like substance found in varying degrees in most fruit, usually in the skins, pips and membranes. Combined with fruit acid and sugar, pectin makes a good setting agent. Some fruit contains little pectin, however, so it must be added during cooking. You can usually buy it in granular form in 13g sachets. The same applies to fruit acid: extra can be added by using lemon juice. There is a special jam-making sugar available that contains pectin, but I never use this, as it takes so long to dissolve and you never know exactly how much pectin you're using.

Equipment

You don't need lots of new equipment; just have the following to hand:

- A large, sturdy-based pan
- A long-handled spoon (I use a wooden one)
- A ladle
- Some sterilised jars with good-fitting lids; screw-tops or Kilner-type jars are ideal. It's best to have an extra jar around, as quantities can never be precise
- Sticky labels – to remind you what is in the jar and when it was made
- A jam funnel: the only thing I advise buying specially
- A jam-making thermometer: this indicates when jam has reached setting point, so it can be useful, but you'll still need to test for setting to be sure

Choosing the produce

Choose the freshest, ripest, most perfect fruit and vegetables you can. This will guarantee that your preserve will remain fresh and uncontaminated. Successful jam may be made with frozen fruit so long as it is fully defrosted before using. You can make jam with any kind of sugar, but white granulated sugar is probably the most economical.

Working with sugar

Heat the sugar in a roasting pan in the oven for 10 minutes on a very low temperature. This helps the sugar dissolve more quickly in the fruit. To check whether the sugar has dissolved, simply look at the mixture on the back of the spoon; if it looks grainy, it hasn't.

Testing for setting point

Place a saucer in the fridge to test the jam on after boiling. Put a very small amount of jam on your cold plate, allow it to cool, then push it gently with your finger. It should wrinkle and stay in place if setting point is reached. Don't worry if it moves a little; so long as it wrinkles and doesn't run round your finger, it is ready to pot.

Sterilising jars

Wash the jars in hot, soapy water, rinse them well in clean water, then prepare them in one of the following ways.

1. Place the jars on a baking tray and put them in a cold oven. Turn on the heat to 160°C/gas mark 2. When the oven has reached this temperature, turn it off and leave them inside to cool.

2. Put the jars and lids in a baby-feeding equipment sterilising solution for the manufacturer's allotted time.

3. Place jars and metal lids in warm water and bring slowly to the boil. Boil for 5 minutes.

The Easiest Strawberry Jam

Unlike our ancestors, if necessary we can use pectin sachets when making our preserves. This makes jam and jelly-making so much easier.

Makes about 6 x 450g jars of jam

2kg fresh strawberries, hulled and washed
Juice of 1 lemon
1.8kg white granulated sugar
1 x 13g sachet pectin

Tip
The jam does not have a very firm set and may slip out of cakes and sandwiches, but the flavour is wonderful and worth making.

1. Put the fruit and lemon juice into a large preserving pan and cook on a medium heat for 3–4 minutes. Mash some of the fruit with a potato masher as it is cooking.

2. As the juice is released, lower the heat and add the sugar and pectin. Stir until all the sugar has dissolved.

3. Bring rapidly to the boil, and when boiling, set your timer for 4 minutes. As soon as the 4 minutes has elapsed, remove from the heat and leave to cool for 10 minutes.

4. Stir and ladle the jam into prepared, sterilised jars, screw the tops on immediately and label when cool.

Raspberry Jam

Makes about 7 x 450g jars of jam

2kg raspberries, washed
Juice of 1 lemon
2kg sugar

1. Put the fruit and lemon juice in a preserving pan and cook at simmering for 5–6 minutes, or until the juice is running from the fruit.

2. Turn down the heat and add the sugar. Stir until all the sugar has dissolved.

3. Turn up the heat and boil for 6 minutes, then test for setting point (see page 266).

4. If ready, remove from the heat and allow to cool for 10 minutes, then ladle into the prepared, sterilised jars and seal well. When cool, label and date the jars.

Blackberry Jam

This is a jam you can make from gathering a wild harvest. Always pick the blackberries on a warm day to get the best flavour from them.

Makes about 5 x 450g jars of jam

1.5kg blackberries, stems removed, well-washed
80ml water
Juice of 1 lemon
1 x 13g sachet pectin
1.5kg sugar

1. Put the fruit in a large pan. Add the water and lemon juice and heat to simmering. Cook for 6–8 minutes, or until the fruit is tender.

2. Add the sugar and pectin and stir on a low heat until all the sugar has dissolved.

3. Bring to the boil and boil rapidly for 8 minutes, then check for setting point (see page 266).

4. Leave to cool for 5 minutes. Stir and pot the jam into prepared, sterilised jars. Label and date when cool.

Blackcurrant Jam

Makes approximately 4 x 450g jars

1kg blackcurrants
500ml water
1.5kg sugar

1. Put the blackcurrants and water in a large pan; bring to the boil. Reduce the heat and simmer for 30 minutes, or until the fruit is tender.

2. Add the sugar and turn down the heat to low while the sugar dissolves. Stir constantly.

3. Bring to the boil and boil rapidly for 5 minutes. Test for setting point (see page 266).

4. Leave to cool for 5 minutes, stir, then pot the jam into prepared, sterilised jars. Label and date when cool.

Gooseberry Jam

Makes approximately 5 x 450g jars

1.5kg gooseberries, topped, tailed and washed
600ml water
2kg sugar

1. Put the fruit and water in a large pan; bring to the boil, then turn down the heat and simmer for 20 minutes, or until the gooseberries begin to pop.

2. Turn down the heat to low and stir in the sugar. Continue stirring until all the sugar has dissolved.

3. Bring back to the boil and boil rapidly for 10 minutes. Test for setting point (see page 266).

4. Allow to cool for 5 minutes, then stir and pot the jam into prepared, sterilised jars. Label and date when cool.

Plum Jam

Use the freshest plums you can for this jam because they have the best flavour and the highest pectin content, which means you will get a good set.

Makes approximately 5 x 450g jars

1.5kg plums, quartered and stoned
280ml water
1.5kg sugar

1. Put the fruit in a pan. Add the water and bring to the boil, then turn down the heat and simmer for 20 minutes.

2. Turn down the heat and stir in the sugar. Continue to stir until all the sugar has dissolved.

3. Bring to the boil. Boil rapidly for 6–8 minutes. Remove from the heat and test for setting point (see page 266). If not ready, put back on the heat and boil for 2 more minutes.

4. When setting point has been reached, cool for 5 minutes. Stir and pot the jam into prepared, sterilised jars. Label and date when cool.

Making Fruit Jelly

Unlike jam, a jelly is a preserve that contains no pips or seeds, as these will have been strained out in the jelly-making process. The result is clear, fruit-flavoured goodness!

The sugar content of these recipes is not given in the list of ingredients because this depends on the juice yield of the fruit, so you'll need to measure the juice before weighing out the sugar. Use a large jug for this, one that is easy to read for measuring liquids. It is worth making large amounts of jelly because of the time it takes to prepare this preserve. You'll also need a jelly bag with which to strain the fruit and a large clean pan or bowl to catch the juice.

The process of jelly-making is sped up, however, because you don't have to worry about topping and tailing the fruit: any stalks or seeds get strained out. The final yield is also difficult to judge, so an average amount is given in the following recipes as a guide to how many jars you may need. None of the jelly recipes below use any added pectin; this is because they are all high in pectin already, and any extra might cloud the jelly.

Jellies should keep for up to 9 months unopened and should be stored in a cool, dark place.

Blackcurrant Jelly

Makes approximately 7 x 450g jars

3kg blackcurrants
1.3 litres water
Sugar: 80g per every 100ml of juice

1. Cook the fruit and the water at simmering for about 25 minutes, or until the fruit is soft.

2. Pour the fruit into the straining bag positioned over a container to catch the juice. Do not push the pulp through the strainer as this will make the finished jelly cloudy. Leave to strain for 3–4 hours, or until the juice has stopped dripping through the bag.

3. Measure how much juice you have and weigh out the appropriate amount of sugar.

4. Put the juice in the pan over a low heat and slowly stir in the sugar; this will dissolve quicker if you warm the sugar in the oven for 10 minutes at 140°C/gas mark 1. Stir until the sugar is completely dissolved.

5. Bring to the boil and boil rapidly for 5–6 minutes. Test for setting point on a cold saucer as for jam (see page 266).

6. When setting point has been reached, skim off any froth and pot immediately. Label and date when cool.

Cranberry Jelly

Makes approximately 4–5 x 450g jars

1.5kg cranberries
500ml water
Sugar: 80g per 100ml of juice

1. Simmer the cranberries and water for about 2 minutes, or until the fruit is soft.

2. Pour the fruit into the straining bag positioned over a container to catch the juice. Do not push the pulp through the strainer as this will make the finished jelly cloudy. Strain the juice for 3–4 hours, or until it stops dripping through the bag.

3. Measure the juice, then weigh out the correct amount of sugar.

4. Put the juice in the pan with the sugar over a gentle heat and stir until all the sugar has dissolved.

5. Turn up the heat and boil rapidly for 10 minutes. Check for setting point as for jam (see page 266).

6. When setting point has been reached, remove from the heat and cool for 5 minutes before potting and labelling.

Redcurrant Jelly

Makes approximately 6 x 450g jars

2kg redcurrants
600ml water
Sugar: 80g of sugar per 100ml of juice

1. Put the fruit in a pan with the water and simmer for 25–30 minutes, or until the currants are tender. Mash the fruit while it is cooking to help release the juice.

2. Pour the fruit into the straining bag positioned over a container to catch the juice. Do not push the pulp through the strainer as this will make the finished jelly cloudy. Strain the fruit for 4–5 hours until it stops dripping from the bag.

3. Measure the juice and weigh out the necessary amount of sugar.

4. Put the juice and sugar together in the pan and heat gently, stirring constantly, until the sugar has dissolved.

5. Bring to the boil and boil rapidly for 10 minutes, then check for setting point (see page 266).

6. When setting point has been reached, skim the froth from the top if necessary, then pot immediately. Label and date when cool.

Marmalade

Marmalade is made with citrus fruit in much the same way as jam. The whole of the fruit is used: peel, pips, juice and flesh. The pips are removed after cooking the fruit and before the sugar is added, so if you put them in a small square of muslin or a muslin bag and tie it securely, they can be easily removed with tongs.

You can use any oranges to make marmalade, but Sevilles are best: they are very bitter and have an incredible orange flavour; just don't be tempted to eat one like you would a dessert orange! Sevilles have only a very short season, December and January, but they do freeze well, so wash the skins and freeze them whole. Defrost fully before preparing them for marmalade. Marmalade should keep for up to 15 months unopened.

Seville Orange Marmalade

Makes about 8–9 x 450g jars of marmalade

1.5kg Seville oranges
2.5 litres water
Juice of 2 lemons
2.2kg sugar

1. Wash the fruit, cut each orange in half and squeeze out the juice. Put the juice in the pan, and don't waste any of it. Put all the pips in a dish, ready to be tied in a muslin bag or square.

2. Scoop out all the pith and flesh and add it to the pan. If there are some thick bits of pith (most will dissolve in cooking and help the marmalade set), cut them away and put them in the bag with the pips.

3. Cut the peel into thin strips – as thin as you like in your finished marmalade. Put these into the pan along with the other orangey bits.

4. Add the water and put the pips and pith bits in a muslin bag and tie well. Pop them in the pan.

5. Bring to the boil, then turn down the heat and simmer for 2 hours, or until the peel is very soft. Remove the pips bag with tongs and squeeze out all the juice it contains; you will see that it is quite slimy – this is the pectin being extracted.

6. Remove from the heat and stir in the lemon juice and sugar.

7. Put back on a low heat and stir until all the sugar has dissolved.

8. Bring to the boil and boil for 10 minutes, then test for the setting point as for jam (see page 266).

9. When setting point has been reached, leave to cool for 10 minutes, then stir to distribute the peel evenly before potting into prepared jars. Label and date when cool.

Old English Marmalade

Makes about 8 x 450g jars

1.5kg Seville oranges
2.5 litres water
1kg white sugar
1.2 kg brown sugar
1 tablespoon dark treacle

Prepare as in the Seville Orange Marmalade recipe, but after the sugars have dissolved, stir in the treacle and proceed in the same way.

Lemon Marmalade

Makes about 7 x 450g jars

12 lemons
1.5 litres water
1.5kg sugar

1. Wash the lemons and peel off the rind with a potato peeler, leaving as much of the pith behind as you can. Cut the rind into fine shreds and put in the pan.

2. Juice the lemons and add the juice to the pan. Put any pips in a muslin bag, tie it securely, then add this to the pan. Cut up the rest of the lemons, discarding any of the thicker pieces of pith. Add to the pan.

3. Pour the water over the lemons and simmer for 2 hours.

4. Remove the muslin bag with tongs and squeeze out all the juice.

5. Stir in the sugar and put over a low heat, stirring until all the sugar has dissolved.

6. Turn up the heat and bring to the boil. Boil for 15 minutes, then test for setting point (see page 266). Remove from heat while testing, but boil again if necessary.

7. When setting point has been reached, stir and leave to cool for 10 minutes. Stir again and pot into your prepared jars. Label and date when cool.

Lemon Curd

This isn't really a preserve because you have to use it within a month of making it and keep it in the fridge once opened. But it is lovely stuff, and well worth the effort. You will need a large, sterilised 900g jar with a well-fitting screwtop or a similar-sized Kilner topped jar.

Makes 1 x 900g jar

5 lemons
225g butter
5 eggs
450g caster sugar

1. Finely grate the rind of the lemons, taking the zest part only and leave the pith behind.

2. Extract all the juice and put the zest and juice in a double boiler, or in a bowl over a saucepan of simmering water.

3. Add the butter and, once melted, add the sugar and stir gently until it has dissolved.

4. Beat the eggs, without frothing, and remove the bowl of lemon mixture from the heat. Stir the eggs into the lemon mixture and place back on the heat.

5. Stir until the curd thickens into a spreadable mixture.

6. Pour into the jar and seal well. Label with the date made and a use-by date of 28 days after preparation. Once opened, keep in the fridge.

Chutney and Relish

Chutneys and relishes are very easy to make; you can make a chutney within a couple of hours without even having to stand over it. Most recipes ask for all the ingredients to be put in the pan together, heated gently until the sugar has dissolved and boiled for a few minutes, then you can forget about it for an hour or more while it simmers gently and thickens as the fruit and/or vegetables tenderize. You will have to leave it for a couple of days or weeks while all the flavours mature, but it is worth it.

Chutneys thicken as they cook and you will know yours has achieved the correct thickness when it remains on a spoon tipped sideways, and doesn't run off but slides off in a lump. Relishes are finer in texture and often don't need as much cooking as chutneys.

Autumn Chutney

A deliciously sweet chutney that goes well with cold meats and pork pie.

Makes about 5 x 450g jars

1.5kg apples, pears and plums, cored or
   stoned and chopped into small,
   cube-like pieces
80g chopped dates
100g raisins
450g onions chopped finely
2 garlic cloves, chopped
350g soft brown sugar
550ml malt vinegar
1 level teaspoon allspice
1 level teaspoon ground ginger
½ teaspoon white pepper
1 rounded teaspoon salt

1. Put all the ingredients into a large pan over a gentle heat and stir while all the sugar dissolves.

2. Bring to the boil, then turn down the heat and simmer for 1½ hours, or until the mixture has thickened and has gloss. Stir a couple of times during the cooking time.

3. Pot immediately, label and date.

4. Leave to mature for 1 week in a cool, dark place before using.

Mango Chutney

This a chutney that has become more economical to make due to mangoes
now being available in most supermarkets. I tend to buy mine from my local
Asian greengrocer because I can get them at varying states of ripeness.
You need unripe green mangoes for this recipe.

Makes about 1 x 900g jar

3 large green mangoes, peeled and diced
2 rounded teaspoons salt
1 green chilli, chopped finely
3 garlic cloves, chopped
350ml white vinegar
350g soft brown sugar
50g sultanas
1 level teaspoon turmeric
½ teaspoon ground cumin
¼ teaspoon allspice
1 teaspoon salt

1. Put the mangoes in a dish and sprinkle with
the 2 teaspoons of salt. Cover and leave
overnight or for 7 hours.

2. Rinse and dry the mangoes and put them in
the pan with all the other ingredients.

3. Heat to simmering, then continue to simmer
for 40–50 minutes, or until the mixture is the
correct thickness.

4. Pot and seal immediately. Label and date your
chutney once it has cooled.

Tomato Chutney
This is wonderful served with barbecued food.

Makes approximately 2kg

1.5kg red tomatoes, chopped
1 onion, chopped finely
200g soft brown sugar
1 teaspoon mixed spice
½ teaspoon paprika
2 garlic cloves, chopped
2 level teaspoons salt
200ml malt vinegar

Storage
Once opened, store in the fridge and eat within 4 weeks.

1. Put all the ingredients into a large, strong pan but with only half of the vinegar. Simmer gently until all the sugar has dissolved, stirring all the time.

2. Bring to the boil, then reduce the heat and simmer for 30 minutes, stirring occasionally.

3. Add the rest of the vinegar and cook at simmering for a further 35–40 minutes.

4. Turn up the heat and simmer more vigorously until the chutney thickens – about 5 minutes.

5. Pot and seal immediately. Keep for 7 days before consumption.

Green Tomato Chutney

This is a useful chutney to make if you grow your own tomatoes because you inevitably end up with lots of those green beauties that just won't ripen.

Makes approximately 3–3.5kg

1.8kg green tomatoes, chopped
700g onions, chopped
2 Bramley apples, peeled and diced
575ml white vinegar
500g white caster sugar
25g chopped fresh or ½ teaspoon
　　dried ground ginger
½ level teaspoon mixed spice
2 teaspoons salt

1. Put the tomatoes, onions and apples in a large, strong pan with half of the vinegar and bring to the boil.

2. Remove from the heat and stir in the sugar and all the other ingredients except the rest of the vinegar.

3. Place back on a gentler heat, stir until all the sugar has dissolved and simmer for 30 minutes, then add the rest of the vinegar.

4. Simmer for 1 hour, or until the chutney thickens. Stir occasionally.

5. Pot and seal immediately. Leave to mature for 2 weeks before consuming.

Pumpkin and Tomato Chutney

This one of my favourite combinations for chutneys. It goes well with most cold meats and cheese, but especially with cheese flans and pies.

Makes about 2–2.5kg

1kg pumpkin flesh, cut into 1.5cm cubes
500g red tomatoes, chopped
300g onions, chopped finely
50g raisins
50g sultanas
750g brown sugar
580ml white vinegar
2 level teaspoons ground ginger
1 level teaspoon ground cinnamon
1 level teaspoon ground black pepper
2 garlic cloves, chopped
2 level tablespoons salt

1. Put all the ingredients into a large pan over a low heat and stir until all the sugar has dissolved.

2. Turn up the heat and bring to the boil. Stir continuously.

3. Turn down the heat until it is simmering and cook for 45 minutes. The chutney should be much thicker. If not, raise the heat so that it is simmering more briskly and stir until it is thicker. This should take about 4–5 minutes.

4. Stir well and pot immediately. Leave the chutney to mature for 2 weeks before consuming.

Quick Tomato Relish

This is good if you only wish to make a small amount to eat almost immediately.
It only makes about 2 x 450g jar, so you don't have to make loads at one go.
However just double the quantities if you do want more.

Makes about 2 x 450g jars

1 tablespoon olive oil
120g red onions, chopped finely
1 small red chilli, chopped
½ teaspoon onion seeds
450g red tomatoes, chopped finely
100g soft brown sugar
80ml malt vinegar
½ level teaspoon salt

Serving suggestion
Try this sandwich: butter 2 slices of fresh
crusty bread or a large roll and fill it with
slices of creamy Brie, some crispy green
leaves and a large spoonful of this
sweet relish.

1. In a large pan, heat the oil gently and fry the onions and chilli together until the onion is soft.

2. Stir in the garlic and onion seeds.

3. Add all the other ingredients and stir well.

4. Bring to the boil, stirring continuously.

5. Turn down the heat to simmering and cook for 50–60 minutes. The mixture should be thick by this time.

6. Transfer to a prepared screwtop jar (see page 266).

7. Leave for 24 hours before consuming, but this tastes good even if you eat it when it is just cool.

Red Onion Relish

Makes 1 x 450g jar

3 red onions, chopped very finely
1 red pepper, chopped finely
6 tablespoons soft brown sugar
6 tablespoons white-wine vinegar
½ teaspoon salt
1 garlic clove, chopped or grated

1. Put all the ingredients in a pan and heat gently until the sugar has dissolved.

2. Bring to the boil, then turn down the heat and simmer gently for 35–40 minutes, or until thick and glossy.

3. Stir and pot immediately. You can eat this as soon as it is cold.

Pickles

Pickles are an excellent way of preserving a wide range of foodstuffs, from onions and red cabbage to eggs and cucumbers. Apart from vinegar and some spices, they don't contain many ingredients and are very easy to make. As long as the jar they're packed in has a good, secure seal, they will keep well for a year.

A pickle tastes better after it has matured in the vinegar for a few weeks (some recipes say two months).

There are four main types of pickle: cooked, uncooked, sweet vegetable and fruit pickles. When making pickles of any kind, however, DO NOT use pans made of copper: vinegar reacts badly with this metal and spoils the preserve. Any glass jars must have secure lids made of plastic or with a plastic lining; again, this is because vinegar corrodes metal over time, and eventually the pickles would spoil. Glass jars with snap-down lids, such as Kilner jars, are ideal because the lid is glass, any metal is located only on the outside and the lid has a safe rubber seal.

Muslin bags are useful if you're using whole spices and don't particularly want them in your finished pickle. A muslin square gathered up and tied with string works equally well.

Using brine solutions and salt

In addition to vinegar, some pickles depend on brine, especially when using vegetables which keep and taste better if soaked in brine before pickling. This also helps kill off any bacteria that will spoil the look and taste of the finished pickle and cut down its storage life. To make a basic brine solution, mix 120g coarse salt to every litre of water; *do not* use table salt, however, as this will cloud the finished pickle. To use the brine, submerge the fruit or vegetables to be pickled in the brine solution for the time given in the recipe.

Some recipes require vegetables to be salted rather than put in brine. Simply place the vegetable in thin layers in a large dish and salt each layer, finishing with a layer of salt. Don't be afraid to be liberal with the amount, as every part of the vegetables needs covering. This step usually lasts 24 hours.

After salting or brining, drain the brine or remove the salt and rinse thoroughly in cold water. This is best done in a colander under a running tap because the salt clears much more quickly.

Quick Spiced Vinegar
This is ideal for making pickles when time is short.

1 litre malt vinegar
Ready-mixed pickling spice: the correct amount to use should be on the packet

1. Put the vinegar in a double boiler or glass bowl over a pan of cold water. Add the pickling spice.

2. Bring to the boil, then remove from the heat but keep the vinegar bowl in the hot water so that they both cool down together.

3. Strain if you wish and use for your pickles.

Pickled Onions

Makes about 7 x 450g jars

3kg shallots or pickling onions, peeled
1 litre Quick Spiced Vinegar (see above)
Coarse salt for brining (see opposite)

1. Soak the peeled onions in a brine solution for 36 hours.

2. Rinse well and pack into clean, prepared jars.

3. Cover with the vinegar and seal well. Label and date.

4. Leave for at least 2 months before consuming.

Pickled Red Cabbage

I don't think I could eat a meat and potato pie without a side helping of this pickle.

Makes about 5 x 450g jars

1 large red cabbage
About 1 litre Quick Spiced Vinegar
  (see page 285)
Coarse salt

1. Shred the cabbage and layer it in a dish, sprinkling each layer liberally with salt. Leave for 24 hours.

2. Rinse the cabbage thoroughly and pack into jars. Cover with the vinegar and seal immediately.

Storage
This is ready to eat after 5 days, but must be consumed within 3 months if unopened. White cabbage may be prepared in the same way, but it will keep for 2 months.

Pickled Cucumbers

Makes about 2–3 x 450g jars

3 medium cucumbers
580ml Quick Spiced Vinegar (see page 285)
Coarse salt

1. Wash and dry the cucumbers and chop them into thick slices. Layer the slices in a dish and salt each layer liberally. Leave for 24 hours.

2. Heat the spiced vinegar just before needed to just simmering.

3. Drain the cucumber liquid and rinse off the salt. Pack the cucumber into the jars and cover with the hot vinegar. Seal well immediately. Label and date the pickles when cool.

Storage
This will be ready to eat after 5 days and will keep for up to 6 months unopened.

Pickled Cauliflower

Pickled cauliflower tastes best if the vinegar is slightly sweet, so add 2 teaspoons of white granulated sugar per 500ml of vinegar a few days before it is needed. This recipe requires a stronger brine solution that the basic brine used for pickling onions, as it destroys bacteria faster and prevents the cauliflower from going grey.

Makes about 3–4 x 450g jars

4 cauliflower heads
300g coarse salt for brine
1 litre water for brine
1 litre Quick Spiced Vinegar (see page 285)
Sugar: 2 teaspoons per 500ml vinegar,
   added at least 2 days prior to pickling

1. Wash the cauliflower heads well and cut them into small florets.

2. Mix the salt with the water and soak the cauliflower in the brine solution for 24 hours.

3. Rinse well and drain, pat dry with a cloth.

4. Pack into the jars and cover with the vinegar. Seal immediately. Label and date the pickles.

Storage
This is best left for 1 month before consuming and will keep for 6 months unopened.

Toffee, Treats and Sweets

From chewing on treacle toffee on Bonfire Night to nibbling crystallised fruits at Christmas, toffee and sweets are loved by young and old alike – although the older I get the more careful I am about chewing toffee...

Making these sweets is a great joy, and they make excellent gifts for any time of the year: for a house-warming, a birthday and, of course, for Christmas gifts.

Temperatures and stages

A preserving thermometer will help you know when toffee and other sweets have reached the correct stage. A 'firm ball', for example, is around 120°C – which is what you need for the recipe on the next page.

If you don't have a preserving thermometer, however, don't worry: you can still check for readiness in the following way: have a bowl of iced water ready and, after three to four minutes of boiling the syrup, drop a little of the mixture into the water; when it forms a firm ball, the toffee (or whatever type of sweet you're making) is ready.

Also have a large bowl of cold water ready to plunge the pan into when your syrup has finished its boiling time. This will ensure that your sweets don't overcook and become hard.

Similarly the 'soft-ball' stage is about 115°C, or when the syrup dropped in cold water forms a ball that will not hold its shape.

Traditional Toffee

This creamy homemade toffee will taste better than most bought versions.
Always use double cream as it will stand up to the boiling (unlike single cream).

Makes about 36 pieces

250g golden caster sugar
25g butter
225ml double cream
2 tablespoons golden syrup
½ teaspoon vanilla extract
Tip of a teaspoon of cream of tartar

1. Butter an 18cm square tin well and line it with baking paper.

2. Put the sugar carefully into a large, sturdy pan. Add the butter, cream, syrup and vanilla extract. Stir on a low heat until the sugar has dissolved.

3. Stir in the cream of tartar and bring the mixture to the boil.

4. Continue boiling until the mixture forms a firm ball (see previous page), or reaches the desired temperature if you're using a thermometer.

5. Plunge the pan into cold water to stop cooking the toffee. Leave it there for only a few seconds.

6. Pour the toffee into the prepared tin and leave for about 45 minutes to cool, then cut into squares of your desired size.

7. When completely cool, remove the toffee from the tin and wrap each piece in greaseproof paper or coloured cellophane (I buy mine from a large craft centre, but some garden centres also stock it). Store in an airtight tin.

Treacle Toffee

This is a very easy recipe, and if you have been worried in the past
about making toffee, then have a go at this one.

Makes about 48 pieces

500g golden caster sugar or soft brown sugar
4 tablespoons dark treacle
125g unsalted butter
1 x 372g tin condensed milk
3 dessertspoons water

Tip
This can be made a few days before serving
if required.

1. Butter an 18 x 26cm rectangular tin and line
it with baking paper.

2. Put all the ingredients into a large, heavy-based
pan over a low heat. Stir gently until all the sugar
has dissolved. Check the back of the spoon for
sugar crystals; once there are no crystals showing,
the mixture is ready to bring to the boil.

3. Turn up the heat and continue to cook. When
the mixture reaches a rolling boil, continue
boiling for 4 minutes, then begin to test the
temperature either with a preserving thermometer
or with the ice-water method described on page
288. If you have a thermometer, it needs to reach
130°C or a firm-ball consistency. This will good
and chewy, but won't break your teeth!

4. When the right stage has been reached,
remove from the heat and allow the bubbling to
subside before pouring the toffee into the tin.

5. When cool, leave in the tin and cut the toffee
into bite-sized squares (I use a strong fish slice to
cut the toffee as you can lift it easily as well). This
may need to be repeated as the cuts tend to
disappear as it cools. Once completely cold, break
up the pieces and wrap each in greaseproof paper.
Store in an airtight tin until ready to serve.

Fudge

Delicious creamy fudge is a wonderful treat – Paul's favourite, in fact.
This keeps very well in an airtight container for up to 2 weeks in the fridge.

Makes about 48 pieces

450g golden caster sugar
110g butter
1 x 397g can condensed milk
2 tablespoons water
1 teaspoon vanilla extract

Variations
Change the flavour of the fudge by adding
other ingredients at the beating stage.
Try one of the following:

- 2 tablespoons rum and 50g raisins
- 50g chopped glacé cherries
- 40g sieved cocoa powder
- 50g chopped hazelnuts or walnuts

1. Butter a 20cm square tin and line it with
baking paper.

2. Put all the ingredients into a heavy-based pan
and heat slowly, stirring continuously until all
the sugar has melted.

3. Bring to the boil without stirring, then
boil rapidly until the mixture reaches the
soft-ball stage (see page 288), or 115°C if
you're using a preserving thermometer.

4. Remove from the heat, then beat the
mixture with a wooden spoon until the fudge
becomes grainy.

5. Pour into the prepared tin and allow to cool
completely before cutting into cubes.

Old-fashioned Coconut Ice

Most coconut-lovers can never resist this sweet,
and the best news is that it is very easy to prepare.

Makes about 550g

140ml condensed milk
400g white caster sugar
15g unsalted butter
1 tablespoon water
150g desiccated coconut
½ teaspoon vanilla extract
Red food colouring, optional

Storage
This will keep for at least 3 weeks.

1. Butter a 20cm square tin and line the base with baking paper.

2. Put the condensed milk, sugar, butter and water in a heavy-based saucepan over a low heat and stir until the sugar has dissolved.

3. Bring to the boil and continue to boil for 10 minutes, or until the temperature reaches 115°C – the soft-ball stage (see page 288).

4. Remove from the heat and stir in the coconut and vanilla extract.

5. Beat well with a wooden spoon until the mixture is thick and creamy.

6. At this point, if you wish to give half the ice the traditional pink colour, put half of the mixture into the prepared tin and smooth out into a layer. Beat a few drops of red food colouring into the remaining coconut mixture, then spoon this onto the top of the white layer and spread evenly.

7. Leave to cool completely, then slice into bars or squares – however you wish to serve it. Wrap each piece in greaseproof paper and store in an airtight tin.

Peppermint Creams

I made these once with the infant children I teach at school. Rather than
having fresh white sweets, they came out a dirty grey colour. Needless
to say, I mimed eating one – but I don't think they knew!
After air-drying these sweets, they can be dipped into melted chocolate for
an extra-tasty treat. The dough can also be moulded into all kinds of shapes:
little white mice with string tails are fun. The eyes can be candy silver balls;
these are found in the home baking section of a shop or supermarket.
Once you've shaped them, they need to be left to dry as before.

Makes about 25 pieces

2 medium egg whites
450g icing sugar
4 drops peppermint oil
Extra icing sugar, for dusting

Storage
This will keep for about 2 weeks in an
airtight tin – *if* they last that long!

1. Whisk the egg whites until frothy, but not
stiff, in a mixing bowl.

2. Sieve half the icing sugar into the egg whites
and stir in thoroughly.

3. Add the peppermint oil and sieve in the rest
of the sugar and beat well until it forms a stiff
but pliable dough.

4. Knead the mixture for a few minutes.

5. Roll out the dough with a rolling pin, dusting
with a little icing sugar so as the dough doesn't
stick. When it is about 2cm deep, use a small
round cutter to cut out circles.

6. Leave to dry in a cool room for 6–8 hours,
then place in airtight tin.

Golden Honeycomb

Honeycomb is something I remember buying loose by the ounce in a little plastic bag at our local market. Its pleasure to me was the way it fizzed and melted on your tongue. This is remarkably easy to make at home, but it doesn't keep well, as it goes sticky in the air, so make and eat it on the same day. You will need a thermometer for this recipe because it has to reach a very high temperature.

Makes about 250g

150ml cold water
1 tablespoon golden syrup
220g golden granulated sugar
¼ teaspoon cream of tartar
½ teaspoon bicarbonate of soda
1 teaspoon hot water

1. Butter an 18cm square tin.

2. Put the cold water, golden syrup, sugar and cream of tartar into a heavy-based pan over a low heat. Stir with a wooden spoon until all the sugar has dissolved.

3. Turn up the heat and bring the mixture to the boil. Don't stir at this stage.

4. Continue to boil until the mixture reaches 154°C.

5. The next step has to be done very quickly. When the syrup has reached the correct temperature, remove it from the heat. Mix the bicarbonate of soda with the hot water and immediately add it to the toffee mixture, stirring gently. It's fun to watch it fizz and rise.

6. Pour into the prepared tin and allow to cool and set.

7. Cut the honeycomb up as best you can; regular shapes are almost impossible because it cracks and breaks. Eat within 24 hours.

Marzipan

This has always been a sweet treat and dates back in British culinary history to the fifteenth century, when many a banquet was adorned with an elaborate marzipan sculpture. Then it was called *marchpane*.
These days we tend to know it mostly as that layer of almond paste that goes under the icing on a Christmas cake, but you can make delicious sweets and chocolate fillings with marzipan.

Makes about 700g

350g ground almonds
180g caster sugar
180g icing sugar
1 teaspoon lemon juice
½ teaspoon almond extract or
   almond flavouring
1 egg, beaten

1. Put the ground almonds and caster sugar into a bowl. Sieve in the icing sugar.

2. Add the lemon juice and almond flavouring or extract and stir in enough of the egg to make a pliable paste. Knead until smooth, adding a dusting of icing sugar if it goes sticky.

Now it can be used to make many things. Try the following for starters.

- *Make an after-dinner fruit bowl*
  Knead food colouring into small sections of the marzipan to make strawberries, bananas, oranges and apples and dust with a little caster sugar to finish.

- *Marzipan truffles*
  For a luxurious treat, try kneading in 2–3 teaspoons brandy or rum. Roll small, equal-sized pieces into balls, then use a cocktail stick to dip each into melted chocolate. This would make an excellent gift idea for a marzipan-lover.

Butterscotch

This is a rich, buttery, hard toffee that tastes wonderful. It obviously has Scottish origins and was traditionally made by courting couples – but surely having all that hot sugar around wouldn't be conducive to safe 'cuddling'!

Makes about 56 pieces

450g white granulated sugar
150ml hot water
¼ teaspoon cream of tartar
80g unsalted butter, cut into small pieces
½ teaspoon vanilla extract

Storage
This will keep for 4 weeks without going too sticky.

1. Butter a 20cm square tin and line the base with silicone paper.

2. In a sturdy pan, dissolve the sugar in the water over a low heat. Stir gently with a wooden spoon. All the sugar must be dissolved before boiling.

3. Add the cream of tartar and bring to the boil, but do not stir during boiling.

4. When the mixture reaches 116°C, remove from the heat and add the butter – dot it all over the surface so that it melts into the mixture evenly. Do NOT STIR.

5. Put the pan back on the heat and allow to boil until it reaches 138°C.

6. Remove the pan from the heat and stir in the vanilla.

7. Pour the toffee into the prepared tin. Leave to set, but when almost set cut it into rectangles.

8. When completely cold, break up the pieces and wrap them in coloured cellophane. Store in an airtight container.

Toffee Apples
Real Bonfire Night treats and not just for the children.
Ours are grown-up and they still love them!

Makes 8

8 eating apples of your choice
8 lolly sticks

For the toffee
225g soft brown sugar
30g unsalted butter
1 tablespoon golden syrup or honey
5 tablespoons water

1. Wash the apples well to remove any grease; otherwise the toffee won't stick. Push a lolly stick into the centre of each apple, making sure it doesn't go right the way through.

2. Put a bowl of cold water in the fridge so that the toffee will cool quickly.

3. Place all toffee ingredients in a heavy-based pan and put on a low heat until all the sugar has dissolved.

4. Bring to the boil and allow to bubble briskly. When it reaches 140°C, known as the 'soft-crack' stage, it is ready.
If you don't have a thermometer, test for the soft-crack stage as follows: drop a bit of this syrup into a bowl of cold water. It will solidify into threads that, when removed, are flexible, not brittle, and they should bend slightly before breaking.

5. Remove from heat and have your bowl of cold water ready. Dip each apple into the toffee first, coating well, then into the cold water for a few seconds to set.

6. Stand the apples on non-stick paper. When they are completely cool, wrap them in greaseproof paper.

7. Serve within 24 hours.

Peanut Brittle

I remember one of my teachers nibbling this during lessons and wondering
why she could eat sweets and we couldn't. She was, I found out later,
expecting a baby and it was one of her cravings.

Makes about 500g

180g raw, shelled peanuts, chopped
220g granulated sugar
100g soft brown sugar
3 tablespoons golden syrup
75ml hot water
25g butter
¼ teaspoon bicarbonate of soda

1. Butter a shallow rectangular tin – a Swiss roll tin is ideal.

2. Toast the peanuts in the oven for 10 minutes at 190°C/gas mark 5. Keep them in a warm place until needed.

3. Place the sugars, syrup and water in a heavy-based pan and put over a low heat until the sugar dissolves.

4. Bring to the boil and boil – do not stir – until it reaches 154°C or the 'hard-crack' stage. To check this without a thermometer, drop a little of the syrup into a bowl of cold water; it will form hard, brittle threads that break when bent if it's ready. Let the syrup cool in the cold water for a few moments before touching it, however, to avoid burns.

6. Remove from the heat and stir in the butter, peanuts and bicarbonate of soda.

7. Pour into the prepared tin and leave to cool for 10 minutes. Leave to cool completely.

8. Break into pieces and wrap in cellophane or baking paper. Store in an airtight container in a cool, dark place.

Chocolate Truffles

These scrumptious treats are named after the dark-coloured, expensive fungi so well-loved in culinary circles. To tell the truth, I prefer the chocolate ones!

Makes about 350g (about 25 pieces)

For the ganache
200g dark chocolate, at least 70% cocoa solids
25g unsalted butter
180ml double cream

For flavourings (use one or a combination, optional)
• 2 tablespoons brandy or rum
• 1 dessertspoon of any liqueur of your choice
• 1 dessertspoon of instant coffee mixed with a teaspoon of boiling water; leave to cool before adding to the ganache
• ½ teaspoon vanilla or almond extract
• 3 tablespoons ground almonds, hazelnuts or walnuts

For coating
Cocoa powder
Ground almonds
Melted chocolate: white, dark or milk.

1. Put the cream and butter in a bowl over a pan of hot water to warm.

2. Break up the chocolate into small pieces. When the butter starts to melt, add the chocolate. Stir gently to combine everything.

3. When everything has melted and is well-combined, remove the bowl from the heat and leave to cool and set. When cool, put it in the fridge to firm up for an hour.

4. If you want flavoured truffles, stir one of the flavouring suggestions gently into the ganache when you remove it from the heat.

5. Once cooled, make small balls of ganache, either using a melon baller or 2 teaspoons. Try not too handle them too much as the ganache melts very quickly.

6. Dip the truffles in cocoa powder, ground almonds or more melted chocolate: white, dark or milk. Just have fun, both making and eating them!

Drinks, Squashes and Cordials

Like everything else you make at home, when you make your own squashes and cordials you know exactly what you are drinking and giving your family.

In addition to the natural ingredients listed in each recipe, you'll need to have some sterile screwtop bottles ready to hold your drinks so that they will store more successfully.

Sterilising bottles

Glass or sturdy plastic screwtop bottles are the best types to use for squash- and cordial-making. You can even re-use bottles so long as they are washed and then sterilised between uses.

For plastic bottles with plastic lids, this is best done with the tablets or liquid used to sterilise baby-feeding equipment; just follow the manufacturer's instructions.

Glass bottles may also be sterilised using the tablets or liquid, but they can also simply be placed in warm water and brought slowly to the boil, then boiled for 5 minutes. Leave them immersed in the water until you are ready to use them.

Another way is to put the bottles on a baking sheet into a cold oven and set to 160°C/gas mark 2. When the oven reaches the temperature, switch it off and leave the bottles to cool.

All metal lids are best boiled for 5 minutes.

Orange Squash
This is very easy to make and tastes very refreshing on a hot day.

Makes about 1.5–1.7 litres, depending on the juice yield of the oranges

12 medium oranges, washed
1.2 litres water
6 tablespoons sugar

1. Juice the oranges and pour the juice in a jug.

2. Put any pulp in a large saucepan. Peel the outer skin and zest of the oranges away from the pith and add this to the pulp. Make sure no pith is left on the peel, as this will make the squash taste bitter.

3. Add the water to the pan and bring it to the boil. Boil for 3 minutes, then remove from the heat and stir in the sugar. Keep stirring to make sure the sugar has dissolved. Leave to cool.

4. Strain the boiled mixture into the juice, then pour the squash into a bottle, or leave in the jug and cover with foil.

5. Dilute 1 part squash with 4 parts water when drinking.

Storage
This will keep for 5 days in the fridge – *if* you can keep it that long!

Lemon-lime Squash

This has to be my favourite. It is delicious served with ice cubes
and thin slices of lime and lemon.

Makes about 2 litres

7 lemons
8 limes
1 litre water
800g caster sugar

Variation
For Lemon Squash, use 14 whole lemons
instead of the mixture of lemons and limes.

1. Pare the skins of the lemons and limes away
from the pith, making sure you don't take any
pith at all.

2. Put the skins in a pan with the water and
bring to the boil.

3. Continue to boil for 10 minutes, then turn
down the heat and add the sugar. Stir well until
it is dissolved. Leave to cool.

4. Juice the lemons and limes and add the juice
to the cooling mixture. Don't worry about pips
or pulp going in as it is going to be strained.

5. Strain the liquid into a jug, then decant it
into prepared bottles (see page 300).

6. When serving the squash, dilute 1 part squash
with 5 parts water.

Storage
This will keep for 10–12 days in the fridge.

Strawberry and Rhubarb Cordial

This is wonderful as a drink or, when served with
less water, as an ice-cream syrup.

Makes about 1 litre

6 stems rhubarb, washed and
  cut into 1.5cm pieces
230g caster sugar
250ml water
400g strawberries, washed,
  hulled and halved

Storage
This will keep for 3–4 days in the fridge.

1. Put the rhubarb, sugar and water in a pan.
Heat gently, stirring all the time until the
sugar has dissolved.

2. Bring to the boil and cook at boiling for
2 minutes. Remove from the heat.

3. Add the strawberries immediately. Use a
potato masher to crush them into the liquid.

4. Leave for 15 minutes.

5. Push the mixture through a sieve into a
clean jug.

6. Cover and keep in the fridge until needed.

7. When serving, dilute 1 part cordial with
3 parts water.

Elderberry Cordial

If you have lots of elder trees close by, you can make a really cheap cordial that has a very rich, fruity taste. Pick your elderberries on a dry day; the fruit will be fresher-tasting and juicier. Have a large 2-litre jug ready to measure the juice yield.

Makes at least 1 litre

2kg elderberries
Enough water just to cover the fruit
White granulated sugar: 350g
    per 500ml juice
5 whole cloves, optional
A pinch of nutmeg, optional

1. Wash the elderberries but don't remove the stalks. Put them in a pan with sufficient water just to cover the fruit.

2. Heat to simmering and continue to simmer gently for 2–3 minutes. Do not allow the mixture to boil at this stage. Remove from the heat.

3. Strain the liquid into a measuring jug and measure how much juice has been produced. For every 500ml of juice, add 350g sugar.

4. Put the juice and sugar in a pan and heat gently until the sugar has dissolved, then boil for 5 minutes. Add the spices if you are using them.

5. Allow to cool and decant into prepared bottles (see page 300).

6. When serving, dilute 1 part cordial with 4 parts water.

Blackcurrant Syrup

This can be used like a cordial and can be made with other berries,
such as raspberries, gooseberries and blackberries. I use caster sugar to
make this because it dissolves more quickly.

Makes about 1 litre, depending on juice yield

3kg blackcurrants, cleaned, and
  any bad ones discarded
1.8 litres water
Caster sugar: 50g per 100ml juice

Variations
• To make other fruit syrups, do not add
any water at step 1, except for blackberries:
they require 300ml to 3kg of fruit.
• You can make a fruit liqueur by adding
200ml brandy to every litre of syrup for a
special drink.

1. Put the fruit and water in a pan and bring to
the boil. Use a potato masher to crush the fruit.

2. Boil for 1 minute only. Remove from the heat.

3. Strain the pulp from the juice using a
preserving bag over a large bowl. Because you
are not making jelly, a gentle squeeze of the
bag will aid the flow of juice.

4. Measure the juice and weigh out the sugar.

5. In a large pan, heat the juice to body
temperature – NO HOTTER or the flavour
will spoil.

6. Remove from the heat and stir in the sugar
until completely dissolved.

7. Pour the syrup into prepared bottles (see page
300) and screw on the tops.

8. To serve, dilute these syrups 1 part syrup to
3 parts water. Add more water for
young children.

Storage
These syrups do not have a long shelf life
because they are not boiled for long enough, so
consume within 7 days and store in the fridge.

Herbal Teas

I drink lots of herbal teas. I find them more refreshing than ordinary tea, especially in the afternoon. Many herbal teas are made using the flowering heads of plants, whether fresh or dried. Obviously, if you can dry your own, you then have a steady supply on hand all year from which to make tea.

Choosing your flowers

Make sure you collect the flowers of your choice as soon as you can after they bloom. This is less important for rose-petal tea than for elderflower tea, but in any case, try to get the flowers before they have been pollinated; after this, they tend to deteriorate rapidly.

Collect the flowers as early as your schedule will allow – dawn is the best time. Flowers taken at noon are not as good as those taken at dawn, because the essential oils will have evaporated. Also, don't pick them during or just after rain.

Only collect perfect flowers or petals. Don't put up with broken parts, spoiled or rotting petals or hips. After all, the best raw ingredients will make the best tea.

Drying flowers and petals

The easiest way of drying flower heads and petals is to cover a tray with sand, then lay the petals or flower heads on top of this. Put them in the oven at the lowest heat it will allow and leave the door open. An hour or two (or even three) later and the petals will have dried out sufficiently for you to store them in airtight containers, such as jars or cannisters. Do not close the lid of your container, however, until the petals or flowers are completely cool.

Another way of drying flowers in sufficient quantity for teas is to put them in a desiccator, which is a drying machine that allows you to dry almost anything from flowers to strips of meat (ideal for making your own jerky).

You can air-dry your flowers, but while it requires no electricity, air-drying takes a long time, and you have to be sure you have a dry-enough volume of air that will remain dry for at least three weeks. You need a plastic tub lined with kitchen paper, into which you fold your flowers. A loosely fitting lid – enough to keep the contents from blowing away – completes the job. It will take quite some time (up to a month) before the petals will be ready. This method is only really good for petals, as whole flowers can more easily spoil in the time it takes them to dry out.

Each of the following recipes makes 2 cups of tea.

Lemon Balm and Honey Tea

About 15g fresh lemon balm leaves, chopped
370ml boiling water
2 teaspoons clear honey

1. Put the leaves in a teapot and pour on the boiling water. Stir well and allow to brew for 5 minutes. Stir in the honey as it brews.

2. Strain the tea into cups. Keep shaking the pot gently to keep the leaves from clogging the spout.

Lemon and Ginger Tea

Zest and juice of 1 lemon
Tip of a teaspoon ground ginger or
 ½ teaspoon grated fresh ginger
370ml boiling water
2 teaspoons honey

1. Pour the lemon juice and zest into a jug or teapot and add the ginger.

2. Pour on the boiling water and stir in the honey. Brew for 1–2 minutes, then strain into cups.

Elderflower Tea

Although you can make this with either fresh or dried flowers, I tend to use dried elderflowers for the tea because I think the taste is better.

15g fresh or 10g dried elderflowers
370ml boiling water
3 teaspoons honey

1. Put the dried flowers in a teapot and pour on the boiling water. Stir in the honey.

2. Strain the tea into cups to serve.

Chamomile Tea

You can dry chamomile flowers for this tea, then put them in a food processor and chop them finely. Store in a lidded jar or caddy and keep in a cool, dark place.

About 5 fresh flower heads or 2 teaspoons
dried chopped chamomile flowers
350ml boiling water
Honey (optional)

1. Put the dried flowers in a teapot and pour on the boiling water.

2. Brew for 5 minutes and strain into cups.

3. Sweeten with honey if you prefer.

Peppermint Tea

2 teaspoons of fresh mint leaves,
chopped finely
400ml boiling water
Honey (optional)

1. Put the leaves in a teapot.

2. Pour on the water and leave to brew for 5–6 minutes.

3. Add honey if you wish.

Making Beer and Wine

As our grandparents knew, making your own beer and wine is much easier and less complicated than you think. When Diana and I first started out, we read books about fancy wines and felt it was a particularly complicated, messy business. Then we read about how French wines are made and learned that, on a micro-scale, this is very achievable. You won't have châteaux-tasting wines, of course, but so long as what you make is left to mature after bottling, it is very drinkable. These days, we always have a gallon on the 'go'.

Beer is very similar: you can make good home brews very cheaply and consistently.

Winemaking Basics

The basic ingredients you need to make wine are fruit juice, water, sugar and winemaking yeast. While the fruit juice can be derived from 'hedge fruits' such as elderberry and blackberry, I recently started to make wine with red and white grape juice that you can buy in shops. Some are reasonably cheap and make very acceptable-tasting wine, and this has turned out to be the easiest wine I've ever made.

In addition to the natural ingredients, you will also need some basic winemaking and brewing equipment. If you purchase the items listed below from brewing shops, it is much more expensive than buying the same ones from large hardware stores. You will need:

- A plastic lidded bin for mashing the fruit
- At least 2 glass or plastic fermentation jars or demijohns to hold the wine during the fermentation process – one to rack the wine off into when fermentation has occurred
- A large pan – a preserving pan is ideal, as it has a pouring lip
- 2 airlocks and rubber bungs. These stop air from getting into the fermenting wine but still allow gases to escape
- A long plastic siphoning tube to rack the wine into a clean jar
- 1 plastic funnel. This helps when pouring the wine into fermenting jars
- 1 large heatproof jug for dissolving sugar in hot liquid
- At least 6 screwtop or corkable bottles (I prefer the screwtop ones)
- Labels
- 1 nylon or plastic sieve or bag

All equipment must be kept as sterile as possible, just like when you are making preserves. I sterilise all my equipment using sterilising tablets – the same ones used for baby-feeding equipment. Just follow the instructions on the packet.

You can also sterilise glass bottles simply by placing them in warm water, bringing this slowly to the boil, then boiling for 5 minutes. Leave them immersed in the water until you are ready to use them.

Another way is to put the bottles on a baking sheet into a cold oven and set to 160°C/gas mark 2. When the oven reaches the temperature, switch it off and leave the bottles to cool.

Any metal lids are best boiled for 5 minutes.

Useful non-essentials

Some ingredients that aren't essential but which may improve homemade wine are:

- Yeast nutrients (usually vitamin C). This helps the yeast to do its job. Most yeasts already contain the nutrient, however, so read the label on the pack before buying or adding any extra nutrient to it.

- Citric acid, if the fruit you are using is low in acidity. You can get this from winemaking suppliers or brew shops, some of which are now online as well.

- Some wines (mainly red) require the addition of tannins, which give the wine its strength of flavour. This can usually take the form of a cup of strong tea in the list of ingredients.

- Campden tablets. These are winemakers' cleaning tablets. They clean equipment and the wine both before and after fermentation.

- Some fruits that are full of pectin, such as blackcurrants, require a pectin-destroying enzyme. This helps in the fermentation process and it enhances the flavour of wine.

Wine Recipes
All the wine recipes here make 5–6 x 75cl bottles

Elderflower Wine
You may wonder why this wine uses grape juice when it's called 'Elderflower'. Grape juice is added to many fruit wines to boost the flavour – without detracting from that of the fruit.

4 litres white grape juice
2 large elderflower heads, washed
500g sugar
2 rounded teaspoons winemaking yeast

1. Heat 1 litre of the grape juice in a pan until simmering. Remove from the heat and add the elderflowers. Leave until the juice has cooled completely. Strain the juice first into a jug, then into the fermenting jar.

2. Heat 500ml of the grape juice until hot. Remove from the heat and stir in the sugar. Pour into the fermenting jar.

3. Pour all the remaining juice, except for 4 tablespoons, into the jar. Put the 4 tablespoons juice into a warm jug along with 1 teaspoon of the sugar. Add the yeast, stir well and add this mixture to the jar.

4. Shake the jar to allow the yeast to distribute evenly throughout the liquid, then fit the airlock. Follow from step 4 of the Easy Grape-juice Wine instructions (see page 312) to the end.

5. Leave this wine to mature for at least 2 months before drinking.

Easy Grape-juice Wine

This is a very quick way of producing a reasonable wine. It can be left to mature for longer in the fermentation jar if you wish, and you can leave it for up to 6 weeks before bottling. But I usually need the jar for the next batch...

4 litres red or white grape juice
450g white granulated sugar
2 rounded teaspoons winemaker's yeast

1. Heat 500ml of the grape juice in a pan until very hot, but not boiling. Remove from the heat and stir in the sugar until it has completely dissolved.

2. Pour the rest of the juice, except for 3 tablespoons, into your fermenting jar and add all the sugar solution except for 1 tablespoon. Put the tablespoons of juice and sugar solution into a small, warm jug and add the yeast. Stir well and pour into the fermenting jar. Give the jar a swirl to mix the ingredients together. Be careful: it will be heavy.

3. Put a little cool boiled water in the airlock and push it into the rubber bung (this may already be done). Fit the bung securely into the top of the fermenting jar.

4. Leave at room temperature away from draughts and direct sunlight to ferment.

5. The yeast will begin working after a few hours and froth will begin to form on the top of the wine; the airlock will begin popping as the yeast gives off carbon dioxide. This popping sound is the signal that fermentation has begun and it will also let you know when it has finished. At first, there should be a constant popping; then over the next 2 weeks the sound will subside until eventually it will

stop altogether. There is no definite timescale for this first process, but it is usually about 10–14 days.

6. Once fermentation has finished, sterilise the other jar and have the siphoning tube ready.

7. This next step is to get rid of the dead yeast – the 'lees' – at the bottom of the jar. Place the wine-filled jar on an upturned bowl next to the sink and place the empty sterilised fermentation jar in the sink. Remove the bung from the wine and push the siphoning tube into the wine until it reaches about 5cm from the bottom. This prevents the lees at the bottom from going up the tube and spoiling the wine. Suck the other end of the tube until the wine flows through the tube, then place the tube quickly into the clean jar. As the wine flows into the clean jar, steady the end of the tube in the first jar to keep it in place.

8. When the level in the fermented jar is almost above the unwanted yeast, pull out the tube.

9. Put your hand over the neck of the new fermentation jar and shake it thoroughly. This gets rid of any carbon dioxide still present in the wine. Shake 3 times. Again, be careful as it will be heavy.

10. Seal the wine with a clean airlock as in step 3 above.

11. After 1 week, repeat this 'racking off' process into a sterile jar and shake as before.

12. After 1 more week, you may add a Campden tablet if you wish, following the instructions on the pack. This will make sure no yeast particles or bacteria will spoil your wine once it has been bottled. Shake the jar once again, then leave it for 3 days.

13. Sterilise your wine bottles (see page 300). I always have 6 bottles, with screwtops, ready but usually find that I only need 5.

14. After sterilising, rinse the bottles with cool, boiled water and place them in the sink as you did when racking into the clean fermentation jar. Put the wine on the upturned bowl as before and siphon the wine into each bottle. You have to watch this constantly as the bottles fill quickly. Screw on the tops immediately or push in the corks. Dry the bottles, then label and date your wine.

15. Allow the wine to mature for at least 3 months before drinking.

Making Fresh Fruit Wines

You'll need to prepare the fruit to extract the juice, and this is when your plastic lidded bin comes in useful. The preparation steps below apply to all fruit-based wine recipes listed in this chapter. All fruit wines benefit from being left in the bottle for at least three months.

Fruit Winemaking Steps

1. Clean the fruit, removing any damaged bits, and mash it down in a large pan with a potato masher.

2. Add the designated amount of water and ingredients such as pectin destroying enzyme, tannin or citric acid, but NOT sugar, dried fruit or yeast; those come at a later stage.

3. Pour the mixture into the lidded plastic bin and leave it for 24 hours at room temperature.

4. Place the yeast in a jug with the yeast nutrient (if using) and 100ml warm water. Stir and leave it for 10 minutes.

5. Stir the yeast mixture into the fruit mixture in the plastic bin. Add any dried fruit the recipe calls for now. Mash the fruit again with a potato masher. Cover and leave it for 48 hours at room temperature.

6. Stir in the sugar and leave it to rest again for 24 hours.

7. Using a jug, scoop the mixture from the bin and strain through a sieve into a large pan.

8. Pour the strained mixture into a fermentation jar using the jug and a funnel.

9. Top up with white grape juice if the fruit is light, or red grape juice if it is dark fruit.

10. Fit an airlock and allow the wine to ferment in a warmish place, away from sunlight.

11. After fermentation is complete, follow steps 6–15 of the Easy Grape-juice Wine recipe on page 312.

Apple Wine

3.5–4kg apples
3 litres water
1 teaspoon citric acid
1 teaspoon pectin-destroying enzyme
200g sultanas
2 rounded teaspoons winemaking yeast
800g sugar

1. Wash the fruit and cut it into small cubes.

2. Place these in the bin together with the water, citric acid and enzyme. Mash the mixture. Continue from step 3 in Fruit Winemaking Steps (page 314). Add the sultanas with the yeast at step 4.

Blackcurrant Wine

1kg blackcurrants
4 litres water
1 teaspoon pectin-destroying enzyme
200g raisins
2 rounded teaspoon winemaking yeast
1kg sugar

1. Wash and place the fruit in the bin and add the water and enzyme. Mash down and continue from step 3 in Fruit Winemaking Steps (page 314).

Plum Wine

2kg plums
1 teaspoon pectin-destroying enzyme
1 teaspoon citric acid
3 litres water
500g raisins
About 150ml (1 small cup) of strong tea
2 rounded teaspoons winemaking yeast
1.3kg sugar

1. Cut the plums into small pieces, catching all the juice, and put them in the bin. Add the stones for flavour if you wish, but they must be removed before the yeast is added. Continue from step 3 in Fruit Winemaking Steps (page 314), making sure you add the tea before the yeast goes in.

Rhubarb Wine

2kg rhubarb, chopped into 1cm pieces
Juice and zest of 1 lemon
1 teaspoon pectin-destroying enzyme
3.5 litres water
250g sultanas
2 rounded teaspoons winemaking yeast
1.3kg sugar

1. Put the fruit, juice and zest of the lemon and water in the bin and continue from step 3 in Fruit Winemaking Steps (page 314).

Gooseberry Wine

2kg gooseberries
3.5 litres water
1 teaspoon pectin-destroying enzyme
250g sultanas
2 rounded teaspoons winemaking yeast
1kg sugar

1. Wash the gooseberries and put them in the bin with the water. Continue from step 3 in Fruit Winemaking Steps (page 314).

Blackberry and Raspberry Wine

We make this with wild fruit we gather in the hedgerows near us. If you use wild fruit, wash it thoroughly and bring it to the boil first before adding it to the fermentation bin.

1kg mixed blackberries and raspberries
3 litres water
2 rounded teaspoons winemaking yeast
1kg sugar

1. Put the fruit and water into the bin and continue from step 3 in Fruit Winemaking Steps (page 314).

Mead

Mead is essentially an alcoholic drink made from fermented honey, and it must be left to mature for 6 months or it tastes very strange. If you keep bees, this will be a very inexpensive drink to make.

1.5kg honey – set, clear or
  a combination of both
4 litres hot water
3 level teaspoons winemaking yeast
Juice of 2 lemons
50ml strong tea
1 Campden tablet

1. Put the honey into a large pan and stir in the water. Allow to cool to body temperature.

2. Put 3 tablespoons of the honey-water into a jug and stir in the yeast.

3. Pour the lemon juice and tea into the fermenting jar and add half of the honey-water.

4. Pour the yeast mixture into the jar and add the rest of the honey-water.
Swirl to mix.

5. Put in the bung and add a little water to the airlock.

6. Leave in a warmish place until fermentation has finished.

7. Rack off twice, shaking well each time, and leaving 5 days in between each racking.

8. Add the Campden tablet to kill any stray yeast or bacteria, then bottle as normal.

9. Leave in a cool, dark place for at least 6 months before drinking.

Brewing Beer

Home-brew kits are excellent and allow you to make very good beer easily and quite cheaply. We tend to make our own brown ale from a can bought from our local brew shop. A pint of brown ale costs approximately 40p. We use powdered glucose rather than sugar, as this imparts a better flavour to the ale.

Brown Ale

You'll notice that we use plastic bottles to store this, which may at first sound less than 'eco-friendly'. The green thing about using plastic lemonade bottles is that you don't need to use any strong chemicals to sterilise them because they're already sterile. And if you drink the lemonade, you're actually reusing them.

Makes about 23 litres (40 pints)

About 23 litres (40 pints) of water
1 can of brown ale concentrate
1kg glucose
Beer-brewing yeast; this can vary from make to make, so read how much yeast is required on the packet

1. Pour 2.8 litres of hot water into the fermenting bin and stir in the brown ale concentrate. Fill the can with some of the hot water and swirl it around to remove any dregs. Pour this back into the bin.

2. Add the glucose and the rest of the water.

3. Stir in the yeast well and put on the lid.

4. Leave in a warm place for days 7–10 to allow fermentation to take place.

5. Siphon into glass or plastic bottles: we tend to buy 12 cheap bottles of lemonade, store the lemonade in another vessel (or discard it) and add 1 level teaspoon of sugar, then siphon the beer straight into the bottles (they will be already sterile), screw on the tops and leave them in a cool place for at least a month to mature.

Bitter Beer
A very simple way of making cheap, good-tasting bitter beer.

Makes about 15.3 litres (27 pints)

1 can hopped malt extract concentrate
   for bitter beer
Water to make up to 15.3 litres
250g glucose
1 rounded teaspoon brewers beer yeast

1. Warm the can of concentrate in a bowl of hot water for 4–5 minutes; this makes it easier to pour. Pour the concentrate into the fermenting bin and add 4 pints of hot water. Fill the can with hot water, swirl, then add this to the bin as well.

2. Stir in the glucose and the rest of the cold water to make up the 15.3 litres of water.

3. Stir in the yeast well and put on the lid. Leave for 24 hours and skim off the froth. Cover and leave in a warm place. Stir every day, skimming off the froth with each stirring. This should stop after about 5 days.

4. Leave for another 5–6 days, then siphon the bitter into glass or plastic bottles, seal well and label.

5. Leave in a dark place at room temperature for 3–4 weeks before drinking.

Ginger Beer

This is the old-fashioned brew that is alcoholic and really warms you on a cold autumn evening. Be very careful where you store your ginger beer as it ferments quickly; do keep checking it. My grandad made this just after the Second World War and thought during one night the Third World War had started: all the corks blew out on his home brew, hitting the ceiling of the larder with some force! For this and the nettle beer recipe that follows, use strong glass bottles: the ones with lever-type lids are best as they are most secure.

Makes about 4 litres (7 pints)

25g fresh ginger, chopped
450g sugar
Rind and juice of 1 lemon
20g cream of tartar
4 litres boiling water
2 level teaspoon winemaking yeast

1. Put the ginger, sugar, lemon rind and juice and cream of tartar into a large pan, then pour on the boiling water. Cover and leave to cool.

2. Put 3 tablespoons of the ginger mixture into a small cup, add the yeast and stir well. Add this back to the rest of the ginger mixture. Cover and keep in a warm place for 24 hours.

3. Skim off any froth and siphon the beer into 8–9 strong beer bottles or 2 x 2-litre stone jars. Cork securely.

4. Leave in a cool place. The beer will be ready to drink after 3 days.

Nettle Beer

This is a good-flavoured, inexpensive beer to make. Use only the nettle tops to make it –
and don't forget to wear gloves when gathering them!

Makes about 4 litres (7 pints)

1kg nettle tops, washed well
4 litres water
Rind and juice of 2 lemons
20g cream of tartar
500g soft brown sugar
2 teaspoon winemaking yeast

1. Put the nettles in a pan with the water and bring to the boil. Boil for 15 minutes.

2. Add the lemon rind and juice, cream of tartar and sugar. Stir well and leave to cool.

3. When the mixture is just warm, blend 3 tablespoons of it with the yeast. Stir this back into the nettle mixture, cover with a lid and do not remove for 3 days. Leave in a warm place.

4. Strain the liquid into a large jug and use a funnel to fill glass beer bottles; you'll probably have to do this in batches. Close the bottles securely.

5. Mature for 7 days before drinking.

Mulled Wine

This is traditionally drunk at Christmas time and it is a Christmas Eve treat in our house, while the last of the presents are being wrapped and the mince pies are being made.

Serves 6

1 litre red wine
Zest and juice of 1 lemon and 1 orange
2 large tangerines with 6 cloves stuck in the skin
3 small cinnamon sticks
100ml brandy, optional
2–3 tablespoons brown sugar, optional

1. Place all the ingredients in a pan and heat to just boiling.

2. Reduce the heat and simmer for 5 minutes, then remove from the heat.

3. Serve hot in heatproof glass mugs or large wine glasses.

Mulled Ale

In 'olden times' this drink was served during the winter months to travellers who were cold and weary after a long journey. It warmed and fortified them.

Makes 2 servings

2 large eggs
600ml dark ale
A little grated nutmeg
25g unsalted butter
3 teaspoons soft brown sugar, or to taste

1. Beat the eggs with a little of the ale and all the grated nutmeg in a large bowl.

2. Add the butter and sugar to the rest of the ale and heat it in a saucepan over a medium heat. When hot (not boiling or even simmering), whisk into the egg mixture.

3. Reheat the ale in the pan until hot and serve straight away.

Index

GOOD HOME COOKING
Diana Peacock

Tired of eating bland, ready-made meals and packaged and processed food? Let *Good Home Cooking* be the answer to your prayers. You'll learn how to make tasty, healthy food, and discover that what you make is not only better-tasting than anything you can buy, it's cheaper, too!

Good food shouldn't be a luxury; it's a right, and this book will show you how to make simple, inexpensive recipes that ensure you eat well every day of the week. From light snacks to hearty main courses and home baking, you will find out how a cleverly stocked store-cupboard and some simple recipes mean tasty family meals, whatever your budget.

Here you can create everything from light bites and tasty treats to hearty main courses, while learning just how easy it is to prepare food from fresh ingredients with fantastic results every time. In addition, you can also discover how to make your own pickles, baked beans, bread, butter, yoghurt, cream and cottage cheese… even sausages and bacon – and all without having to buy any expensive equipment.

With almost 300 tried-and-tested recipes, *Good Home Cooking* is a must for anyone who wants to eat good, fresh, local, homemade food, whatever their income. It is essential reading for anyone who wants to provide their family with the best food possible.

ISBN 978 1 905862 30 6

THE URBAN HEN
Paul Peacock

Thousands of backyard poultry keepers are springing up all over the country, experiencing afresh the joys of their first hen, their first egg, their first happy chuckle in the morning garden.

Keeping poultry in the city brings with it not only joys but responsibilities. *The Urban Hen* is the perfect companion for the city poultry keeper and shows you how to maintain a happy, healthy garden or backyard flock in towns and cities everywhere.
In this book you'll discover how to:

- find the best poultry for the small garden – and how to house them properly
- feed your birds, tune in to their daily needs and enjoy your own eggs
- avoid annoying the neighbours by showing that it is possible to keep poultry without attracting unwelcome pests
- recognise healthy happy birds and learn their daily routine
- recognise poorly hens – and how to treat them or get help
- incubate and care for fertilised eggs and raise chicks

ISBN 978 1 905862 27 6